Introduction to International Humanitarian Law

Curtis F.J. Doebbler

CDP

CDPublishing

Introduction to
International Humanitarian Law
Curtis F.J. Doebbler

Published and Distributed by

CD PUBLISHING
Washington, DC, USA | Mumbi, India
Fax: +1-206-984-4734
Email: Sales@cdpublishing.org
Website: http://cdpublishing.org

ISBN: 978-0-9743570-6-5 (pbk)
Stock number: IHR0014 (ebook)

Typesetting:
MS Word 2003/Adobe Indesign CS/Bodoni MT (OTF)/10-12pt.

Printed in the United States of America, Palestine and India.
Printed on acid free paper meeting ANSI/NISO Z39.48-1992 paper quality standards.

Generic Cataloguing Data:
Doebbler, Curtis, F.J. 1961-
   viii/214 pp, 15.25 cm X 22.86 cm
   Introduction to International Humanitarian Law/ by C.F.J. Doebbler
   Includes index and selected readings.
   Library of Congress Classification: KZ6471 .D6 2005
   Dewey Decimal Classification: 341.48 – dc22
   Keywords: 1. international humanitarian law, 2. international law, 3. international relations, 4. law, 5. politics, 6. war, I. Title

Library of Congress Control Number: 2006920738

Introduction to
International Humanitarian Law

Curtis F.J. Doebbler
Professor of Law
An-Najah National University

CD Publishing

2005

Table of Contents

Abbreviations

ACHR	American Convention on Human Rights
art(t)	article(s)
Bk	Book
Ch	Chamber (of ICTR or ITCY)
Chap	Chapter
Comm	Commission
CRC	Convention on the Rights of the Child
CTA	Central Tracing Agency
Doc(s)	Document(s)
ECHR	European Convention on Human Rights
ECTS	European Credit Transfer System (academic credits)
ed(s)	editor(s)
GAOR	(UN) General Assembly Official Record
GCI-IV	Four Geneva Conventions from 1949
HRC	(UN) Human Rights Committee
ICC	International Criminal Court
ICJ	International Court of Justice
ICL	international criminal law
ICCPR	International Covenant of Civil and Political Rights
ICRC	International Committee of the Red Cross
ICTR	International Criminal Tribunal for Rwanda
ICTY	International Criminal Tribunal for (Former) Yugoslavia
IHL	international humanitarian law
IHRL	international human rights law
ILR	International Law Reports
LL.M.	masters degree in law
NGO	non-governmental organization
NL	The Netherlands
No(s)	Number(s)
PI-II	Two Additional Protocols from 1977
PIL	public international law
POW(s)	Prisoner(s) of War
OAS	Organization of American States
Res.	Resolution
T. Ch.	Trial Chamber (of ICTR or ITCY)
UN	United Nations
UNESCO	UN Education, Social and Cultural Organization
UNGA	United Nations General Assembly
UNTS	United Nations Treaty Series
USA	United States of America
v.	'and' (distinguishing two or more parties in a case)

Acknowledgments

This book was written while teaching at An-Najah National University. Its realization is due to the support and understanding of the university, especially Dr. Rami Hamdallah, President of the University, and Professor Maher Natsheh, Vice-President of Academic Affairs.

I also benefited tremendously from my students both at An-Najah National University and at Pristina University whose insightful and insistent enquires frequently required my careful consideration of material relevant to this book.

And, as usual, everyone at CD Publishing has once again been very supportive and helpful in the production of this book.

Most of all, however, this book is product of the hardship and suffering of the people of Afghanistan, Iraq and Palestine. As an American, I must acknowledge my country's contribution to the infliction of the scourge of war on these people. This acknowledgement is all the more painful, because each of these wars are widely believed to have been wars of aggression against the respective populations of Afghanistan, Iraq and Palestine started illegal either by the United States or continued with the United States' explicit support. How we can act with such inhumanity against others for only our own selfish interests, I will never understand. But because we do, it is imperative that we also do everything in our power to mitigate the injury we cause and to ultimately strive for justice. Something I hope I will never forget.

CFJD
September 2005

Preface

The audience of this book is students, particularly students of international law. Others who will be interested include students of history or political science; practitioners who are seeking to further their knowledge of the law; politicians seeking to acquire a basic understanding of the law applicable in an armed conflict; and any other individuals striving to better understand the field of international law applying during wartime.

This book can be read alone or used in a basic course on international humanitarian law. While there are many similar books, this book attempts to provide an unique perspective characterized by its critical understanding of the law. Rather than attempting to touch on all aspects of the law, it deals with a well-considered selection of topics and materials so as to provide the reader the basics of the law without engaging him or her too deeply in too many of the complexities of law.

It also contains excerpts from the basic texts of international humanitarian law so as to provide a self-contained introduction to the law. It is hoped that this work will provide readers an introduction that will stimulate further study of the law for which there are a increasing multitude of excellent works available and for which this might be the first step.

This book is dedicated
to the Victims of War
in Afghanistan, Iraq,
and Palestine.

Introduction

International humanitarian law (IHL) is the law that governs the conduct of armed conflict. It is thus law concerning the most inhumane activities of human beings against each other.

The purpose of the law is to ensure that even when engaged in their most horrific activities, human beings maintain a minimum degree of respect for each other.

Usually it concerns the conduct of soldiers and protects other soldiers who have been in some way incapacitated, those who try to assist the victims of war, and civilians from undue harm.

It also provides a common means of evaluating the valour of soldiers in the field by providing basic rules to which every soldier must adhere when fighting a war. In this way, apparently, at least a minimally fair fight will be guaranteed.

International humanitarian law does not prohibit war—although the individual perhaps most responsible for its modern creation hoped it would—but rather governs conduct in war.

The Contents of this Book

This book examines international humanitarian law with the goal of providing students a brief overview of the law, its institutions, and its application in practice.

Chapter One considers the 'History and Development of IHL' by reviewing some of main actors and actions taken in the nineteenth and twentieth century that led to the development of contemporary IHL. Discussed will be the most important events in the history and development of IHL starting from how the law evolved from different cultural, religious and social practices; to how it has progressed through the most basic restrictions on states' ability to wage war; to more detailed provisions concerning how individual soldiers and their commanders must act in an armed conflict even of a non-international nature. This excursion will take us from a brief look at the pre-18th century practices right up to how the ICC has begun to function and how states and non-state actors have applied IHL in recent conflicts.

Chapter Two provides an Introduction to 'Basic Concepts of IHL 'discussing the nature and goals of IHL, the Martens Clause, military necessity, proportionality, subsidiarity, legality, state and individual responsibility, command responsibility, the characterization of an armed conflict, categories of IHL, Article 3 common to the four Geneva Conventions, grave breaches, protecting powers, occupation and occupying powers, detaining powers, *hors de combat*, protected persons, fair trial, the duty to punish offenders, and immunity and impunity.

Chapter Three explores the 'Relationship between IHL to PIL, ICL and IHRL.' The Chapter discusses how IHL became a part of public international law (PIL) and the emergence of its later relationship to international human rights law (IHRL) and more recently international criminal law (ICL). We look at how ICL has borrowed from IHL and how IHRL and ICL tribunals have applied or otherwise used IHL for the interpretation of the instruments the tribunals are applying.

Chapter Four provides an 'Introduction to the Rules of IHL' that concentrates on rules of law and the instruments in which they are found. We start by understanding when these rules apply, to whom they apply, and generally what types of acts are prohibited by different actors. We will also discuss some of the basic substantive rules such as the prohibition of attacks on civilians and civilian targets, the treatment of prisoners of war, and the need to allow relief supplies to reach protected persons.

Chapter Five looks more particularly at the Hague law 'Restricting the Means and Methods of Warfare.' Although no longer restricted to the instruments adopted at The Hague, this law still refers to the rules that restrict the means and methods that states may use to conduct armed conflicts. Although this law has gradually been merged with the Geneva law under contemporary IHL, the distinction is an appropriate one to highlight the different protections provided by the law and how they operate. We will try to understand how states must evaluate the weapons they use and how they use them in an armed conflict. Also discussed is the Washington convention on chemical weapons and the Ottawa convention on landmines.

Chapter Six looks at the law protecting individuals or the Geneva law 'Concentration on the Individual.' Focusing on the four Geneva Conventions and their two Protocols we will delve into a deeper examination of what the various provisions mean by looking at those relating to the duty to ensure respect for the law, the protection of civilians, the protection of prisoners of war, the protection of relief agencies, medical personnel and religious personnel, and the duty to punish grave breaches.

Chapter Seven looks at the 'Forums for the Application of IHL.' Discussed will be the various tribunals in which IHL is applied and interpreted. We will look at the provisions of the statues of these bodies as well as the case of the *Prosecutor v. Dusko Tadiç* before the ICTY, as an example of the application of rules of IHL. The discussion will focus on the different jurisdictions of the various tribunals and the different types of IHL that they interpret and apply.

Chapter Eight examines the role of Non-State Actors in the development and application of IHL. Our focus will be on the International Committee of the Red Cross, but we will also look at projects associated with the International Criminal Court. We will see how non-state actors have helped to shape the law as well as how they participate in ensuring it is respected.

Finally, the Conclusion speculates about the direction of international humanitarian law in an ever-changing international society. In doing so means are suggested by which today's student of IHL might influence the development of the law and what might be a valuable direction for the development of the law.

Readers should use this *Introduction to International Humanitarian Law* as an aid to understanding the most fundamental aspects of the law. But is should be understood that it provides only a basic glimpse into the law and should be followed up with much more detailed reading of treaties, cases, articles and other books on the subject. At the same time, readers will benefit significantly if they seek to apply the law to the events they observe around them. As society has unfortunately not yet extinguished the scourge of war, the opportunities still exist to observe contemporary armed conflicts.

Activity

Describe three situations of armed conflict that occurred during your lifetime. Did they involve two or more states? Do you know what laws applied to the parties to the armed conflict? Can you list some laws that were broken?

Chapter One
The History of IHL

International humanitarian law is a relatively recent creation of the international community in name alone. The principles and practices upon which this law is based can trace the modern law back to the 19th century.

Ancient Norms and Practices

The ancient practices that are part of contemporary humanitarian law can be found in the authoritative texts of both warriors and religions. Sun Tzu's *The Art of War* from almost 2500 years ago tells about how captives are to be treated well and cared for (Chap. II, §19). The 200 years-old *Bible* (2 Kings 6: 20-23), the almost 1500 year-old *Quran* (47:5; 79:9), and the approximately 3800 year-old the Code of Hammurabi (Laws 27, 32 and 34) all tell of the virtues of treating the enemy with mercy and respect. The equally ancient Hindu *Book of Manu* (7th Book: §§90-93) places limits on means and methods of warfare.

The principles in these texts are also found Hugo Grotius treatise on international law, *De jure belli ac pacis, in* 1625 that describes the existing legal limits of warfare. These limits include the rights of prisoners of war (Bk. III, Chap. 7), limits on the means and methods of warfare (Bk. III, Chap. 12), and protections for general population (e.g. Bk. III, Chap. 5 concerning the prohibition on the desecration of graves). Without these limits, Grotius postulates, man could not survive. Limiting warfare by law, according to Grotius, was necessary.

The practice of states also confirms the existence of humanitarian practices that are today part of IHL. UNESCO in a book entitled *International Dimensions of Humanitarian Law* (Henry Dunant Institute, Geneva, 1988) has documented the rich and diverse cultural heritage of principles of IHL.

The Contemporary Antecedents

The modern practice and *opinio juris* of states also indicates support for IHL. Recently the ICRC's *Customary International Humanitarian Law* (several volumes published by the ICRC in Geneva and by Cambridge University Press in Cambridge, UK and edited by Jean-Marie Henckaerts and Louise Doswald-Beck 2005), which took more than a decade to complete, has documented contemporary state practice and *opinio juris*. This works lists the numerous rules of IHL that are supported by state practice and *opinio juris* to the extent that they can be referred to as customary international humanitarian law.

Most contemporary IHL, however, is found in treaties. And these treaties are so widely ratified that there is no need to have recourse to the more difficult to ascertain customary international law. This contemporary treaty law can be traced back to 1863.

The person perhaps more responsible than any other was Henri Dunant, a Swiss businessman. During the Napoleonic wars of the latter 19th Century Dunant was struggling in neutral Switzerland to make a living. Having heard of business opportunities in Algeria he sought out permission from Louis-Napoléon Bonaparte himself to do business there. In the course of his attempts to find Napoleon, Dunant traveled to Northern Italy where some of the fiercest battles of the Napoleonic wars were taking place. As he approached the battleground of Solferino in northern Italy where Napoleon, he believed, was leading his army, he was prevented from traveling further by the fighting. He took refuge in the village of Castiglione. It was in this village, close to the battle front, that he witnessed the scares of war.

It has been recounted, mainly by stories passed down by word of mouth and journalists, that Dunant volunteered to help tend to the wounded in a small church in Castiglione. He employed his business skills to organize the relief effort with volunteer nurses and laypersons. He saw maimed soldiers arrive he became shocked at human beings' inhumanity towards each other. While he was in the church, dressed in his business apparel, soldiers of Napoleon's army entered the church. They were dismayed that both enemy and their own soldiers were being treated. The commanding officer sought to put an end to this and demanded that the enemy not be treated. Dunant intervened. He argued forcefully that every injured person must be treated. Apparently intimidated by Dunant's formidable business attire, the military commander may have believed him a special envoy from Napoleon. As a consequence the military commander withdrew allowing the treatment of all the wounded to continue.

This story indicates the core principles of impartiality and neutrality that are suppose to characterize both IHL and the Red Cross Movement. Dunant was so touched by what he witnessed in Castiglione that when returned to Geneva he wrote an emotive account entitled *Un souvenir de Solferino* (A Memory of Solferino) which was published in 1862. In this book he recounts what he had witnessed and urges humankind to end the scourge of war and to protect victims of war.

Dunant also began to tirelessly pursue an agreement between states to protect persons made *hors de combat* in wars. He was mainly interested in protecting soldiers as they—not civilians as today—accounted for the overwhelming majority of the wartime causalities in the 19th century. To further his effort he and four colleagues from the Geneva business community formed the International Committee for Aid to the Wounded. This Committee was the forerunner to what was to become the International Committee of the Red Cross (ICRC) and the stimulus to the Red Cross Movement which consists of the ICRC, the Federation of Red Cross and Red Crescent Societies, and the national Red Cross societies. While all of these are NGOs, they play a special role in relation to armed conflicts and have a special character. This is especially true of the ICRC that has responsibilities under the four Geneva Conventions.

It is important to note that Dunant saw IHL as a means of ending all armed conflicts. For him there was no strict distinction between *jus ad bellum* (laws prohibiting recourse to armed force) and *jus in bello* (IHL). Both of these areas of law should be employed for the same overall goal of banning wars forever, he argued. This view was not popular. Even during Dunant's lifetime he himself felt the consequences of those who doubted that war could be ended. As Dunant campaigned for an end to all wars he became increasing unpopular with his colleagues. When Dunant pleaded for the ICRC to intervene to protect soldiers on both sides of a war in which Swiss public opinion was sympathetic to only one side, Dunant was banished from the ICRC, the organization that he began. Had it not been for an enterprising journalist that stumbled upon him living in secluded retirement in a small Swiss village, the world may never have heard of Henri Dunant. As a consequence of his rediscovery, however, his work drew so much attention that he was awarded the first Nobel Peace Prize, ostensibly for his commitment to peace and ending all wars as much as for his humanitarian efforts to ensure the application of law during wars.

At around the same time that Henri Dunant was encouraging a world wide movement to protect victims of war, a German-American named Francis Lieber was preparing *Instructions for the Government of Armies of the United States in the Field* (1863) at the request of American President Abrahim Lincoln and in the mist of a civil war. The instructions were to be based on the customs and practice of states. These 157 articles of instructions included the principle of distinction between combatants and civilians or non-combatants. They, however, also allowed such means of warfare as starvation (art. 17) and the taking of hostages (arts. 54 and 55).

The result of Dunant's work was the Geneva Convention for the Amelioration of the Condition of the Wounded in Armies in the Field, Geneva of 22 August 1864. This Convention was drafted by states called together in a diplomatic conference that Dunant and his colleagues had convinced the Swiss government to host. This treaty concentrated on protecting soldiers injured in war and was the first modern elaboration of the principle of protecting wounded and sick.

Within months two addition instruments were elaborated. The Additional Articles relating to the Condition of the Wounded in War from 20 October 1864 added some protections to persons involved in wars at sea. The Saint Petersburg Declaration Renouncing the Use, in Time of War, of certain Explosive Projectiles adopted on 11 December of the same year limited means and methods of warfare. This latter instrument gave rise to a trend of norm setting initiated by Russia and relating to the means and methods of warfare.

At the end of the 19th century and the beginning of the 20th century this trend was continued by Russian Czar Nicholas III who called for the convening of a series of Hague conferences to discuss means of resolving disputes peacefully and mitigating the inhumanity of war. These conferences took place from 1899 to 1907 and resulted in a series of Hague Conventions. Among the most well know was the Fourth Hague Convention, whose annexed regulations served as the primary instrument of IHL during World Wars I and II.

The Fourth Hague Convention respecting the Laws and Customs of War on Land and its annexed Regulations concerning the Laws and Customs of War on Land was adopted on 18 October 1907 and ratified by the majority of the states in the international community. It contains the basic rules of land warfare, including detailed rules for occupying armies. The definition of occupation in article 42 remains an accepted statement of this condition under international law. Article 42 states that "[t]erritory is considered occupied when it is actually placed under the authority of the hostile army. The occupation extends only to the territory where such authority has been established and can be exercised." The Regulations also limit the means and methods of warfare prohibiting the "bombardment by whatever means, of towns, villages, dwellings, or buildings, which are undefended...." In addition they provide for the rights of prisoners of war and the sick and wounded.

The Regulations and the Fourth Hague Convention to which they are attached are joined by twelve other Hague conventions and a Declaration prohibiting the use of balloons to drop bombs. Although these instruments provide for some rights of *hors de combat* their general focus is on the means and methods of warfare. For this reason they are known as the Hague law—as compared to the law of Geneva, which focuses more on the protection of the individual. Today, however, this description is somewhat misleading as treaties negotiated in other cities have now made substantial contributions to both areas of the laws of war.

In the aftermath of World War I two treaties were adopted limiting some of the weapons that had been used during that war. The Treaty relating to the Use of Submarines and Noxious Gases in Warfare was adopted in Washington, D.C., in the United States on 6 February 1922 and the Protocol for the Prohibition of the Use of Asphyxiating, Poisonous or Other Gases, and of Bacteriological Methods of Warfare was adopted in Geneva on 17 June 1925. Both of these treaties address concerns related to the use of chemical weapons that had arisen from the use of mustard gas in World War I.

Between the first and second World Wars several treaties were also adopted concerning naval warfare. One such treaty was the Convention on Maritime Neutrality adopted in Havana on 20 February 1928. This treaty established the rights and responsibilities of both neutral and belligerent states on the high seas during a war. The Geneva law was supplemented by two additional treaties protecting *hors de combat* that were adopted in Geneva. The Convention for the Amelioration of the Condition of the Wounded and Sick in Armies in the Field and the Convention relative to the Treatment of Prisoners of War both adopted on 27 July 1929 added more details to the provisions of the 1864 Geneva Convention and the Hague treaties.

In 1935 a new type of treaty was adopted protecting property of cultural and historic value, the Treaty on the Protection of Artistic and Scientific Institutions and Historic Monuments. Although such protections are found as far back as the Lieber Instructions and again in the Hague Treaty of 1899, these protections were not the subject of a dedicated treaty. This effort was to be followed up in 1954 when the Convention for the Protection of Cultural Property in the Event of Armed Conflict was adopted at The Hague on 14 May 1954 at a conference convened under the auspices of UNESCO.

A 1937 agreement adopted in Nyon, Switzerland was an attempt to mitigate the damage done by submarine attacks on merchant ships. By this time, however, World War II was underway and much of IHL proved inadequately up to the challenge presented by yet another world war.

In the aftermath of World War II the countries that had fought in the war again set about trying to repair the damage to the IHL. Again lead by Switzerland their main effort included the adoption of four Geneva Conventions:

1. Convention on the Amelioration of the Condition of the Wounded and Sick in the Armed Forces in the Field, *signed* at Geneva, 12 August 1949, *entered into force* 21 October 1950, 6 *UST* 3114, *TIAS* No. 3362, 75 *UNTS* 31. This treaty provides for basic protections for medical personnel, medical buildings, medical transports, religious personnel, the sick, and the wounded who are attached to a state's army.

2. Convention on the Amelioration of the Wounded, Sick, and Shipwrecked Members of the Armed Forces, *signed* at Geneva, 12 August 1949, *entered into force* 21 October 1950, 6 *UST* 3217, *TIAS* No. 3363, 75 *UNTS* 85. This treaty provides for basic protections for medical personnel, medical buildings, medical transports, religious personnel, the sick, the wounded and the shipwrecked who are attached to a state's army and who are injured at sea.

3. Convention Relative to the Treatment of Prisoners of War, *signed* at Geneva, 12 August 1949, *entered into force* 21 October 1950, 6 *UST* 3316, *TIAS* No. 3364, 75 *UNTS* 135. This treaty provides for an elaborate set of protections for prisoners of war, including details about how they are to be treated in detention, procedural guarantees for trial, provisions governing their labour while in detention, and provisions for their release, among other rights.

4. Convention Relative to the Protection of Civilian Persons in Time of War, *signed* at Geneva, 12 August 1949, *entered into force* 21 October 1950, 6 *UST* 3516, *TIAS* No. 3365, 75 *UNTS* 287. This treaty protects the basic rights of civilians effected by an armed conflict. It provides for some basic rights that apply to all civilians in all situations of armed conflict as well as rights that apply in occupied territories.

All four of these Geneva Conventions contain a common article 3 that covers non-international armed conflicts. It is the only article in these treaties expressly relating to non-international armed conflicts, nevertheless some provisions of these treaties are now recognized as customary international law.

These four treaties have been ratified by almost every country in the world and are the foundation of IHL today. While they do not cover completely new areas of the law, they provide much more detail in their 429 articles and additional annexes. The provisions of these four treaties will be discussed in more detail below.

On 8 June 1977, two Protocols additional to the original four Geneva Conventions were adopted. Although the two additional protocols do not enjoy as wide adherence as the four Geneva Conventions, they include important developments in the law. Some of the provisions of these protocols are now customary international law. As such they are binding even on states that have not ratified the protocols.

The Protocol Additional to the Geneva Conventions of 12 August 1949, and relating to the Protection of Victims of International Armed Conflicts, or Protocol I, adds especially to the protection of civilians and installations that are of importance to civilians. Its 102 articles provide for greater protection for relief workers, women and children, and civil defense personnel. It limits the means and methods of warfare by protecting civilian installations from attack, prohibiting indiscriminate attacks, and protecting objects indispensable to the survival of the civilian population. It also contains provision for a Fact-Finding Commission to address the lacuna of a body to authoritatively interpret the law and determine when violations have taken place.

The Protocol Additional to the Geneva Conventions of 12 August 1949, and relating to the Protection of Victims of Non-International Armed Conflicts, or Protocol II, is much shorter and deals with the difficult and controversial area of civil wars. Its 28 articles supplement article 3 that is common to all four Geneva Conventions and which is the only article in those treaties specifically applying to non-international armed conflicts. Most controversial of all is the definition of non-state actors and the types of conflicts that are covered by Protocol II.

Article 1 defines the material field of application of the Protocol as all armed conflicts that are not covered by Protocol I "and which take place in the territory of a High Contracting Party between its armed forces and dissident armed forces or other organized armed groups which, under responsible command, exercise such control over a part of its territory as to enable them to carry out sustained and concerted military operations and to implement this Protocol." The second paragraph of article 1 then excludes "situations of internal disturbances and tensions, such as riots, isolated and sporadic acts of violence and other acts of a similar nature, as not being armed conflicts."

Although article 2 states that the Protocol applies to "all persons affected by an armed conflict" as described above. This definition was the result of significant debate and compromise. It is clear, however, that it applies *ratione personae* both civilians and combatants, as long as the latter meet the requirements of article one.

It is also apparent that these two protocols, like the four Geneva Conventions they supplement, were intended to ensure that as many people as possible are protected by IHL. About 150 states have ratified both protocols as of the turn of the century.

While the four Geneva Conventions and their two Protocols are the most significant steps in the development of IHL they are not the last ones.

Since 1977, for example, the Convention on Prohibitions or Restrictions on the Use of Certain Conventional Weapons Which May be Deemed to be Excessively Injurious or to Have Indiscriminate Effects was adopted on 10 October 1980. This treaty limiting the means and methods of warfare has been supplemented by several protocols. Other recent treaties include the International Convention against the Recruitment, Use, Financing and Training of Mercenaries adopted on 4 December 1989; the Convention on the prohibition of the development, production, stockpiling and use of chemical weapons and on their destruction adopted on 13 January 1993; the Convention on the Prohibition of the Use, Stockpiling, Production and Transfer of Anti-Personnel Mines and on their Destruction adopted on 18 September 1997 (also known as the Ottawa Convention); and, most recently, the Convention on cluster munitions (also known as the 'Cluster Bombs Convention' or the 'Oslo Convention') adopted on 30 May 2008.

In addition, significant strides have been taken to ensure respect for IHL by the adoption of the statutes of two ad hoc tribunals for the former Yugoslavia and Rwanda, respectively, and the 1998 adoption of the Statute of the International Criminal Court. These latest developments of tribunals or courts to apply IHL, among other sources of law, have spawned a whole new field of law referred to as international criminal law. The object of this law is to hold individuals responsible for their most serious crimes—crimes that violate international law—including IHL.

The modern trend in the latter part of the first decade of the 21st century is to ensure respect for the law by holding individuals responsible. It is a trend that has had mixed results, however, as the most powerful countries claim they are above the law. Senior government officials in the United States, for example, have argued that their President can suspend the Geneva Convention unilaterally and in turn this has severely injured the reputations of these treaties among individuals everywhere in the world. The affected individuals now frequently ask why they should apply IHL when America claims to be able to use the law as a weapon in its vague wars against others, instead of respecting the law as a limitation of its actions and as a rule of international law.

Activity

Think about the history of IHL that has been described. Can you think of a specific contribution to the rules of warfare that emanates from your cultural, ethnic, or social background? If you can, describe it to others and see if they agree with you that it is based on your cultural heritage. Then listen as they do the same.

Chapter Two
Basic Concepts of IHL

Nature and goals of IHL

International humanitarian law strives to humanize war. On the one
hand this may be seen as making war more palatable even though few
proponents of the law would encourage wars. Indeed, Henri Dunant, one
of the leading proponents of modern IHL, sought to use the rules of law
as a step towards ending all wars for all time. Such a view today would
undoubtedly be seen as unrealistic by even staunch supporter of IHL.
One may well ask if this pessimism is justified. And one might also ask
if it would not be valuable for modern day proponents of IHL to follow
in Henri Dunant's footsteps by at least employing *jus ad bellum* to avoid
wars with the same enthusiasm that they have recourse to *jus in bello*
once a war starts.

Few proponents of IHL have done this. Even the ICRC, which has
called Henri Dunant its father for more than a century, has refused to
condemn recourse to war or to seriously campaign to prevent wars. This
is true surely not because the ICRC seeks to promote wars merely to
give itself work, but more likely because of the pervasive fatalism in the
international community that leads to the conclusion that war cannot
be avoided.

Proponents of IHL stress that this law applies irrespective of the illegality
or legality of the armed conflict. The claim to ensure this then must

not be combine with judging the legality of the war. Thus although the overwhelming majority of the world's leaders and international lawyers condemned the United States' aggression against the Iraqi people that started in March 2003, the ICRC and many other staunch proponents of IHL refused to condemn the war as illegal. Somewhat inconsistently, however, many of these same proponents of IHL did condemn the Iraqis who took up arms to fight for their independence against a foreign and oppressive occupier.

Why do many international lawyers often make an effort to distinguish *jus ad bellum* from *jus in bello*? A frequently heard claim is that to do otherwise might jeopardize the application of IHL. This reason, however, could equally apply to arguments claiming that all criminal procedure laws are illegitimate because they make it more difficult to convict criminals. Other reason might be more linked to the vest interests of some of the proponents of IHL. As the Iraq example demonstrates, it may be difficult for these senior individuals and established organizations to risk the funding and support of countries and other elites who benefit from armed conflicts. These individuals and organizations often need the support of these elites to do their work. Speaking out against powerful countries that use force might lose them this support. Groups like the Iraqi Resistance, the Palestinians, and the Kosovars make for easier targets as they lack full access to international forums in which they can authoritatively challenge such politicalization.

Whatever the explanation may be, the principle that IHL applies in all armed conflicts—regardless of their legality—is a fundamental principle.

Martens clause

Another fundamental principle is the Martens clause. The Martens clause appears in the preambles of Hague Conventions of 1899 and 1907 and in article 1(2) of Additional Protocol I to the four 1949 Geneva Conventions. In this latter instrument the Martens clause reads: "In cases not covered by this Protocol or by other international agreements, civilians and combatants remain under the protection and authority of the principles of international law derived from established custom, from the principles of humanity and from dictates of public conscience."

In essence the Martens clause restates a common principle of international law: that states obligations that are not expressly extinguished continue in force. In other words, even a state that has not ratified any human rights treaty remains bound by the rules of customary international law. The International Court of Justice has found this to be the case holding that the principle expressed in the Martens clause is customary international. *Advisory Opinion on the Legality of the Threat or Use of Force of Nuclear Weapons*, Advisory Opinion, No. 95, (8 July 1996) at para 84.

Military necessity

Military necessity requires the evaluation of the means and methods of warfare. Military necessity is a professional. It requires that the officer commanding an attack or sometimes even a soldier carrying out an attack decide if their is a legitimate military objective to be achieved, and if the means or methods applied of achieving this objective will cause the least harm to non-combatants or facilities necessary to their survival. It is also part of the wider considerations of proportionality. The very creation of rules of IHL has given rise to lengthy debates on the relative value of military necessity in relation to the dictates of humanity. This has been true since the drafting of the first Geneva Conventions in the 1860's to the most recent instruments of IHL. Article 23(g) of the 1970 Hague Regulations recognizes the principle of necessity as prohibiting destruction or seizure of "the enemy's property, unless such destruction or seizure be imperatively demanded by the necessities of war'. The Hague Convention on the Protection of Cultural Objects from 1954 calls for both a standard of "imperative military necessity" as well as "unavoidable military necessity." The latter apparently imposes a heavier burden on the attacker. Although the principle remains a pertinent part of IHL, instruments such as the two Additional Protocols of 1977 have taken it into account and determined that some attacks are absolutely prohibited, regardless of their military value or necessity. This appears to be the trend in the development of the law, but not always in the practice of armies in the field. See further Chapter Five.

Proportionality

Proportionality provides a measure for deciding whether an armed attack has been taken into consideration the protection of non-combatants particularly civilians. The test requires (1) that the soldiers of the state planning an attack always consider the possibility of civilian casualties, (2) that the consideration takes into account the absolute prohibitions of attacking civilians and installations necessary to the survival of the civilian population, (3) that only the means and methods necessary to accomplish a legitimate military objective are used, including weapons chosen when possible because they will limit and possible civilian casualties, and (4) that when a military installation is attacked the military advantage is weighed against the possibility of any civilian casualties with due regard being given to other existing alternatives. The principle of proportionality is alluded to in article 57 of the First Protocol to the four Geneva Conventions. It might be suggested that military commanders are under a duty to keep records of the considerations they have taken into account when planning an attack if they wish to have the benefit of the doubt concerning their decisions. In other words, the burden is on the attacker to show that his or her attack is proportional to the military advantage claimed or reasonably thought to be gained. See further Chapter Five.

Subsidiarity

Subsidiarity is merely the requirement that one not resort to a means of method of warfare that might injure protected persons even if there is an argument of military necessity until all other alternatives have been considered, tried and exhausted. The principle plays a role in applying both the considerations of necessity and proportionality by emphasizing on the need to have exhaustively considered alternatives. Whether this is realistic in the heat of battle may be questioned. Many problems have arisen concerning the application of the principle of subsidiarity even when there is sufficient time and conditions in which to plan an attack.

Legality

The principle of legality might seem obvious to lawyers. It means that action must be based on law. In the application of IHL this means, among other things, that a state cannot justify an action that violates IHL for reasons such as its domestic law. Although domestic politicians, and sometimes even domestic judges, may argue that their domestic law allows an action that violates IHL this can never be the position of an international lawyer. Regardless of its domestic law, international law remains in force for a country that has agreed to it or when the consensus of the international community has formed a rule of customary international humanitarian law. The legality of states' actions must thus be evaluated on the basis of their conformity with IHL.

State and individual responsibility

Unlike international human rights law that is based almost entirely on state responsibility and international criminal law that is based almost entirely on individual responsibility, IHL is based on both of these forms of responsibility. The primary obligations under both the Geneva Conventions and customary international humanitarian law are those of states. Article 1 common to all four Geneva Conventions reads unequivocally that states "undertake to respect and to ensure respect for the present Convention in all circumstances." This is an example of state responsibility.

Through international criminal law, responsibility for war crimes is individual. This means that before the International Criminal Court, for example, only individuals can be charged and the prosecutor must prove that each individual charged played a part in the perpetration of a war crime. Individual responsibility is also sometimes imposed in several treaties of IHL (art. 49, GCI; art. 50, GCII; art. 129, GCIII; art. 146, GCIV; and art. 85, PI). Article 6, paragraph 2, subparagraph b, of Additional Protocol II, protecting the victims of non-international armed conflicts, for example, states that individuals may only be prosecuted on the basis of individual responsibility. This also means that there can be no collective responsibility for acts committed by one or more members of a group.

There was a serious concern with collective penalties in the aftermath of the Second World War. In this war it was frequent for occupation powers to take hostages to prevent disorders and attacks on occupation soldiers. This practice was roundly condemned. Nevertheless, even as late as 2005, United States soldiers in Iraq have been accused of similar actions against civilians. Such actions violate article 33 of the Fourth Geneva Convention protecting civilians that not only states that "[n]o protected person may be punished for an offence he or she has not personally committed," but also condemns "[c]ollective penalties" together with "measures of intimidation" and "terrorism."

Command responsibility

The collateral to individual responsibility is command responsibility. Although an apparent exception to the principle of individual responsibility, it is better viewed as a form of individual responsibility particular to members of the military. It is a responsibility that attaches to seniority of rank in the military. The elements of command responsibility are explained by article 87 of Additional Protocol I protecting the victims of international armed conflicts. It specifies several duties of commanders. First, they must suppress and report breaches of IHL. Second, they must ensure that their subordinates are aware of the rules of IHL. Third, they must take action to prevent violations of IHL whenever possible and in all cases initiate the punishment of the perpetrators. Rather than contradicting the principle of individual responsibility, command responsibility therefore adds to the obligations that commanders have by virtue of their rank.

Characterization of armed conflicts

For IHL to apply an armed conflict must exist. This is a *de facto* determination whereby the intensity of the use of force must be evaluated.

It is not, however, necessary that there be a formal declaration of war or any other type of recognition of a state of war. In one case before the Inter-American Commission on Human Rights, the question arose as to whether or not the use of force by rioting prisoners constituted an armed conflict. The prisoners, who were mainly members of a rebel movement had been joined by colleagues from outside the prison. The state had argued that an armed conflict existed in order to justify its use of force and derogation from some human rights provisions. The Commission appeared to agree based on a superficial evaluation of the degree of the use of force by the rebels, but also to allow it to apply IHL. *Juan Carlos Abella v. Argentina*, Case No. 11, 137, Annual Report 1997, OAS Doc. OAE/Ser.L/V/II.98, Doc.7 rev (13 April 1998). The Inter-American Court later decided that the Commission could find the state liable for its violations of international human rights law but not IHL, thus avoiding the determination of whether or not an armed conflict existed. *Las Palmeras Case*, Judgment on Preliminary Objections of 4 February 2000, Ser. C, No. 67 (2000).

The ICTY has also had to consider the question of whether an armed conflict existed. *Prosecutor v. Dusko Tadiç*, Case No. IT-94-1-AR72, App. Chamber (decision of 2 October 1995) at para. 70. The Appellate Tribunal of the ICTY defined an armed conflict as existing "whenever there is a resort to armed force between States or protracted armed violence between governmental authorities and organized armed groups or between such groups within a State."

An armed conflict may be international or non-international. When an armed conflict involves two or more states it is said to be an international armed conflict. An authoritative determination as to whether an armed conflict is international was made in *Prosecutor v. Dusko Tadiç*, Case No. IT-94-1-AR72, App.Ch of the ICTY (2 October 1995).

The ICTY's Appellate Tribunal had to decide if the armed conflict taking place in Bosnia and Herzegovina in the 1990s constituted an international or a non-international armed conflict. The crucial test for the Tribunal was the "degree of control" of the Serbian government over the Bosnian-Serb participants in the armed conflict. The Tribunal decided that an armed conflict did exist because of the substantial support provided to the Bosnian-Serbs by the Serbian government in Belgrade.

A non-international armed conflict can be defined as any armed conflict that is not international. In other words, the requirement of a sufficient degree of force must be met and not more than one state must be involved.

In practice determining whether or not the use of force has achieved a level sufficient to classify the violence as an armed conflict is a difficult task. The case of *Juan Carlos Abella v. Argentina*, Case No. 11, 137, Annual Report 1997, OAS Doc. OAE/Ser.L/V/II.98, Doc.7 rev (13 April 1998)) cited above is perhaps the best example of such a determination, although it appears to be based on a superficial evaluation of the degree of force used by the rebels. An easier situation might be the American civil war of 1863-1865, which was fought between the various United States, but even the parties to this war had links to other governments that might allow one to argue that it had an international nature.

The determination as to whether an armed conflict is international or non-international is relevant for deciding the *corpus* of law that applies. In an international armed conflict, for example, all the provisions of the four Geneva Conventions will apply. In a non-international armed conflict only common article 3 applies. Similarly the more lengthy and elaborated First Additional Protocol applies to international armed conflicts, while the much briefer Second Additional Protocol applies to non-international armed conflicts.

Categories of IHL

The law called IHL or the laws of war is frequently divided by academics into the Hague law and the Geneva law. Although not based on the geographical distinctions that they seem to represent, they do provide a useful understanding of the difference between the law governing the means and methods of warfare and the law dealing with the protection of civilians and other non-combatants. It should be recognized, however, that in reality both categories of law seek to protect individuals.

The Hague law refers to the law that was first promulgated between 1899 and 1907 in a series of conferences organized in The Hague, the Netherlands (Den Haag, Nederland). This law concentrated more on the control of the means and methods of warfare then on the protection of civilians. One reason for this was that civilians were not the major casualties of war at this time.

The Geneva law refers to the law promulgated in Geneva, Switzerland in 1949 or the four Geneva Conventions. These convention have as their main object the protection of *hors de combat*, civilians, and other enumerated protected persons. There is little in these conventions about the means and methods of warfare. These conventions were promulgated in response to a recognized gap in the law.

Occasionally, one will also see a reference to the 'New York' law. This refers to international criminal law or the law relating to the punishment of war criminals promulgated by the United Nations—which is headquartered in New York. The adoption of the Statute of the International Criminal

Court in Rome, Italy in 1998, perhaps make 'the Rome law' a more fitting title for this area of the law.

Common Article 3 to the four Geneva Conventions

Article 3—identical in all four Geneva Conventions—is a statement of the customary international humanitarian law that applies to non-international armed conflicts. *Case Concerning Military and Paramilitary Activities in and against Nicaragua (Nicaragua v. United States)*, [1986] *ICJ Reports* 14 (27 June 1986) at para. 114. While the rest of the provisions in the four Geneva Conventions only apply to international armed conflicts, article 3 applies expressly to non-international armed conflicts.

The following acts are prohibited at all times by common article 3 in all types of non-international armed conflicts—even those not involving any states:

(a) violence to life and person, in particular murder of all kinds, mutilation, cruel treatment and torture;

(b) taking of hostages;

(c) outrages upon personal dignity, in particular humiliating and degrading treatment;

(d) the passing of sentences and the carrying out of executions without previous judgment pronounced by a regularly constituted court, affording all the judicial guarantees which are recognized as indispensable by civilised peoples.

In practice many states have been fearful of admitting the application of common article 3 believing that it would constitute a *de facto* recognition of armed opposition to the government. This view appears contrary to the express words of article 3 that state that the application of its "provisions shall not affect the legal status of the Parties to the conflict." Rebel groups and national liberation movements by comparison have usually welcomed its application.

Grave breaches

Grave breaches are found in specific articles in each of the four Geneva Conventions and the first Additional Protocol (art. 50, GCI; art. 51, GCII; art. 130, GCIII; art. 147, GCIV; and artt 11 and 85 PI).

In all cases grave breaches are defined as willful killing, torture or inhuman treatment, including biological experiments, willfully causing great suffering or serious injury to body or health, and extensive destruction and appropriation of property, not justified by military necessity and carried out unlawfully and wantonly. In each case the offense must be carried out against a person protected in the particular Convention to be a grave breach of that treaty. Prisoners of war and civilians are also protected against being compelled to serve in the forces of the hostile Power, or being willfully deprived of the rights of fair and regular trial. Civilians are additionally protected against unlawful deportation or transfer or unlawful confinement and being taken hostage.

State parties are obliged to "enact any legislation necessary to provide effective penal sanctions for persons committing, or ordering to be committed, any of the grave breaches;" "to search for persons alleged to have committed, or to have ordered to be committed, such grave breaches;" and to "bring such persons, regardless of their nationality, before its own courts" or "hand such persons over for trial to another" state party provided "a *'prima facie'* case" has been made out.

Protecting powers

All four Geneva Conventions describe "protecting powers" as playing a special role for ensuring respect for IHL during an armed conflict. The protecting power is to be designated at the onset of the armed conflict. In practice this has not worked as states fail to nominate a protecting power. Instead, the fallback clauses found in article 10 of the first three Geneva Conventions and article 11 of the Fourth Geneva Convention have been used to provide for an alternative. These clauses call upon the parties to accept the services of any humanitarian organization to assume the humanitarian functions to be preformed by the protecting power.

Occupation and occupying powers

Occupation is a *de jure* situation brought about by *de facto* control over the territory of another state. Article 42 of the 1907 Hague Regulations states that "[t]erritory is considered occupied when it is actually placed under the authority of the hostile army." Article 43 of the same Regulations make it clear that the occupying power does not acquire sovereignty over the people of the territory, but merely a type of temporary custodianship based on its superior military power. As a result the occupying power "shall take all the measures in his power to restore, and ensure, as far as possible, public order and safety, while respecting, unless absolutely prevented, the laws in force in the country." Moreover, an occupying power "is forbidden to force the inhabitants of territory occupied by it to furnish information about the army of the other belligerent, or about its means of defense" (Art. 44). The Fourth Geneva Convention, Part III, Section III (articles 47 to 78) also provides rules governing occupation.

Detaining powers

According to article 12 of the Third Geneva Convention prisoners of war are in the hands of the detaining power. This power is the state, not the soldiers that capture the prisoners. This state is the detaining power. Moreover, the detaining power remains responsible to take all necessary steps to protect a prisoner of war even if the prisoner is transferred to another state. Thus if a prisoners' rights are violated, even by a third party, the original detaining powers can incur state responsibility for a violation of international law. Pictet, J., (ed.), *Commentary: III Geneva Convention Relative to the Treatment of Prisoners of War* 135-36 (ICRC 1958). When one of more states—for example, a coalition of states—act together to capture a person, all of the states may be considered detaining powers.

Hors de combat

This French phrase refers to persons who have been injured so they are no longer able to participate as combatants in an armed conflict. Although it may sometimes be difficult to determine whether or not a combatant has become *hors de combat* one clear sign is a combatant who is surrendering. A feigned surrender will itself violate IHL, as will attacking the person trying to surrender whether they are injured or not.

Protected persons

The phrase 'protected person' appears in article 86 of the 1929 Geneva Convention. Under the four Geneva Conventions there are numerous categories of persons who are protected (art. 8 in GCI, GCII, and GCIII, and art. 9 in GCIV).

Protected persons include injured or *hors de combat*, soldiers who are seriously ill, soldiers who are surrendering, shipwrecked members of the armed forces, prisoners of war, relief workers of recognized humanitarian relief organizations, members of the ICRC carrying out their duties under the four Geneva Conventions, and last but perhaps most importantly, civilians. Civilians may be classified in several categories some of which are entitled to enhanced protections, such women, pregnant and lactating women, children, religious personnel, medical personnel, judges, refugees, internally displaced persons, stateless persons, and journalists.

All of these categories of persons are protected under IHL and should not be the object of attack. This does not mean that they can never be injured in an attack. Where military necessity and proportionality dictate that a military installation be attacked, protected persons may be injured (such casualties are sometimes derogatorily referred to as collateral damage).

Fair trial

While only one of many legal principles in the four Geneva Conventions and one found regularly in international human rights instruments the right to a fair trial it is worthy of emphasis if only because of how it has been abused in recent years.

The military trials of Guantánamo detainees and the trial of members of the Iraqi regime all illustrate violations of fair trial. In the former case the detainees were denied access to courts, lawyers of their own choosing, facilities to prepare a defense, and even humane treatment while in custody. Nevertheless, despite these serious violations of the right to fair trial, the United States government brought many of the detainees before special military commissions that were set up to be able to deal with them without providing the guarantees that others in America, including members of the military, would enjoy.

In the case of the Iraqi prisoners, the violations of due process were even more widespread. Detainees were not charged for months, they were not allowed access to lawyers, to courts, to their family, to the evidence against them, to the charges against them, to an independent and impartial tribunal, and they were regularly abuses by their captors. The treatment they received was hard to understand considering that the detaining power, the United States and some of its allies, claimed that they had overwhelming evidence against the detainees. In such a case, common sense would dictate that the prosecuting state would be careful to provide due process.

Even more detrimental to the rule of law is the fact that in both cases the willful denial of fair trial to prisoners of war was a grave breach of the Third Geneva Convention (art. 130). Despite this fact, no action was taken to bring any official to justice for this grave breach. This itself constitutes a violation of IHL (see arts. 129-131 of GCIII).

Duty to punish offenders

The identical provisions on grave breaches in each of the four Geneva Conventions place "[e]ach High Contracting Party ... under the obligation to search for persons alleged to have committed, or to have ordered to be committed, such grave breaches, and shall bring such persons, regardless of their nationality, before its own courts. It may also, if it prefers, and in accordance with the provisions of its own legislation, hand such persons over for trial to another High Contracting Party concerned, provided such High Contracting Party has made out a *prima facie* case." (GCI, art. 49, GCII, art. 50, GCIII, art. 129, GCIV, art. 147)

This is a duty *aut judicare aut dedere*. It means that states must either prosecute the accused or to ensure that the accused is tuned over to another state that will prosecute him or her where a *prima facie* case has been made that a grave breach has been committed.

This is the strongest and clearest obligation of implementation under IHL. It has been relied upon indirectly by the UN Security Council in the case of the two *ad hoc* international criminal tribunals for the former Yugoslavia and Rwanda and by the international community more generally in the case of the International Criminal Court (ICC). In each of these cases, however, the obligation to try or extradite international criminals, including war criminals, is based on a treaty or resolution of international criminal law. In each of these cases the obligation is also limited. For example, only states that have ratified the ICC Statute are bound to turn over individuals to the ICC, but even these states may be able to avoid this obligation if another international obligation requires otherwise (art. 98, ICC Statute). Such a situation may arise when a state that has ratified the ICC Statute also has an extradition treaty with a non-state party.

The United States government has taken advantage of this situation to enter into agreements (known as "Article 98 agreements") with dozens of state parties to the ICC Statute requiring the extradition of American citizens to the United States. As article 98 was not intended to block the apprehension and bringing of international criminals before the Court, but to provide states the ability to respect pre-existing international obligations, it may be questioned whether states who entered into such agreements are acting in good faith to execute their treaty obligations under the ICC Statute.

Immunity and impunity

Immunity and impunity are related concepts, but they are not the same.

Immunity refers to the ability of a person to avoid legal liability because of their characterization or position as recognized under international law. Heads of State, for example, generally have immunity. Immunity for war crimes, genocide, crimes against humanity, and the crimes of aggression is prohibited. Thus immunity plays little or no role in application of IHL.

Impunity refers to the failure to punish violators of the law. Rather than being a principle of international law it is a description of a condition that exists when states fail to implement the law. Impunity is a major problem as concerns the application of IHL because few bodies exists that are able and willing to enforce the law. Moreover, despite the clear statement in common article 1 of all four Geneva Conventions that all state parties must ensure respect for the law, few states have taken this obligation seriously.

In recent years, one of the major international efforts has been to end impunity for violations of international law by individuals. For example, in the United Kingdom, Chilean General Augusto Pinochet was brought to court to face extradition proceedings. Although he was eventually released for health reasons, his immunity was later withdrawn when he returned to Chile. Many states now have laws that allow the prosecution of war criminals. And some, like Belgium and Spain, have attempted to use them in internationally prominent cases. The United States has also used its military power to capture international war criminals from weaker states, but not without sometimes committing equally egregious war crimes in the process, which it then has failed to adequately prosecute. Most notably the already mentioned International Criminal Court, which has more than a hundred and twenty state parties as of January 2005, is a means of ensuring that all international criminals can be tried.

Unfortunately, however, this enthusiasm has not been shared by all countries. Some of the most important states, that harbour some of the most hideous war criminals, remain outside the new system of international criminal justice and thus above the law.

* * *

These selected basic principles of international humanitarian law are the language by which the law is given meaning. They are the basis for both state and individual obligations under IHL. And they help us to understand the meaning of the law and how it should be applied.

Activity

Make a list of the basic principles of IHL and describe what they are and how you would explain them to a group of military officers training in the basic principles of IHL.

Chapter Three
PIL, IHRL, ICL, AND IHL

The relationship between IHL and general public international law (PIL) is as old as these two branches of law themselves. Twenty three years before the state, the traditional subject of international law, came into existence after the Peace of Westphalia in 1648, Hugo Grotius had postulated rules for the intercourse between states that included rules governing warfare. Thus the first writings on public international law include rules of warfare drawn mainly from the already existing practice of states.

Contemporary IHL is today usually viewed as a type of PIL. Consequently the general rules of state responsibility and treaty interpretation that have developed under PIL apply equally to IHL. Conversely this means that states' legal obligations under PIL may be based upon treaties of IHL. Documents of public international law such as the United Nations International Law Commission's Draft Articles on the Responsibility of States for Internationally Wrongful Acts provide for rules to help us understand how IHL applies. Other treaties that are part of the corpus of public international law that are of particular relevance to the IHL include the Vienna Convention on the Law of Treaties, the Charter of the United Nations, and the Statute of the International Court of Justice.

There can also be little doubt that there exists a close relationship between international human rights law (IHRL) and international humanitarian law. It is, however, a relationship that is often misunderstood. Sometimes lawyers believe that the two bodies of law attempt to achieve different aims, that one excludes the other, or, that one is not at all relevant to the other.

There is a similarity in the purposes of IHL and IHRL. These common goals include that of installing some humanity in an often inhumane world. Dunant's ability to champion both types of laws is evidenced by his belief that there was a common ground and a single spirit of humanity. His life is evidence that both IHL and IHRL have similar attributes that can be appreciated by an individual who is imbued with that spirit of humanity. This common purpose can be found in the shared objectives and purposes that have guided the development of both IHL and IHRL.

From the Convention for the Amelioration of the Condition of the Wounded in the Field, adopted by an inter-governmental conference held in Geneva on 5 August 1864 to more modern instruments such as 1996 Amended Protocol on Prohibitions or Restrictions on the use of Mines, Booby-Traps and Other Devices, much of IHL has been directed at protecting the individual human being. The protections of individuals range from prohibiting attacks against medical personnel and wounded in the 1864 Geneva Convention; to the more elaborate provisions of the 1949 Geneva Conventions, particularly the Fourth Geneva Convention Relative to the Protection of Civilians Persons in Time of War (GCIV), and the two 1977 Protocols securing for individuals respect for their persons, honour, family rights, religious convictions, manners, customs and property (art. 27(1) of GCIV); prohibiting discrimination (art. 21 of GCIV); prohibiting violence against civilians (art. 13 and 27 of GCIV); prohibiting reprisals against civilians (art. 33(3) of GCIV); prohibiting collective penalties (art. 33(2)); and prohibiting hostage taking (art. 33(1) and 34 of GCIV).

All of these rights have their parallels in universal and regional IHRL treaties, especially the International Covenant of Civil and Political Rights (ICCPR), 999 *UNTS* 171, which entered into force on 23 March 1976 and which over 150 states have ratified. For example, the ICCPR protects the rights to privacy and private life (art. 17); the rights to religious and cultural freedom (art. 18); contains a prohibition of discrimination (artt. 2 and 26); and prohibits torture, cruel, inhuman and degrading treatment (art. 7). Moreover, some instruments of IHRL specifically refer to states' duties to respect IHL, such as article 22 of the African Charter on the Rights and Welfare of the Child, OAU Doc. CAB/LEG/24.9/49 (1990), *entered into force* 29 November 1999.

The first instruments of IHL were written and ratified while war was still a legitimate tool of international affairs between states. It was not until the Kellogg-Briand Pact in 1928 that war was even theoretically condemned as illegal. In more contemporary times, war appears to be considered something that we are unable to prevent. Thus, IHL was created in the hope of adapting an inhuman situation to the more humane tendencies of human beings. It is this aspect of IHL that the International Court of Justice referred to in its *Advisory Opinion on the Illegality of the Threat or Use of Nuclear Weapons*, 1996 *ICJ Reports* 225 at 240, para. 25 and to which the Inter-American Commission of Human Rights was referring in its finding in *Abella v. Argentina*, Inter-Am. H.R. Comm. Report No. 55/97 at para. 161. Both bodies found that they could have recourse to IHL in order to consider killings taking place in a situation of armed conflict. It is, however, wrong to conclude that they were applying every source to which they referred. While the ICJ could indeed apply all the sources of international law falling under article 38(1) of its Statute, the Inter-American Commission could only apply the instruments of the Organization of American States to which the states before it were parties. This was made clear when the Court considered the preliminary objections of the government of Columbia in the *Las Palmeras Case*, Judgment on Preliminary Objections of February 4, 2000, Inter-Am. Ct. H.R. (Ser. C) No. 67 (2000). The Inter-American Court held that "[t] he fact that States members of the Organization of American States must observe the Geneva Conventions in good faith and adapt their domestic legislation to comply with those instruments does not give the Commission competence to infer State responsibility based on them."

Just as IHL law applies in times of war, IHRL usually applies in time of peace and indeed, may, on occasion, be derogated from during an armed conflict. The right of derogation is provided for in specific articles of some human rights treaties. These articles require that a state seeking to derogate from its human rights obligations provide notice in writing, including its reasons for derogation, the provisions being suspended, and the date when the suspension would be terminated. While this right exists, it has been rarely used. Thus, despite there having been well over a hundred wars since 1945—many between states who are parties to IHRL treaties—there have only been a handful of examples of derogations. In addition, some claims that a national emergency exists, like that of the Greek Generals' military junta in 1967, have been rejected as invalid.

Additionally, there are some important exceptions to instruments that allow the right of derogation. One of the most prominent is the African Charter of Human and Peoples' Rights. In the case of *Commission Nationale des Droits de l'Homme et des Libertés v. Chad*, Communication 74/92, AHG/Res. 250 (XXXII) (10 July 1996), decided just two days after the ICJ decision in the *Nuclear Weapons Case*, the African Commission on Human and Peoples' Rights unequivocally held that

> [t]he African Charter, unlike other human rights instruments, does not allow for states parties to derogate from their treaty obligations during emergency situations. Thus, even civil war in Chad cannot be used as an excuse by the State violating or permitting violations of rights in the African Charter.

Thus, avoiding the application of human rights by derogations is impossible for the fifty-three states that have ratified the African Charter on Human and Peoples' Rights. Another instrument prohibiting derogation from any of the human rights therein is the Convention on the Rights of the Child (CRC), UN G.A. Res. 44/25, annex, 44 UN GAOR Supp. (No. 49) at 167, U.N. Doc. A/44/49 (1989), which is ratified by 191 states—more than any other convention of either IHL or IHRL. The CRC contains thirty-nine articles providing for the human rights of children. Thus, in total there is a substantial number of international human rights provisions from which the right to derogate is denied.

Other exceptions are the non-derogable human rights. Among these is the right to life in the ICCPR. The ICJ recognized the non-derogable nature of this right in the *Nuclear Weapons Case* stating that "[i]n principle, the right not to be deprived of one's life applies also in hostilities" (para. 25). Other non-derogable rights include the prohibition of torture, freedom from slavery, freedom of religion and conscience, the right to equality before the law, the right not to be convicted of a crime that was made such *ex post facto*, the right not to be imprisoned for a contractual breach, the rights of the family, the right to a name, the right to a nationality, the right to participate in government and the rights of children.

Even where IHL applies there is often a Martens clause that expressly preserves the application of other laws, including IHRL. This clause first appeared in the 1907 Hague Convention, but has since reappeared in most IHL treaties thereafter. In Additional Protocol I the Martens clause reads:

> [i]n cases not covered by this Protocol or by other international agreements, civilians and combatants remain under the protection and authority of the principles of international law derived from established custom, from the principles of humanity and from the dictates of public conscience.

This clause echoes a general principle of international law that holds that a rule of international law continues to apply unless a later rule of law expressly derogates from it. In so far as treaties are concerned—the source of most IHRL—this rule is confirmed by the Vienna Convention on the Law of Treaties, UN Doc. A/CONF.39/27, *entered into force* 27 January 1980, in articles providing for the binding force of treaty obligations and the rule stating that other existing international legal obligations are not effected when a state withdraws from a treaty (Art. 43).

As a result of the above principles and provisions, IHRL has been applied in cases of armed conflict in such cases as *Loizidou v. Turkey*, 108 *ILR* 443 (1996), by the European Court of Human Rights, *Abella v. Argentina*, Report No. 55/97, para. 159, by the Inter-American

Commission of Human Rights, and *Commission Nationale des Droits de L'Homme et des Libertés v. Chad*, Communication 74/92, OAU Doc. AHG/ Res. 250 (XXXII) (10 July 1996), by the African Commission on Human and Peoples' Rights. And while on rare occasions IHL applies in times of peace. For example, use of the red cross and red crescent emblems is limited in even times of peace according to article 44, paragraph 2 of the Second Geneva Convention from 1949.

To most international lawyers, it is not the mere theory, but the practice of the law that counts. In this perspective, it is important to determine who is applying the relevant law. Although this may change somewhat with the establishment of the International Criminal Court, in practice there are many more cases brought before tribunals that must apply specific rules of IHRL.

Human rights are usually applied by international human rights bodies with mandates limited to certain treaties. These bodies must apply the IHRL to which their mandate is limited. Thus, the Human Rights Committee (HRC), the IHRL body created under the ICCPR, must apply the ICCPR and cannot decide to apply even general principles of public international law instead. Thus, if a case concerning the threat or use of nuclear weapons arises before the HRC, this body will be forced to apply the ICCPR. Even if the HRC turns to other areas of law for assistance, the HRC will have to decide whether the right to life in article 6 of the ICCPR is violated. Confronted with a practical, not theoretical case, such as the ICJ was in 1996, the HRC could not decide to turn to IHL to restrictively interpret article 6 of the ICCPR, at least not as easily as the ICJ. Instead, it is suggested, the HRC would first have to examine article 6, its drafting history, its own comments and expressions of views and other similar evidence. Only when this provided no way forward, could the HRC turn to IHL for assistance in interpretation as did the Inter-American Commission. Any other decision making process would be contrary to the HRC mandate under the ICCPR. This mandate, in the case of individual communications, is defined by article 1 of the Optional Protocol to the ICCPR that limits these communications to those concerning violations of the ICCPR. Similar limitations appear in article 44 of the ACHR and article 25 of the ECHR.

Finally, mention must be made of the relationship between IHL and the new field of international criminal law (ICL) that is in the early stages of its development. This relationship is characterized by the use of substantive obligations from IHL as the definitional basis of obligations under ICL. Thus the Statutes of the ICTY, ICTR, and ICC prohibit war crimes based, expressly in some cases, on obligations created by IHL treaties. In the Statute of the ICTY, for example, both the protection of individuals against attacks on their human dignity as well as prohibitions of some means and methods of warfare form the basis of international crimes. Sometimes new crimes related to war are prohibited such as the recruitment of children under 15 years-of-age, which is prohibited by article 8 of the Statute of the ICC.

It is also important to note that genocide—a crime that requires taking certain types of steps to destroy an ethnical, religious, racial or national group in whole or in part—is often considered a war crime although it is itself outlawed by a separate treaty that is often described as *sui generis* (*see* Convention on the Prevention and Punishment of the Crime of Genocide, 1021 *UNTS* 78 (1951)).

Activity

Divide into three groups. The first groups of individuals will represent governments (respondent). The second group of individuals will represent other individuals (applicant). The third group of individuals will represent judges of an international human rights tribunal. Work in each group to formulate arguments as to <u>why</u> and <u>how</u> the Court should use international humanitarian law in a case involving a riot at a prison in which about fifty foreign and national rebels from outside the prison—whose goal is to overthrow the existing government—assist the prisoners in taking over the prison. The respondent and applicant may liberally interpret these very general facts to support their arguments. The judges must provide some criteria for their decision making process. You will be told which regional or universal human rights treaty you are to apply as your point of reference.

Chapter Four
The Basic Rules of IHL

International humanitarian law consists of treaty law and customary law. Treaties are written agreements between states that reflect the explicit consent of the state parties. Like all treaties, those concerning IHL are to be interpreted in accordance with the rules of international law governing treaty interpretation. These rule are most importantly reflected in the Vienna Convention on the Law of Treaties (VCLT) from 1980 that has been ratified by the overwhelming majority of states in the international community and which in large part reflects rules that are customary international law.

The basic rules of treaty interpretation are found in articles 31 and 32 of the VCLT. These rules state that treaties should be interpreted in good faith in accordance with the ordinary meaning to be given to words in the context that they are used and in light of the object and purpose of the treaty (art. 31, VCLT). The context, article 31(2) says, is provided by the text, the preamble and any annexes to the treaty as well as any agreements or declarations that were made by all or some of the parties to the treaty. Attention may also be had to subsequent treaties, practice, relevant rule of international law, or a special meaning that the parties intended.

Article 32 of the VCLT provides for recourse to supplementary means of interpretation including the preparatory work and circumstances of conclusion of the treaty. Supplementary materials may be consulted to confirm a meaning resulting from the application of the rules in article 31 or when application of the usual rules still leaves a term "ambiguous" or "obscure" or "leads to a result which is manifestly absurd or unreasonable" (art. 32, VCLT). In the context of the four Geneva Conventions and their two Additional Protocols among the most important supplementary materials are the Commentaries that were promulgated the ICRC between 1952 and 1958. These materials explain the provisions of the above-mentioned treaties article by article.

Treaties create legal obligations between states and their violation gives rise to state responsibility. Thus when a state, one of its military personnel, or any other person over whom the state exercises sufficient control, violates a rule of international humanitarian law the state is internationally responsible. This responsibility entails at least the duties to restore the situation to that which existed before the violation took place in as far as this is possible and to provide compensation to any injured party. Failure to take these responsibilities seriously significantly devalues the rule of international law and promotes lawlessness around the world.

Customary international law is harder to discern, but just as legally binding as treaty law. Customary international law is traditionally said to consist of state practice and *opinio juris*. State practice is how states act in their international relations with each other. *Opinio juris* is the reason that states give for their actions. Both state practice and *opinio juris* must be present to form customary international law. That is, state must act in a certain way and they must manifest the opinion that they are bound to so act based on a legal obligation. The significant number of ratifications that the four Geneva Conventions enjoy is a good indication that the rules therein have entered the corpus of customary international law.

The recent publication compiled by Jean-Marie Henckaerts and Louise Doswald-Beck for the International Committee of the Red Cross (ICRC) entitled *Customary International Humanitarian Law* enumerates the rules that are considered customary international humanitarian law in the view of the many leading international lawyers who contributed to the publication. This project took almost a decade to complete and was finally published in early 2005. The basic rules that are discussed below are all listed in this study together with many more.

In both the case of treaties and customary international humanitarian law a state's actions are subject to the general rules of public international law relating to state responsibility. These rules are codified in International Law Commission's Draft Articles on the Responsibility of States for Internationally Wrongful Acts (ILC Draft Articles) (adopted in 2000 and sent to the UN General Assembly). The most basic of these rules establish that a state is responsible when (1) there is an act or omission attributable to the state and (2) when that act or omission violates and international legal obligation of the state.

The element of attributability is a matter of determining whether the acts of individuals are under the effective control of a state. The ILC Draft Articles indicate that certain acts or omissions are assumed to be attributable to a state. Such acts include the acts or omissions of a state's officials, members of its military, persons acting on the specific instructions of a state's government, other governments acting on the specific instructions of a state's government, among other types of acts and omissions.

The element of an international obligation is determined by examining the treaties a state has ratified and the rules of customary international law that are relevant to the action or omission in question.

It is through the application of these basic rules of the public international law of state responsibility that we can determine if a state has violated IHL.

Basic Rules

States have many international legal obligations under IHL. All of the rules cannot be enumerated in this book. And while the basic rules will be discussed in this Chapter, other Chapters will discuss many more rules. This starting point is one of the 'Basic Rules' of IHL.

In 1983 the ICRC published the *Basic Rules of the Geneva Conventions and their Additional Protocols*. While only the opinion of an NGO it lists seven basic rules that form an adequate basis for starting the discussion of the rules of IHL. Illustrations of all of these rules can be found in the four Geneva Conventions and their two Additional Protocols.

The seven rules listed by the ICRC are:

1. Persons who are *hors de combat*, prisoners of war, or combatants who do not otherwise take direct part in an armed conflict are entitled to respect for their physical and moral integrity and must be treated humanly in all circumstance. This is the overriding goal and rule of IHL. Otherwise put: combat is restricted to combatants.

2. It is forbidden to kill or injure an enemy that has surrendered or who is *hors de combat*. This principle expresses a basic dictate of humanity that is at the foundation of the Red Cross Movement and the work initiated by Henri Dunant. It is also a rule that can be found in some of the most ancient rules of warfare.

3. Wounded and sick must be cared for and those caring for them must be respected and protected. This includes not only medical personnel,

but also hospitals, field hospitals, clinics and all the employees of these establishments as long as they do not take up arms. This general rule is an accumulation of numerous detailed rules found in all four of the Geneva Conventions and the Additional Protocols.

4.   Prisoners of war must be protected by the power detaining them and allowed to correspond with their families and receive adequate care and relief. This rule forms the basic protection of prisoners of war that is elaborated in Hague Regulations of 1907 and which has been specified in more detail in the Third Geneva Convention relative to the Treatment of Prisoners of War.

5.   Every person is entailed to due process, fair trial, humane treatment, and to be held only individually responsible for violation of the law. This rule reflects the basic principles of international human rights law that have been incorporated into IHL.

6.   The means and methods of warfare are limited by the requirements of the law and the general principles of necessity, proportionality, and subsidiarity. This rule encompasses the fundamentals of the Hague law.

7.   Attacks shall be directed against military objects only and civilians shall be protected from attack. Again this rule embodies a foundational principle of IHL and must be interpreted by taking into account the general principles of necessity, proportionality, and subsidiarity.

While these seven rules by no means express the full breath of IHL, they do provide a set of rules that if memorized assist in understanding the more complex and numerous provisions of IHL.

The Sources of IHL

The above rules of IHL are both found in treaties and are part of customary international humanitarian law. We will concentrate on the treaty law as it is easier to find and to understand. Additionally, the major treaties of IHL have been ratified by almost every country in the world.

The treaties that will be discussed in the following two chapters can be put in two categories. The first category concerns those treaties restricting the means and methods of warfare. The second category includes those treaties concentrating on protecting individual's basic human rights.

In the first category, which is sometimes referred to as the Hague law, we will discuss several of the Hague Conventions of promulgated between 1899 and 1907. We will also discuss the Saint Petersburg Declaration

Renouncing the Use, in Time of War, of certain Explosive Projectiles dating all the way back to 1868 and the Washington Treaty relating to the Use of Submarines and Noxious Gases in Warfare from 1922. Neither of these emanated from The Hague, but both are examples of a growing body of law relating to the means and methods that may be used in an armed conflict. We will also examine some of the most recent instruments of IHL such as the Convention on Prohibitions or Restrictions on the Use of Certain Conventional Weapons Which May be Deemed to be Excessively Injurious or to Have Indiscriminate Effects from 1980 and the Convention on the Prohibition of the Use, Stockpiling, Production and Transfer of Anti-Personnel Mines and on Their Destruction from 1997. Of relevance will also be the jurisprudence of the International Court of Justice in its *Advisory Opinion on the Legality of the Use and Threat of Nuclear Weapons* that considered that the use of nuclear weapons would almost certainly violate international humanitarian law.

In the second category the focus will be on the four Geneva Conventions from 1949 and their concentration on protecting individuals.

The First Geneva Convention for the Amelioration of the Condition of the Wounded and Sick in Armed Forces in the Field protects combatants injured in battles on land. It contains 64 articles and two annexes.

The Second Geneva Convention for the Amelioration of the Condition of Wounded, Sick and Shipwrecked Members of Armed Forces at Sea protects combatants incapacitated from continuing to participate in an armed conflict while at sea. It is the shortest of the four treaties and contains 63 articles and one annex.

The Third Geneva Convention relative to the Treatment of Prisoners of War protects combatants who have been captured. It contains detailed rules as to how they should be treated and what should happen to them once and armed conflict ends. It contains 143 articles and five annexes.

And the Fourth Geneva Convention relative to the Protection of Civilian Persons in Time of War protects non-combatants in armed conflicts and in times of occupation. It is the longest of the four Conventions and contains 159 articles and three annexes.

The four Geneva Conventions have been ratified by 191 states as of September 2003. Two Additional Protocols that were promulgated in 1977 to cover some of the gaps left by the 1949 treaties have enjoyed less support. Nevertheless, in Africa where the most armed conflicts have taken place over the last several decades, almost every country has ratified both the four Geneva Conventions as well as the two Protocols. Some notable exceptions are Eritrea, Somalia, and Sudan who have not ratified the Additional Protocols.

The First Additional Protocol extends the four Geneva Conventions to wars of national liberation, without prejudice to the recognition of the legitimacy of national liberation movements. This treaty is ratified by one hundred and sixty one states. This treaty extends the protections of the four Geneva Conventions to all medical personnel, hospitals and hospital ships (artt. 8-31). It creates an obligation to search for missing persons (art. 33). It adds to the protections of the civilian population that are found in the fourth Geneva Convention from 1949 (artt. 68-71). It provides for the protection of civil defense organizations, both their personnel and their activities (artt. 61-67). And it adds specificity to states' obligations to implement IHL (artt. 80-91) and expressly classifies breaches as war crimes to which individual responsibility attaches.

The Second Additional Protocol extends the protections in non-international armed conflicts that are found in common article 3 of the four Geneva Convention. This treaty is ratified by 156 states. This treaty strengthens the fundamental guarantees for non-combatants (art. 4). It also establishes more detailed guarantees of due process and fair trial for persons prosecuted in connection with an armed conflict (artt. 5 and 6); regulates the movement of civilians (art. 17); protects sick, wounded, and shipwrecked persons (art. 7); protects religious personnel, and medical personnel, units, and means of transport (artt. 9-11); and restricts the use of the red cross emblems (art. 12).

The two Additional Protocols to the 1949 Geneva Conventions, especially the first, will be discussed in both chapters because they contain obligations relevant to both categories.

The Rule of Non-Discrimination

There are some rules that are customary international law and found numerous instruments of IHL. These rules in include the principle of non-discrimination.

Non-discrimination is found in common article 3 of all four Geneva Conventions, among other places. Common article 3 states that "[p]ersons taking no active part in the hostilities, including members of armed forces who have laid down their arms and those placed 'hors de combat' by sickness, wounds, detention, or any other cause, shall in all circumstances be treated humanely, without any adverse distinction founded on race, colour, religion or faith, sex, birth or wealth, or any other similar criteria." This rule is also stated in article 16 of the Third Geneva Convention and article 13 of the Fourth Geneva Convention. It is also a rule of customary international humanitarian law.

The Rule of Distinction

Parties to an armed conflict of either an international or non-international nature must distinguish between combatants and civilians. This rule was first enunciated in the Declaration of St. Petersburg in 1863 and has more recently been repeated in articles 48, 51(2) and 52(2) of the First Additional Protocol.

The rule is usually stated as a prohibition of attacking civilians. It requires states to only attack military objects and not to attack civilians or objects necessary to the survival of civilians. It is a rule that appears to have achieved the status of customary international law. It is also the basis of a war crime under international criminal law (art. 8(2)(e)(i) of the ICC Statute). More details about this rule can be found in Chapter Five dealing with restrictions on the means and methods states may use to wage war.

The principle of distinction forms the basis for other rules prohibiting indiscriminate attacks, requiring attacks be proportional to a legitimate military objective, requiring precautions be taken when carrying out attacks, and that the collateral effects of an attack be mitigated.

Activity

Draft a basic list of the ten most important rules of IHL in appropriate language that can be carried with all soldiers in the field. Be prepared to justify why you have included the ten rules that are on your list and why you have stated them in the language that you have used.

Chapter Five
Means and Methods of Warfare

Restricting the means and methods of warfare means balancing military necessity against the protection of non-combatants from the harm brought about by the waging of war. This can be seen in the preamble to Hague Convention on Land Warfare of 1899 and the annexed Regulations on Land Warfare of 1907 which claim to have "been inspired by the desire to diminish the evils of war, as far as military requirements permit." Article 23 of the Regulations also indicates how this works in practice by prohibiting the destruction or seizure of enemy property, "unless such destruction or seizure be imperatively demanded by the necessities of war."

Ultimately the concept of military necessity might be traced back to the 1863 Lieber Instructions which speak about it as a defense to violations of the law.

Even more ancient is the recognition that the means and methods of warfare must be limited. Hugo Grotius in *De iure belli ac pacis*, published in 1625, called for *temperamenta belli* or the need to limit means of warfare. In 1907, the Hague Regulations repeated this in Article 22 unambiguously stating that "[t]he right of belligerents to adopt means of injuring the enemy is not unlimited," but failing to define this interdiction in greater detail.

On 13 January 1969, the United Nations General Assembly adopted Resolution 2444 (XXIII) calling for limits on the means and methods of warfare. But this general principle has not been incorporated into the four Geneva Conventions from 1949. It was not until the First Additional Protocol in 1977 that governments agreed to state in unequivocal language that "the right of the Parties to the conflict to choose methods or means of warfare is not unlimited" (art. 35). This article then goes on to state in two subsequent paragraphs of the article that

> 2. It is prohibited to employ weapons, projectiles and material and methods of warfare of a nature to cause superfluous injury or unnecessary suffering.

> 3. It is prohibited to employ methods or means of warfare which are intended, or may be expected, to cause widespread, long-term and severe damage to the natural environment.

The ICRC *Commentary* to this article stresses in very strong language that "[c]ontrary to what some might think or wish, in law there are no exceptions to this fundamental rule" (Sandoz, Y., Swinarski, C., and Zimmermann, B., (eds.), *Commentary on the Additional Protocols of 8 June 1977 to the Geneva Conventions of 12 August 1949*, ICRC, Geneva (1987) at 391). And it goes on to warn that "[i]f one were to renounce the rule, by which Parties to the conflict do not have an unlimited right, one would enter the realm of arbitrary behaviour, i.e., an area where law does not exist, whether this was intended or not. It is quite another matter to determine the actual scope of the principle, and the specific rules and practices implied by it, which may differ with the times, depending on the prevalent customs and treaties. These variations do not affect the principle itself but its application." (*Id.*)

Prohibited Means of Warfare (Weapons)

Prohibited means of warfare are weapons that cause superfluous injuries and unnecessary suffering; cannot adequately discriminate between combatants and civilians; or cause severe long-term environmental damage.

The first efforts to control the means of warfare are found in several instruments going back to the Saint Petersburg Declaration of 1868 and forward to the 1980 Weapons Convention.

The 1868 Saint Petersburg Declaration Renouncing the Use, in Time of War, of certain Explosive Projectiles, although short, defined in detail the types or projectiles or missiles prohibited as "any projectile of a weight below 400 grammes, which is either explosive or charged with fulminating or inflammable substances."

The Hague Peace Conferences between 1899 and 1907 also adopted a series of declarations aimed at limiting weapons that cause superfluous injuries and unnecessary suffering. These declarations were sometimes confusingly in the form of legally binding treaties. In these declarations states agreed to ban the dropping of bombs from hot air balloons, to denounce the use of asphyxiating or deleterious gases, and to abstain from the use of bullets which expand or flatten easily in the human body. Each of these declarations, however, stated they were only binding when both parties to an armed conflict had adhered to them.

After the First World War states took new steps to ban certain types of weapons. The 1922 Treaty relating to the Use of Submarines and Noxious Gases in Warfare banned "the use in war of asphyxiating, poisonous or other gases, and all analogous liquids, materials or devices" and even declared this ban customary international humanitarian law (art. 5). A 1925 Protocol for the Prohibition of the Use of Asphyxiating, Poisonous or Other Gases, and of Bacteriological Methods of Warfare also limited the *use* of poisonous gases. This treaty was attached to a treaty supervising arms trade and banning the production of poisonous gases that never entered into force, although the just mentioned Protocol did enter into force.

The above mentioned instruments prohibited the use of certain types of weapons, but did not ban the production and stockpiling of these weapons. To address these deficiencies states adopted the Convention on the Prohibition of the Development, Production and Stockpiling of Bacteriological (Biological) and Toxin Weapons and on their Destruction in 1972 that was simultaneously opened for signature in London, Moscow and Washington. In 1993 these limitations were strengthened by the Convention on the prohibition of the development, production, stockpiling and use of chemical weapons and on their destruction.

Around the same time, another reflection of the cold war mentality was the adoption of the first treaties that attempted to limit nuclear proliferation. While still in force for many counties, the most dangerous nuclear power, the United States has disavowed several of these treaties and has even used low level nuclear weapons. It has also, more worryingly, threaten to use more serious nuclear weapons. One must wonder whether a ban on nuclear weapons can do anything more than provide the United States a military advantage if this country refuses to fully participate in the regime? This question is especially troubling given that the United States is the only country ever to use nuclear weapons.

There has also been concern about small caliber weapons. In 1979-1980 the United Nations Conference on Prohibitions or Restrictions on the Use of Certain Conventional Weapons Which May be Deemed to be Excessively Injurious or to Have Indiscriminate Effects failed to reach agreement on a protocol limiting such weapons.

The modern expression of these prohibitions is found in the Convention on Prohibitions or Restrictions on the Use of Certain Conventional

Weapons Which May be Deemed to be Excessively Injurious or to Have Indiscriminate Effects opened for signature and ratification in Geneva on 10 October 1980. This umbrella treaty serves a coordinating function for its several protocols, at least two of which every state party must ratify when becoming party to the main treaty.

The first Protocol on Non-Detectable Fragments entered into force in 1983 and prohibits "any weapon the primary effect of which is to injure by fragments which in the human body escape detection by X-rays." The second Protocol on Prohibitions or Restrictions on the Use of Mines, Booby-Traps and Other Devices from 1980 was the first to ban landmines, perhaps the weapons most threatening to civilian populations today. This protocol has been amended in 1996 and is now accompanied by the 1997 Ottawa Convention on the Prohibition of the Use, Stockpiling, Production and Transfer of Anti-Personnel Mines and on their Destruction. A third protocol bans incendiary weapons and a fourth protocol bans blinding laser weapons. A deficiency of the Ottawa treaty is the absence of a mechanism by which to ensure it is implemented by the state parties.

The 1907 Hague (VIII) Convention Relative to the Laying of Automatic Submarine Contact Mines restricts the use of such mines and of torpedoes when they have "the sole object of intercepting commercial shipping" (art. 1). The International Court of Justice held this Convention to have been violated by the United States' laying of mines in Nicaragua's territorial waters. *Case Concerning Military and Paramilitary Activities in and against Nicaragua (Nicaragua v. United States)*, [1986] *ICJ Reports* 14 (27 June 1986).

As new and more dangerous and more deadly weapons continue to be created it is likely that the law will expand in an attempt to protect civilians. Can the law, however, really keep up with the weapons research laboratories of the United States and other weapons exporters?

Prohibited Methods of Warfare

Since time immemorial up until the 19th century there were few restrictions on the methods of warfare. Instead states were free to use whatever methods would best defeat the enemy. While it is true that even Hugo Grotius recognized some limits on the methods of warfare, his arguments were not completely convincing to states and their leaders. These sovereigns were concerned with winning wars at any cost. Even the torture or starvation of a population of an enemy was considered acceptable as a method of warfare.

The 1907 Hague Regulations prohibit the treacherous killing of an enemy in article 23(b). Treachery is defined as the "improper use of a flag of truce, of the national flag or of the military insignia and uniform of the enemy, as well as the distinctive badges of the Geneva Convention" (art. 23(f)). Article 24 of the same instrument, however, allows ruses of war. The Regulations also prohibit the killing or mistreatment of *hors de combat* (art. 23(c)); to declare no quarter be given (art. 23(d)); to destroy the property of the enemy, unless required by military necessity (art. 23(g)); and to compel the nationals of an enemy state "to take part in the operations of war directed against their own country" (art. 23(h)).

Reprisals against the persons or property of an enemy state are also prohibited both under customary IHL and in several treaties. The first treaty provision prohibiting reprisals appeared in the Second Geneva Convention relative to the Treatment of Prisoners of War, 118 *L.N.T.S.* 303, from 27 July 1929. This has now been most comprehensively codified in seven articles of the First Additional Protocol (artt. 20, 51(6), 52(1), 53, 54(4), 55(2), 56(4)) and is found in articles in all four Geneva Conventions (art. 46, GCI; art. 47, GCII; art. 47, GCIII; and art. 33(3), GCIV).

In the 20th century efforts were also made to limit naval warfare. Several of the Hague Conventions dealt with different aspects of naval warfare such as a prohibition on laying automatic contact submarine mines on the open seas (Hague VIII), capture at sea (Hague XI), and neutrality at sea (Hague XIII). An attempt was also made to put submarine warfare, a relatively new phenomena, under controls because it threatened some established naval powers as well as general commercial shipping routes. Thus the 1907 Hague VII treaty was complemented by a 1922 Treaty relating to the Use of Submarines and Noxious Gases in Warfare that (art. 3) and a 1936 Procès Verbal concerning Part IV of the 1930 London Treaty that never entered into force, protected merchant vessels from attack. Attempts to lay down broad rules for warfare at sea have not been so successful thus only non-binding instruments exist (which do profess to state rules of customary international law) such as the 1913 Oxford Manual on the Laws of Naval War and, the more recent, 1994 San Remo Manual on international law applicable to armed conflicts at sea

The First Additional Protocol also prohibits attacks that will cause severe damage to the environment (artt. 35(3) and 55). The Convention on the prohibition of military or any hostile use of environmental modification techniques from 1976 emphasizes and details these protections. According to this treaty each state party "undertakes not to engage in military or any other hostile use of environmental modification techniques having widespread, long lasting or severe effects as the means of destruction, damage or injury to any other State Party." Environmental modification techniques are defined as "any technique for changing—through the deliberate manipulation of natural processes—the dynamics, composition or structure of the Earth, including its biosphere, lithosphere, hydrosphere and atmosphere, or of outer space." The 1961 Treaty on Outer Space prohibits the use of outer space for the positioning of certain weapons. It is relevant to point to that these obligations are objective and are violated whether or not a state intended to violate them, if acts attributable to the state do in fact violate the prohibitions.

An area that has received more concentrated effort since the Second World War is the protection of cultural property. In 1954 a treaty was adopted under the auspices of UNESCO. The Convention for the Protection of Cultural Property in the Event of Armed Conflict and its two protocols contain detailed rules for protecting cultural property. Cultural property for the purposes of this treaty includes "(a) movable or immovable property of great importance to the cultural heritage of every people, such as monuments of architecture, art or history, whether religious or secular; archaeological sites; groups of buildings which, as a whole, are of historical or artistic interest; works of art; manuscripts, books and other objects of artistic, historical or archaeological interest; as well as scientific collections and important collections of books or archives or of reproductions of the property defined above; (b) buildings whose main and effective purpose is to preserve or exhibit the movable cultural property defined in sub-paragraph (a) such as museums, large libraries and depositories of archives, and refuges intended to shelter, in the event of armed conflict, the movable cultural property defined in subparagraph (a); (c) centres containing a large amount of cultural property as defined in sub-paragraphs (a) and (b), to be known as 'centres containing monuments'..." (art. 1). Protected property is to be designated in an International Register (art. 12 of the Regulation for the Execution of the Convention for the Protection of Cultural Property in Event of Armed Conflict annexed to the Convention) and marked by a blue and white emblem (art. 6 of the Convention). Such cultural property is protected from "any act of hostility" (art. 9 of the Convention).

Also prohibited are attacks on protected persons—civilian, relief workers, and medical personnel—as well as protected places—cultural objects, hospitals, schools, undefended towns, installations necessary to the survival of the civilian population, and installations that may cause danger to the civilian population such as dams and nuclear power plants. Attacks that cause damage to the environment are also prohibited both under article 55 of the First Additional Protocol from 1977 and by the Convention on the prohibition of military or any other hostile use of environmental modification techniques, annexed to U.N.G.A. Res. 31/172 (10 December 1972).

Today although such excesses are prohibited, they still unfortunately occur. For example, during the 1990s the United States in coordination with many states of the United Nations imposed sanctions on Iraq that have been scientifically shown to have been responsible for killing as many as 500,000 children. International Study Team, *The Humanitarian*

Impact in the Aftermath of the Gulf War (1991). Nevertheless, the most notable developments in law emphasize the prohibition of such actions. For example, article 54 of the First Additional Protocol and article 14 of the Second Additional Protocol, clearly prohibit starvation as a method of warfare. This prohibition is also undoubtedly today part of customary IHL.

Similarly, the bombing of "towns, villages, dwellings, or buildings which are undefended is prohibited" (art. 25 of the Hague Regulations of 1907). Nevertheless, such bombings take place. The NATO allies, for example, bombed both the undefended Chinese Embassy in Belgrade as well as the undefended Radio B92 building during it campaign to force the Serbian army to withdraw from Kosovo in 1999. There are similar examples from the United States' wars of aggression against Afghanistan (2001) and Iraq (1991) and (2003) and by both sides in the war between Eritrea and Ethiopia that flared up in 2000.

The 1922 Treaty relating to the Use of Submarines and Noxious Gases in Warfare, which has been mentioned above because it prohibited means of warfare, also banned methods of warfare. This treaty prohibited submarines from attacking merchant vessels if the vessels agreed to be inspected. A similar treaty was agreed to in 1937, The Nyon Agreement, which extended the prohibition on the attacks on merchant vessels to other types of military sea-going vessels.

At the end of the eighties the international community turned its attention to mercenaries—soldiers without any particular national allegiance who are fighting because they are paid to fight. In 1989, states adopted the International Convention against the Recruitment, Use, Financing and Training of Mercenaries. This treaty contains an elaborate definition of 'mercenary' and makes them as well as their financing, use or training an international crime and an act that entails state responsibility.

A 2000 Protocol to the Convention on the Rights of the Child (CRC), the most widely ratified human rights treaty in the world, rises from 15 to 18 the age from which children may participate in an armed conflict. The Protocol has not yet enjoyed the same wide support as the CRC, and neither is ratified by the United States.

One method of warfare that is encouraged by IHL is that the commanding officer of an army that is about to attack should give warning to the civil authorities of a city or town to be attacked. Unfortunately, this has not received an enthusiastic response from the commanders of armies in the field who feel that they can gain the advantage of surprise by failing to warn the enemy.

Military Necessity, Proportionality, and Precaution in Attacks

The test of whether a means or method of war is allowed is often a test of whether or not the act is militarily necessary or proportional to the harm that may be caused to non-combatants.

As indicated in Chapter Two the test of military necessity means that a commander or soldier involved in an attack must decide (1) if their is a legitimate military objective to be achieved, and (2) if the means or method of achieving this legitimate military objective are those that will cause the least harm to individuals who are not combatants or to facilities necessary to their survival.

The principle of proportionality is often used to characterize the test of military necessity. It is perhaps better to view the test of proportionality as part of the test of military necessity. It requires an attacker not only identify a military objective and the least harmful means or method of attack, but also to balance the degree of harm that might be done in relation to military advantage gained. This test may be viewed as a further restriction on an attacker's ability to attack a military object when harm to non-combatants might result because it requires an additional evaluation of the necessity of the attack. Or it may be viewed as a mitigation or even replacement of at least part of the test of military necessity when it allows an attacker to merely evaluate whether or not the military advantage to be gained justifies an attack.

The test or proportionality is stated by the ICRC in its seminal work in *Customary International Humanitarian Law* in the Rule that "[l]aunching an attack which may be expected to cause incidental loss of civilian life, injury to civilians, damage to civilian objects, or a combination thereof, which would be excessive in relation to the concrete and direct military advantage anticipated, is prohibited" (Rule 14 in Henckaerts, J-M., and Doswald-Beck, L., *Customary International Humanitarian Law: Volume 1: Rules*, 46-50 (2005)). It should be recognized, however, that there is no uniformity of interpretation concerning the test of proportionality. It is a complex test that is likely to require significant analytical skills on behalf of lawyers advising governments or judges determining the legality of an attack when non-combatants are harmed.

Precautionary Principle and the Environment

A general principle of law that is of increasing importance to evaluating the legality of attacks that cause harm to the environment. The principle itself emanates from the realm of environmental law. It requires that a state take due precautions to ensure that its attacks do not cause undue harm to the environment, especially long-term or irreversible harm.

The central feature of this principle is the duty to act prior to an attack. In practice this will often require that a state put into place rules or instructions for its armed forces that require them to take into account the harm that may accrue to the environment. Therefore, when the environment is harmed by an attack, a state that can not prove that it has taken precaution in advance of the attack will be international responsible for a violation of international humanitarian law.

The precautionary principle is most succinctly stated in Principle 15 of the Rio Declaration on the Environment adopted in 1972. It has been incorporated into IHL by the interpretation of state practice by the International Court of Justice (in both the *Nuclear Tests Case* in 1974 and the *Nuclear Weapons Advisory Opinion* in 1996).

Activity

You are a military commander with the following resources to your disposal and a United Nations Security Council mandate supported by all the Member States (with the exception of the USA which has withdrawn from the UN) to invade the United States to prevent it from taking over the world and making everyone in the world speak English and salute the American flag, as its President has announced is its intention.

You have at your disposal 1,550,000 soldiers, 15,000 jet fighters, 1000 bombers that drop between 5 kilogram and 5000 kilogram bombs, 2000 highly accurate smart bombs, 7000 nuclear bombs, 120,000 500 kilogram bombs, 100 5 kilogram bombs, 2500 5000 kilogram bombs, 5500 heavy armored tanks, 15,000 vials of anthrax, 25,000 mustard gas canisters, 1,500,000 land mines, as well as 2200 drone unmanned airplanes, 120 battleships, 12 aircraft carries, 15 submarines.

Assume the enemy has 750 nuclear weapon silos, 2500 military bases, 2500 response batteries, 200 air bases, 750,000 soldiers, 3000 heavily armed tanks, 2,000,000 anti-tank landmines, 1500 battle ships, 25 aircraft carriers, and 350 submarines.

Which means and methods of warfare are lawful for you to employ and how will you employ them to quickly knock out the United States' capacity to respond while minimizing civilian casualties?

Can you attack a nuclear power plant, a museum or a church in New York City? Can you attack a hospital which has 100 soldiers out of 500 patients in it if the soldiers are merely hiding, but not attacking from it. Can you use tear gas or lasers weapons to blind the enemy in an assault?

Chapter Six
Protecting the Individual

The major contribution of IHL in recent years has been its contribution to the protection of individuals. This law originated in its codified form in the first treaties of IHL and has been most comprehensively articulated in the four Geneva Conventions and their two Additional Protocols.

Fundamental Guarantees

The fundamental guarantees of IHL might be said to start with article 3 common to all four Geneva Conventions. Although by its express words this article applies "[i]n the case of armed conflict not of an international character." Article 3 has been held to reflect rules of customary international law by the International Court Justice. *Case Concerning Military and Paramilitary Activities in and against Nicaragua (Nicaragua v. United States)*, [1986] *ICJ Reports* 14 (27 June 1986) at para. 114. As such, it applies to all armed conflicts and prohibits the following acts against non-combatants, including those who are *hors de combat*:

(a) violence to life and person, in particular murder of all kinds, mutilation, cruel treatment and torture;

(b) taking of hostages;

(c) outrages upon personal dignity, in particular humiliating and degrading treatment;

(d) the passing of sentences and the carrying out of executions without previous judgment pronounced by a regularly constituted court, affording all the judicial guarantees which are recognized as indispensable by civilized peoples.

It also requires that the "wounded and sick shall be collected and cared for."

But while this solitary article applies to non-international armed conflicts or civil wars, the majority of the protections accorded protected persons only apply in international armed conflicts.

Each of the four Geneva Conventions provides for some basic fundamental guarantees. The first Geneva Convention provides that sick and wounded ex-combatants must be treated humanely (at. 12) and given medical assistance. Similarly medical personnel attached to the armed forces or assisting in the medical treatment of wounded and sick ex-combatants, must not be attacked.

All four Geneva Convention and the two Additional Protocols require that protected persons be treated in a non-discriminate manner in respect to their rights (art. 12, GCI; art. 12, GCII; art. 16, GCIII; art. 27, GCIV; art. 9, PI; art. 2(1), PII) and that women be treated "with all consideration due to their sex" (*see* e.g. art. 14, GCIII).

Civilians Generally

The Fourth Geneva Convention prohibits certain acts against the civilian population in attempt to protect civilians as far as possible from the horrors of war. These protections are non-derogable and cannot even be suspended by the protected person themselves.

According to all four Geneva Conventions all protected persons are protected against willfully killing, torture, inhumane treatment, non-consensual biological experiments, great suffering, and injury to body or health.

Protected persons under the first, second and fourth Geneva Conventions also enjoy protection from the destruction of their private property in a manner not justified by military necessity (art. 50, GCI, art. 51, GCII, and art. 147, GCIV). Violation of this prohibition is a grave breach and a serious war crime.

Civilians, like prisoners of war (art. 130, GCIII), may further not be compelled to serve in the armed forces of a hostile power (art. 147, GCIV) or deprived of fair and regular trial (art. 147, GCIV).

Civilians may not be unlawfully deported or transferred, unlawfully confined or taken hostage (art. 147, GCIV).

Although the modifier 'unlawful' is not clearly defined, it may be considered with certainty to at least prohibit deportation, transfer, or confinement without any reason being given. Pictet, J., (ed.), *Commentaries: IV Geneva Convention Relative to the Protection of Civilian Persons in Time of War*, ICRC: Geneva (1958) at 599.

The possibility of creating protected zones for civilians is considered in articles 14 and 15 of the Fourth Geneva Convention and articles 56, 60 and Annex I of Additional Protocol I. In these zones all military activity are prohibited.

Civilians are also protected by provisions of Additional Protocol I that prohibits, when these acts result in death or serious physical injury, attacking civilians, indiscriminate attacks, attacks against targets containing dangerous forces, non-defended locations, and misuse of a protective emblem (art. 85, PI). This same article protects a person who is *hors de combat* from being the object of attack.

Article 85 of the first Additional Protocol also prohibits, when these acts are committed willfully, the transfer by an occupying power of parts of its own civilian population to occupied territories, the unjustifiable delay in the repatriation of prisoners of war, *apartheid*, and other practices involving outrages to personal dignity.

Violations of the above provisions constitute grave breaches which must be punished by the state under whose responsibility they fall.

Sick and Wounded Combatants

When a combatant is wounded, sick, surrenders, or is captured, he or she is considered to be prevented from taking part in the armed conflict. As a result of this condition the individual become *hors de combat* and enjoys protections from attack that he or she did not have as a combatant. This general principle, which also includes those who have been shipwrecked, is found in article 12 of First and Second Geneva Conventions.

The possibility of creating protected zones for *hors de combat* is provided for in article 23 and Annex I of the First Geneva Convention. These zones insulate the protected persons from attack.

Detainees and Prisoners

The treatment of prisoners of war (POWs) is governed by the Third Geneva Convention. This Convention provides that all POWs are in the hands of the detaining power not the soldiers who captured them (art. 12). The terms of the Convention apply from the time that a POW falls into the power of an enemy until the time of his release and repatriation (art. 5).

The protections of the Third Geneva Convention are extensive. There is a general obligation to protect detainees (art. 19) and a requirement that a POW be treated humanely (art. 13) and without discrimination (art. 16). There are also limits on how POWs can be questioned (art. 17), the right for POWs to retain private property (art. 18), the right for POWs to be kept in quarters no less than those of the soldiers of the capturing army (art. 25), the right to adequate food (artt. 26 and 28), clothing (art. 27), and adequate medical care (artt. 29-31), respect for a POWs religion (artt. 34 and 35), the right to have access to intellectual and sports activities while in captivity (art. 38), the right to work and benefits from one's work (artt. 18, 28, 49-51, 57, and 59-62), the right to receive humanitarian relief (artt. 72, 74, and 75), and the right to correspond with family and others, including lawyers (artt. 71, 74, 76, and 77). POWs who escape of attempt to escape are protected from harsh penalties (artt. 42, and 91-93). POWs also have an unequivocal right to be released and repatriated without delay after the cessation of active hostilities (art. 118).

While these rights of POWs may be limited for reasons of administration and security, limitations that make these rights illusory or *de minimus* violate the Third Geneva Convention and are war crimes.

The Fourth Geneva Convention provides for the treatment of civilian internees—civilians who are being interned or detained "only if the security of the Detaining Power makes it absolutely necessary" (art. 42). Article 11 of Additional Protocol I adds to the protections accorded and internees in the Fourth Geneva Convention (artt. 79-143). In particular, medical experimentation, physical mutilation and assault are prohibited.

Medical and Religious Personnel

Medical and religious personnel that belong to the armed forces or accompany the armed forces of a country are protected from attack by articles in three of the four Geneva Conventions (artt. 40 and 41, GCI; art. 42, GCII; art. 20, GCIV). The two Additional Protocols extend this protection to medical personnel whether or not they are attached to, or accompanying, a military unit. Additional Protocol I provides this protection in articles 8, 14 and 15. Article 16 of this Protocol also protects individuals on medical missions. Additional Protocol II provides this protection to medical personnel in non-international armed conflicts in articles 9, 10, and 11.

Medical Transports and Facilities

Not only medical personnel, but also medical transports or transports of medical goods and medical facilities are provided significant protections in three of the four Geneva Conventions and the two Additional Protocols (see artt. 19, 36, 39, 42, and 43, GCI; artt. 22, 24-27, 38, 39, 41, and 43, GCII; artt. 18, 21, and 22, GCIV; artt. 15, 16 and 18, PI, and art. 11, PII). These protected units or facilities must not be attacked and must be respected and protected by both the state to which they belong and an attacking or occupying state's armed forces. Medical transports may be by land, sea, or air. Medical facilities or medical units include not only buildings such as hospitals and medical stores, but also blood transfusion units, blood storage units, medical testing equipment and facilities, stretchers, surgical apparatus, medicines, dressings, etc. In every case these units or facilities must be assigned to strictly medical purposes or they may lose their protection. The protection these units or facilities enjoy also mean that when territory is occupied by a state the medical units and facilities must be respected and allowed to continue to serve their purpose of contributing to medical care (art. 14, PI).

Registration

Each of the four Geneva Conventions requires the registration of certain protected persons. Creating Registers for some protected groups of persons is an important part of protecting these persons. The groups that have protection to date and for which a registration requirements exists are *hors de combat*, shipwrecked persons, prisoners of war, children who have been separated from their parents, and detained or interned civilians. It is important that these persons are always registered by the party under whose power they come and that this information is provided to the protecting powers or the ICRC. When they are not registered or are hidden from these observers then these already vulnerable persons are rendered even more vulnerable.

Registration also contributes to the protection of cultural property. Article 13 of the Regulations for the execution of the Convention for the protection of cultural property in event of armed conflict makes provision for an International Register of Cultural Property Under Special Protection that is to be protected once registered.

Emblems and Symbols

Emblems and symbols play an important part in IHL. By marking facilities or transport vehicles with the proper emblem they are protected from attack. Conversely, misuse of the protective emblems are serious offenses (see artt. 44, 53, 54, GCI; artt. 44-45, GCII; artt. 18, 37, 38, 66, 85, and Annex I, PI, art. 12, PII, and artt. 6, 10, 12, and 17 of the 1954 Hague Convention on the protection of cultural property). The most well known of these emblems may be the Red Cross or Red Crescent (the Israeli Red Cross's Star of David does not enjoy similar protection because it is unilateral used and never agreed upon by other states). These two emblems are, however, not the only ones that provide protection.

There are emblems to protect cultural property, to protect civil defense organizations, to protect objects that are dangerous to the civilian population. While these emblems provide protection from attack, it is not allowed to attempt to protect military objects by using these emblems or by using human shields. Such actions are serious violations of IHL.

Children

Children enjoy special protection both under IHL and under international human rights law during wartime. The following are some of the special protections afforded children.

Perhaps most importantly children under 15 should be prohibited from participating in an armed conflict (art. 77, PI). Article 38 of the Convention on the Rights of the Child (CRC) extends this protection to non-international armed conflicts. Additional Protocol II goes even further by absolutely prohibiting both indirect and direct participation (art. 4(c), PII). A Protocol to the CRC from the year 2000 raises the age of allowed participation in an armed conflict to 18 years of age.

Special evacuation and special protective zones may be established for children trapped by an armed conflict (artt. 14, 17, 24(2), 49(3), and 132, GCIV; art. 78, PI; and art. 4(3)(e), PII).

Children must be provided with special assistance and care that is commensurate to their age and vulnerabilities (artt. 23, 24(1), 38(5), 50 and 58, GCIV; artt. 70(1) and 77(1) and (3), PI; and art. 4(3)(d), PII).

The detaining or occupying power must ensure the education of children under its control (art. 24(1), 50, and 94, GCIV; art. 78(2), PI; and art. 4(3)(a), PII).

An effort must be made to identify unaccompanied children and to reunite them with their parents or guardians (artt. 24, 25, 26, 49(3), 50, and 82, GCIV; artt. 74, 75(5), 76(3) and 78, PI; and artt. 4(3)(b) and 6(4), PII).

And arrested, detained or interned children must be treated as children that require special protections, including an exemption for the death penalty (artt. 51(2), 68(4), 76(5), 82, 85(2), 89, 94, 119(2) and 132, GCIV; art. 77(3)-(5), PI; and artt. 4(3)(d) and 6(4), PII).

In addition to these special provisions the Convention on the Rights of the Child continues to apply in full to children in an armed conflict. This treaty provides a wide range of legally binding rights that are non-derogable—that is, all the rights apply at all times without exception.

Redress for Victims of Violations

Although every violation of IHL is considered to be serious and may create either state or individual responsibility, the most serious violations of the law are considered grave breaches and states have a special obligation to prevent grave breaches and to ensure that individuals who commit them are punished.

Despite these duties, only article 91 of Additional Protocol I calls for compensation for individuals who have been victims of violations of IHL. More recently, Article 75 of the ICC Statute that entered into force in 2002 allows for the Court to make orders for compensation or restitution.

Activity

Examine an international armed conflict of which you are aware and describe what laws were broken and how. Concentrate on violations of individuals' rights or protections under IHL. If you use an armed conflict that you have already identified, provide a more detailed description of the violations.

Chapter Seven
War Crimes

War crimes have existed at least since the adoption of the four Geneva Conventions protecting wounded soldiers, shipwrecked, prisoners of war, and civilians. For that reason the four Geneva Conventions from 1949 and their two protocols from 1977 have served as the basis of the long list of war crimes included in the statues of the ICTY, ICTR and ICC.

A summary of crimes categorized as war crimes in these treaties can be seen in article 8 of the Statute of the International Crime Criminal Court which is likely to be among the primary forums for applying IHL in the future.

In international armed conflicts war crimes include:

(i) willful killing;

(ii) torture or inhuman treatment, including biological experiments;

(iii) willfully causing great suffering, or serious injury to body or health;

(iv) extensive destruction and appropriation of property, not justified by military necessity and carried out unlawfully and wantonly;

(v) compelling a prisoner of war or other protected person to serve in the forces of a hostile Power;

(vi) willfully depriving a prisoner of war or other protected person of the rights of fair and regular trial;

(vii) unlawful deportation or transfer or unlawful confinement;

(viii) taking of hostages;

(ix) intentionally directing attacks against the civilian population as such or against individual civilians not taking direct part in hostilities;

(x) intentionally directing attacks against civilian objects, that is, objects which are not military objectives;

(xi) intentionally directing attacks against personnel, installations, material, units or vehicles involved in a humanitarian assistance or peacekeeping mission in accordance with the Charter of the United Nations, as long as they are entitled to the protection given to civilians or civilian objects under the international law of armed conflict;

(xii) intentionally launching an attack in the knowledge that such attack will cause incidental loss of life or injury to civilians or damage to civilian objects or widespread, long-term and severe damage to the natural environment which would be clearly excessive in relation to the concrete and direct overall military advantage anticipated;

(xiii) attacking or bombarding, by whatever means, towns, villages, dwellings or buildings which are undefended and which are not military objectives;

(xiv) killing or wounding a combatant who, having laid down his arms or having no longer means of defence, has surrendered;

(xv) making improper use of a flag of truce, of the flag or of the military insignia and uniform of the enemy or of the United Nations, as well as of the distinctive emblems of the Geneva Conventions, resulting in death or serious personal injury;

(xvi) the transfer, directly or indirectly, by the Occupying Power of parts of its own civilian population into the territory it occupies, or the deportation or transfer of all or parts of the population of the occupied territory within or outside this territory;

(xvii) intentionally directing attacks against buildings dedicated to religion, education, art, science or charitable purposes, historic monuments, hospitals and places where the sick and wounded are collected, provided they are not military objectives;

(xviii) subjecting persons who are in the power of an adverse party to physical mutilation or to medical or scientific experiments of any kind which are neither justified by the medical, dental or hospital treatment of the person concerned nor carried out in his or her interest, and which cause death to or seriously endanger the health of such person or persons;

(xix) killing or wounding treacherously individuals belonging to the hostile nation or army;

(xx) declaring that no quarter will be given;

(xxi) destroying or seizing the enemy's property unless such destruction or seizure be imperatively demanded by the necessities of war;

(xxii) declaring abolished, suspended or inadmissible in a court of law the rights and actions of the nationals of the hostile party;

(xxiii) compelling the nationals of the hostile party to take part in the operations of war directed against their own country, even if they were in the belligerent's service before the commencement of the war;

(xxiv) pillaging a town or place, even when taken by assault;

(xxv) employing poison or poisoned weapons;

(xxvi) employing asphyxiating, poisonous or other gases, and all analogous liquids, materials or devices;

(xxvii) employing bullets which expand or flatten easily in the human body, such as bullets with a hard envelope which does not entirely cover the core or is pierced with incisions;

(xxviii) employing weapons, projectiles and material and methods of warfare which are of a nature to cause superfluous injury or unnecessary suffering or which are inherently indiscriminate in violation of the international law of armed conflict, provided that such weapons, projectiles and material and methods of warfare are the subject of a comprehensive prohibition;

(xxix) committing outrages upon personal dignity, in particular humiliating and degrading treatment;

(xxx) committing rape, sexual slavery, enforced prostitution, forced pregnancy, enforced sterilization, or any other form of sexual violence;

(xxxi) utilizing the presence of a civilian or other protected person to render certain points, areas or military forces immune from military operations;

(xxxii) intentionally directing attacks against buildings, material, medical units and transport, and personnel using the distinctive emblems of the Geneva Conventions in conformity with international law;

(xxxiii) intentionally using starvation of civilians as a method of warfare by depriving them of objects indispensable to their survival, including willfully impeding relief supplies as provided for under the Geneva Conventions; and

(xxxiv) conscripting or enlisting children under the age of fifteen years into the national armed forces or using them to participate actively in hostilities.

In non-international armed conflicts the general point of reference for war crimes is common article 3 of all four Geneva Conventions. This article has been held to reflect customary international law by the International Court of Justice. *Case Concerning Military and Paramilitary Activities in and against Nicaragua (Nicaragua v. United States)*, [1986] *ICJ Reports* 14 (27 June 1986) at para. 114. This common article is elaborated by Additional Protocol I to the four Geneva Conventions. Unlike international armed conflicts, in non-international armed conflicts civilians not taking part in the armed conflict are generally the only types of protected persons. There, however, some exceptions such as the crimes denoted in xii and xiv below.

The crimes prohibited in non-international armed conflicts include (again from article 8 of the ICC Statute):

(i) violence to life and person, in particular murder of all kinds, mutilation, cruel treatment and torture;

(ii) committing outrages upon personal dignity, in particular humiliating and degrading treatment;

(iii) taking of hostages;

(iv) the passing of sentences and the carrying out of executions without previous judgment pronounced by a regularly constituted court, affording all judicial guarantees which are generally recognized as indispensable;

(v) intentionally directing attacks against the civilian population as such or against individual civilians not taking direct part in hostilities;

(vi) intentionally directing attacks against buildings, material, medical units and transport, and personnel using the distinctive emblems of the Geneva Conventions in conformity with international law;

(vii) intentionally directing attacks against personnel, installations, material, units or vehicles involved in a humanitarian assistance or peacekeeping mission in accordance with the Charter of the United Nations, as long as they are entitled to the protection given to civilians or civilian objects under the international law of armed conflict;

(viii) intentionally directing attacks against buildings dedicated to religion, education, art, science or charitable purposes, historic monuments, hospitals and places where the sick and wounded are collected, provided they are not military objectives;

(ix) pillaging a town or place, even when taken by assault;

(x) committing rape, sexual slavery, enforced prostitution, forced pregnancy, enforced sterilization, and any other form of sexual violence;

(xi) conscripting or enlisting children under the age of fifteen years into armed forces or groups or using them to participate actively in hostilities;

(xii) ordering the displacement of the civilian population for reasons related to the conflict, unless the security of the civilians is involved or imperative military reasons so demand;

(xiii) killing or wounding treacherously a combatant adversary;

(xiv) declaring that no quarter will be given;

(xv) subjecting persons who are in the power of another party to the conflict to physical mutilation or to medical or scientific experiments of any kind which are neither justified by the medical, dental or hospital treatment of the person concerned nor carried out in his or her interest, and which cause death to or seriously endanger the health of such person or persons; and

(xvi) destroying or seizing the property of an adversary when such is not imperatively demanded by the necessities of the conflict.

These two lists of war crimes are more extensive than the list of various crimes against humanity found in instruments of international criminal law. Although not every crime is described in detail, a few general comments about the nature of these crimes follow.

First, war crimes, whether committed against combatants or civilians, can be committed by any individual. There is no requirement that the accused be a combatant. The ICTR in *Prosecutor v. Kayisheme and Ruzindana*, Case No. ICTR-95-1-T, ICTR T. Ch. II (21 May 1999) at para. 175, did, however, emphasize that "[i]f individuals do not belong to the armed forces, they could bear the criminal responsibility only when there is a link between them and the armed forces."

Second, an armed conflict must be proven and it must be proven that the accused knew that there was an armed conflict. This knowledge is part of the intention or *mens rea* needed to commit a war crime.

Third, international courts have relied on the jurisprudence of national courts for the interpretation of particular war crimes. For example, the trial court in the *Tadić Case* (jurisdiction decision of 10 August 1995) at para. 125, relied on a decision of the Nigerian Supreme Court to interpret the prohibition of killing or wounding treacherously a combatant (i.e. art. 8(2)(b)(xi) of the ICC Statute) to apply to rebels who feign civilian status to carry out an attack. *See Puis Nwaoga v. The State (Nigeria)*, 52 *ILR* 496 (1979).

Fourth, war crimes can be committed in both non-international and international armed conflicts. The limitation on war crimes in the Statute of the ICTR to an internal or non-international armed conflict is due to the nature of the events over which the ICTR has jurisdiction and is not intended to in any way suggest that war crimes cannot be committed in international armed conflicts. Indeed, international law prohibits even more types of inhumane acts in international armed conflicts.

Fifth, war crimes can be committed anywhere on the territory of states party to an armed conflict. They do not have to be committed only where fighting is taking place.

And sixth, as concerns war crimes in international armed conflicts it is important to recognize that a duty already exists requiring all the states that have ratified the four Geneva Conventions to prosecute or extradite every person accused of a war crime. Although the 1977 Additional Protocol I has extended the definition of war crimes, the ICC Statute uses only the more limited definition from the 1949 Geneva Conventions.

When an armed conflict breaks out, the list of war crimes and used to judge the legitimacy of actions of combatants. As a consequence the respect that combatants enjoy from other soldiers, even their enemy, is usually based in part on their respect for the basic rules of war. In the past this regime of honor was not implemented in any serious way. With the advent of international criminal law, there is today a much greater chance that war crimes will be punished. Unfortunately, the

United States, which is the country that has engaged in the most wars of aggression in recent years, has gone to extremes to avoid the jurisdiction of the ICC. To fulfill the promise of preserving minimum standards of humanity through the rule of law in wartime. Americans will also have to be held responsible for their numerous war crimes in Afghanistan and Iraq. If they are not, the enforcement of responsibility for war crimes is likely to remain an unjust illusion.

Forums for Applying IHL

As the above lists of war crimes indicates, the relatively recently created ICC is likely to be the primary forum for applying IHL in the near future. This Court can try individuals from any of the state parties or any individual who commits a crime on a state party's territory (art. 12, ICC Statute). The lengthy Statute of the ICC provides for arrest warrants, investigations, prosecution, and punishment.

As of January 2005 approximately 120 countries had ratified the ICC Statute, but some very important countries such as the United States have not only refused to ratify it, but have encouraged other states not to adhere to it. The United States has done this by entering into agreements with dozens of states that are then, by virtue of article 98 of the ICC Statute, obliged to extradite American citizens to the United States and not to turn them over to the ICC. It may be questioned whether by entering into such agreements state parties to the ICC Statute are acting in good faith to abide by their treaty obligations.

Article 90 of Additional Protocol I applying to international armed conflicts provides for an International Fact-Finding Commission with the authority to establish when violations of IHL have occurred. States party to the treaty must make an additional declaration accepting the competence of the Fact-Finding Commission. While the Commission was formed after twenty states agreed to accept its competence, it has never played an important role in making determinations of violations. If it does begin to pay a role its unique procedures may become an issue. In making determinations about respect for the law, the Commission functions through Chambers that consist of seven members, five of which are from the International Fact-Finding Commission and two of which are *ad hoc* and appointed by each party to the conflict, but may not be either's own nationals. Furthermore, the findings of the Chamber are merely recommendations and can only be made public if the parties agree.

International human rights law forums might also indirectly provide a forum for applying IHL. The African Commission on Human and Peoples' Rights, for example, has held that the human rights in the African Charter of Peoples' and Human Rights are non-derogable even in time of war. *Commission Nationale des droits de l'Homme et des libertes v. Chad*, Comm. No. 74/92 (1996). Other human rights treaties allow derogation from some, but not all human rights. Among those rights that are non-derogable is the right to life, which under IHL is the prohibition of the arbitrary killing of protected persons. Decisions of many human rights bodies, however, are not binding and often difficult to implement.

Perhaps the oldest and most frequently used forums for applying IHL are domestic courts. In 1880, the *Oxford Manual of The Laws of War on Land* was drafted as a guide for states' domestic legislation. Today the four Geneva Conventions require state parties to implement some provisions of these treaties in domestic legislation. Article 146 of the Fourth Geneva Convention, for example, requires the "High Contracting Parties undertake to enact any legislation necessary to provide effective penal sanctions for persons committing, or ordering to be committed, any of the grave breaches of the present Convention."

India is an example of a state that has passed a special law providing for the criminalization of grave breaches, the protection of the Red Cross and other emblems that are protected by the Geneva Conventions, and the legal actions by prisoners of war and other internees. Geneva Conventions Act, 1960, *Gazette of India*, Extraordinary, Part II-Sec. 1, No. 7, 12 March 1960. *Also see, for example*, the Canadian Geneva Conventions Act, 1965, *Revised Statutes of Canada* (R.S., c. G-3), Criminal Code, *R.S.C., 1985*, c. C-46, ss. 6(2), 7(3.71)(a)(i), (ii), (iii), (b), (3.72), (3.74), (3.76), 15, 25(1), (2), (3), (4), 736, and art. 75bis of Swiss Penal Code.

Domestic courts prosecuting wars have not always found this task straight forward. In *Regina v. Finta*, [1994] 1 *S.C.R.* 701, the Supreme Court of Canada upheld the constitutionality of the War Crimes Act, while finding that the high standard of proof required for a conviction had not been met and that a jury could reasonable have acquitted the defendant, as it had done. And in Switzerland a Bosnian accused of war crimes was acquitted for lack of evidence. *Military Tribunal, Division 1 (Tribunal militaire de division I)* (unpublished), Lausanne (18 April 1997).

Successful prosecutions have taken place in Belgium, for example, where a soldier participating in the Belgian mission in the Congo (now the Democratic Republic of the Congo) was found guilty of murdering a woman and eventually sentenced to three years imprisonment. *Case of Sergeant W before the Brussels War Council*, 18 May 1966, partially reported in the *Revue Juridique du Congo*, 1970, p. 236, and in the *Revue de Droit pénal et de Criminologie*, "Chronique annuelle de Droit pénal militaire," 806 (1970). The United States government has also prosecuted some of its nationals for war crimes committed in Afghanistan and Iraq, but even those convicted have often received only *de minimus* sentences.

National laws also frequently criminalise the misuse of the Red Cross emblem, prohibiting its commercial use even in peace time. *See, for example,* Art. 294 of the Ethiopian Penal Code of 1957 and the Croatian Law on the Protection of the Red Cross Name and Emblem.

The Application of IHL & ICL

Despite being temporary institutions with limited mandates the ICTY and the ICTR have developed a significant corpus of jurisprudence concerning war crimes and the punishment of individuals who commit them.

In their jurisprudence or case law these two bodies have interpreted some important principles of the law and have applied the law to practical situations. Below is a summary of some of their most important findings related to individual responsibility for war crimes.

Can Everyone Commit War Crimes?

In *Kayishema and Ruzindana,* Case No. ICTR-95-1, ICTR T. Ch. II, 21 May 1999 at para. 175, the ICTR held that civilians "could bear the criminal responsibility only when there is a link between them and the armed forces." In the aftermath of World War II Hirota, the Japanese Foreign Minister, was found guilty of war crimes for the 'Rape of Nanking'. More recently, in *Prosecutor v. Jean-Paul Akayesu,* Case No. ICTR-94-T, ICTR T. Ch. II, 2 September 1998, the ICTR found Mr. Akayesu, a civilian government official, guilty of war crimes because he directly assisted the military by allowing them to use his office, carrying a rifle, and wearing a military jacket.

What Constitutes an International Armed Conflict?

The determination as to whether or not there is an international armed conflict is a matter of finding two or more states to be involved in the conflict. This in turn has sometimes seemed to be the question as to whether or not a can be held responsible for its involvement.

In the case of *Military and Paramilitary Activities in and against Nicaragua (Nicaragua v. US), ICJ Reports* 14 (1986), the International Court of Justice had to decide upon the responsibility of the United States for acts carried out by militants or rebels against Nicaragua, but who were based in Honduras. These rebels had been receiving substantial amounts of assistance from the United States and their actions were often supervised and coordinated by the United States. The Court, however, found that these links were not enough. The court held that in addition the sate to which responsibility is to be apportioned must have provided specific instructions concerning the unlawful acts in question. It is important to recognize that the standard the Court was using was aimed at determining state responsibility for specific actions, not merely for participation in an armed conflict.

In the *Prosecutor v. Dusko Tadiç*, Case No. ICTY-94-A, App. Ch. (15 July 1999) at para. 84, the ICTY Appellate Court held that a state is engaged in an armed conflict when it exercises effective control over armed forces engaged in the armed conflict and when there is a relationship of dependence and allegiance. This case appears to set a lower threshold for a state's involvement, than does the *Nicaragua Case*.

The standards are, however, likely reconcilable. One manner of reconciling them is recognizing the different question they addressed. The *Nicaragua Case* was about state responsibility, while the *Tadiç Case* was about individual responsibility and mere state involvement in an armed conflict—not responsibility for action undertaken in the armed conflict. Additionally, in the *Tadiç Case* the Appellate Tribunal recognized that there is a different test for states that are bordering each other, as were Serbia and Montenegro and Bosnia and Hercegovina. By comparison the United States and Nicaragua were some distance from each other. Whether this distinction makes sense in a world of high speed communications and transportation is open to debate.

Examples of the Interpretation of War Crimes

War crimes may be committed by omission or by action. After World War II a Japanese officer was found guilty of conspiring to commit war crimes because he disregarded the POW status of a captured combatant in violation of IHL. *Case of Hideki Tojo*, cited in Röling, B.V.A., and Rüter, E.F., (eds.), *The Tokyo Judgment*, University Press of Amsterdam: Amsterdam, NL (1977) at 461-463.

The ICTR and the ICTY have been in the forefront of the development of our understanding of IHL, especially war crimes. As already indicated above, the Additional Protocol I recognizes that violations of IHL are war crimes.

One of the most serious offenses these tribunals have had to confront is willful killing. Obviously this covers the wanton murder of another individual, but unlike domestic law that may provide for some mitigation where the perpetrator does not him or herself actually render the death blow, IHL has little sympathy for those who take even less obvious action. For example, leaving a seriously wounded person to die without summonsing medical care has been held to constitute willful killing. *Prosecutor v. Zejnil Delatic, Zdravko Mucic, Hazim Delic, Esad Landzo (Celebici Case)*, Case No. IT-96-21-T, ICTY T. Ch. II quarter (16 November 1998).

Similarly not only outright physical torture, but also subjecting a person to psychological and physical trauma may be torture according to the ICTY in the *Celebici Case* at para. 1119. And the same case held that the extensive destruction of property includes "systematic economic exploitation of occupied territory" (*id.* at para. 590). Another extension of the definition of an unjustified appropriation of property occurred in the ICTY when it held that stealing from dead bodies constituted this war crime as well. *Prosecutor v. Tihomir Blaskic*, Case No. IT-95-14-T, ICTY T. Ch. I (3 March 2000).

It is not the purpose to provide a comprehensive understanding of the interpretation of war crimes but merely to sketch some of the trends. As these few examples indicate, the international criminal tribunals have expanded in most cases rather than limited the definitions of war crimes. The expansive interpretations have often illustrated a mixture of allegiance to protecting victims balanced against the realities of a political world.

Undoubtedly, future generations of international lawyers will be tasked with developing the law further, but it is fair to say that IHL is likely to be developed largely by international lawyers working through international criminal mechanisms.

Genocide

Genocide consists of threats to life or the taking of life when it is serious and widespread. It is one of the most serious international crimes and it is linked to IHL because acts of genocide will often constitute acts of war and therefore violations of IHL. Genocide is defined in the Convention on the Prevention and Punishment of the Crime of Genocide from 1951. This definition has been adopted by the statutes of the ICTY, ICTR and ICC.

Article 6 of the ICC Statute defines it as meaning any of the following acts committed with intent to destroy, in whole or in part, a national, ethnical, racial or religious group as such:

(a) Killing members of the group;

(b) Causing serious bodily or mental harm to members of the group;

(c) Deliberately inflicting on the group conditions of life calculated to bring about its physical destruction in whole or in part;

(d) Imposing measures intended to prevent births within the group;

(e) Forcibly transferring children of the group to another group.

The first ever conviction of a person for the crime of genocide came in 1998 when former Rwanda Prime Minister Jean Kambanda became the first former government leader to be convicted of the crime of genocide. His conviction by the ICTR was based on his own agreement as to his actions including incitement to violence and failure to act to prevent violence and killings. Mr. Kambanda merely disputed that his actions had constituted genocide because, he claimed, he did not have the intention to destroy an enumerated group in whole or in part. The Court found that his intention could be inferred from his actions and omissions. He was convicted and jailed for life. *Prosecutor v. Jean Kambanda*, Case No. ICTR 97-23-S (4 September 1998).

In *Prosecutor v. Georges Ruggiu*, Case No. ICTR-97-32-I, ICTR, T.Ch. I (1 June 2000), a Belgian employee of *Radio Television Libre des Milles Collines* broadcast messages inciting genocide against Tutsis. He was convicted of genocide for this action. Evidence was also presented that he accused had sometimes protected Tutsis. The Tribunal, however, only considered this evidence as a means of mitigating the punishment, but not as a justification or negation of intention for the actions that constituted genocide.

The *mens rea* required for genocide is one of specific intent or *dolis specialis*. This means that it must be proven that the accused knew or should have known that he was participating in the destruction of a group by committing a prohibited act. The mere intention to kill a person or persons is not enough. The knowledge of a plan to destroy a group may, however, be inferred from the actions of the accused. In *Prosecutor v. Jean-Paul Akayesu*, Case No. ICTR-96-4-T, ICTR, T.Ch. I (2 September 1998), the First Trial Chamber of the ICTR held that the accused had the required *mens rea* because of his intention to participate in the systematic rape of Tutsi women. But in *Prosecutor v. Goran Jelisic*, Case No. IT-95-10, ICTY T.Ch. I (14 December 1999), a senior official at the Luka Camp where hundreds of Bosnian Muslims perished was found not guilty of genocide because his serial killings of detainees was random and could not be linked to an overall plan to exterminate Bosnian Muslims. The prosecutor, of course, also has the burden of proving that an accused acted against a specific a national, ethnical, racial or religious group. This specific *mens rea* of genocide sets it aside from other international crimes such as the crime against humanity of extermination.

The acts that may constitute genocide fall into five categories.

First, there are *killings* that are any actions committed with the intention to cause the death of the victim. An individual may also act in a manner in which he or she should have known that their actions might reasonably result in the death of the victim. Of course, it is not necessary that the victim or victims actually die, only that the accused intended kill his victims or should have known that they might be killed. Killings can take place by acts or omissions.

Second, are acts that constitute deliberate causing of bodily or mental harm. Such harm will have to be determined on a case by case basis. The harm need not be permanent, but must reach a certain level of severity. Rape, forcing a victim to lie down while threatening to drive over her, forcing one victim to beat another, are all acts that have been found to constitute sufficiently grave physical or mental harm to constitute genocide when they are aimed at the destruction of a group in whole or in part.

Third, are acts inflicting conditions of life calculated to bring about the physical destruction of a group. These acts may include depriving members of a group of proper housing, sanitation, clothing, hygiene, food, water, or requiring them to do excessive work. The acts can be aimed at all or part of the group. In an action brought by the former Yugoslavia against the NATO allies because of their bombing which were aimed at forcing Yugoslavian troops out of Kosovo, the International Court of Justice held that the bombings were not enough in themselves to constitute the infliction of conditions of life calculated to bring about the physical destruction of the ethnic Serb population. *Legality of the Use of Force (Yugoslavia v. Belgium and others), Decision on Request for Indication of Provisional Measures* (2 June 1999) at para. 40.

Fourth, are acts that constitute measures intended to prevent births such as forced sterilization, sexual mutilation, force birth control, forced separation of sexes, prohibition of marriages, as well as laws aimed at preventing births. The emphasis is on acts intended to have the prohibited effect of destroying in whole or in part protected groups of persons, whether or not they actually do.

And fifth, are acts that constitute the forcible transfer of children. In the *Akayesu Case*, mentioned above, and *Prosecutor v. Kayisheme and Ruzindana*, Case No. ICTR-95-1-T, ICTR T. Ch. II (21 May 1999), the ICTR held that the forcible transfer of children could be committed by threats that might lead to forcible transfer as well as the acts of transfer themselves.

Activity

Divide into three groups. The first groups of individuals will represent the Prosecutor's Office of the International Criminal Court (ICC). The second group of individuals will represent defendants before the ICC as defense lawyers. The third group of individuals will represent judges of the ICC. A set of facts will then explained to you in writing or orally.

The Prosecutors should then draw up an indictment for war crimes based on the facts. The defense lawyers should draft outlines of their defenses and of motions—submissions concerning procedural rights—that they might make to the Court. The judges must decide in writing what basic principles they will apply and how they will deal with procedural irregularities.

Chapter Eight
Non-State Actors and IHL

Contemporary international humanitarian law owes a great deal to individuals and non-state entities. The International Committee of the Red Cross (ICRC) created by Swiss-businessman-turned-humanitarian Henri Dunant has evolved into perhaps the most respected entity driving the development of the law. Although one must not forget that the law is formed by the actions, *opinio juris*, and agreements of states, one is equally in error to forget the contributions of the non-state actors without whom there would often have been no state action.

The ICRC can trace it roots back to the Red Cross Movement started in 1864 by Mr. Henri Dunant which has been discussed in Chapter One. Today the International Red Cross and Red Crescent Movement consists of its founding body the International Committee of the Red Cross, the International Federation of Red Cross and Red Crescent Societies (founded in 1919) and the National Red Cross and Red Crescent Societies (175 at the end of 1998).

The ICRC is a Swiss NGO with a Statute and governing executive. Its mandate flows primarily from its Statute and the resolutions of International Conferences of the Red Cross and Red Crescent, but unlike other NGOs it also has a unique role assigned to it in several treaties, namely the four Geneva Conventions and the two Additional Protocols.

To be able to fulfill this role 1965, the three parts of the movement adopted a common set of principles to guide their actions. These principles are summarized by the words: humanity, impartiality, neutrality, independence, voluntary service, unity, and universality.

The ICRC's most general responsibility is to take steps to ensure respect for the rules of international humanitarian law. In recent years this has been neither an enthusiastically implemented step nor one with resounding success. In part this is because of the careful balance that the ICRC must make between offending governments and ensuring they maintain necessary cooperation for their activities. The ICRC also promotes awareness of international humanitarian law by disseminating the law and providing training to both civilians and military personnel. Most recently the ICRC has completed a substantial study of customary international humanitarian law that has been published by Cambridge University Press in 2005.

In the field the ICRC's most important role has probably been its visits to places of detention. These visits should allow ICRC delegates to see all the detainees, to talk freely with them without witnesses, and to view the facilities to which they have access. The visits should be allowed at regular intervals and the ICRC should be provided a list of the persons in detention. Although the ICRC usually does not make information about the visits public, it does allegedly use the information it collects to discuss the situation of detainees with the state, including the state party's respect for the four Geneva Conventions.

The ICRC's Central Tracing Agency (CTA) which was created during the Franco-Prussian War of 1870-71 facilitates the restoration of family links by registering individuals in war zones—especially those being detained, by tracing lost persons, by passing on correspondence, by issuing temporary travel documents, and taking action to reunite family members.

The ICRC also provides basic humanitarian assistance, but in recent years this assistance has been overshadowed by the work of the United Nations, especially the World Food Programme, bilateral government aid agencies, and other NGOs.

While the ICRC remains the lead organization in times of armed conflict and as concern the dissemination of IHL, it is not the only body engaged in activities in armed conflict or related to IHL.

Other bodies involved in the dissemination of IHL include educational institutions that offer graduate degrees in this law. Lancaster University in the United Kingdom, for example, offers an LL.M. in International Human Rights and Humanitarian Law. The University Centre for International Humanitarian Law in Geneva, which is a joint undertaking of Universities of Geneva and Lausanne, the Graduate Institute of International Studies in Geneva, and the ICRC, also offers an LL.M. in IHL.

Non-state actors also play a role in monitoring the violations of IHL. The Crimes of War Project (www.crimesofwar.org) and the Institute for Peace and War Reporting (www.iwpr.net) are examples of NGOs that reports on violations of IHL. Even larger NGOs such as Amnesty International and Human Rights Watch have begun to do so in recent years. These reports often play as much if not more of a role in ending violations of IHL and getting redress for the victims because they are public documents. In comparison, the ICRC, which also reports on abuses of IHL, keeps its reports secret in most cases.

Other NGOs report predominately on the situation of the civilian population and the relief efforts being made to assist them. While some reports come from governments acting as bilateral relief organizations, these reports are often supplemented by and sometimes based upon the reports of NGOs working in an area of armed conflict. Medicines sans Frontiers and Medicos del Mundo—both founded by the Frenchman Bernard Kouchner—are two examples of the hundreds of relief organizations that exist today to work in areas of armed conflict. These NGOs provide medical relief, food, medicines, assist with temporary housing, and sometimes also provide a degree of protection to protected populations. The money channeled through these relief organizations to effected populations can amount to hundreds of millions of dollars in a single armed conflict. Sometimes the number of NGOs providing relief is seen as so numerous that they are considered an industry that survives off the hardship of others. In part this criticism is aimed at the fact that many of these NGOs are staffed by individuals from rich developed countries who are earning many times more than the local wage and who—locals sometimes claim—are benefiting from the devastation caused by their militarily powerful countries either directly or indirectly through the sales of arms. Some of these NGOs have tried to mitigate this criticism by speaking out against wars or "man-made" disasters (as opposed to natural disasters).

Humanitarian relief NGOs have sometimes provided the most reliable documentation of the scourges of war on humankind. After the 1991 Gulf War in Iraq, for example, a group of scientists from a variety of disciplines came together to form the International Study Team and published the most in-depth study of the effects of war on civilians ever produced. The study showed how not only an estimated tens of thousands of civilians had died in the relatively short armed conflict, but how hundred of thousands of civilians—mainly women and children—would perish in the following months and years. The study—which was carried out in Iraq without any interference from the Iraqi government and with the support of numerous governments, NGOs and universities, including Harvard University in the United States and Nijmegen University in the Netherlands—examined the aftermath of the armed conflict from a multidisciplinary perspective. It reviewed civilian casualties, the impact of the war on women and children both in terms or mortality and nutrition, and food distribution capacity among other things. For almost a decade this study also it served as the baseline for the provision of humanitarian assistance to Iraq.

In recent years and particularly in more politically volatile armed conflicts—such as the United States' wars of aggression against Islamic countries—individuals have also begun reporting on violations of IHL, when the larger NGOs have shied away from doing so. The armed conflict in Iraq, which began in March 2003, is an example. In this armed conflict, uruknet.info has included reporting on violations of IHL among its topics of reporting. This organization works with many individuals who are in Iraq to provide an alternative perspective on the war—from the point of view of the Iraqis who are suffering its consequences. Its writers include well-established journalists and academics as well as less known figures. Although this organization is often accused of being anti-American, similar to Henri Dunant, one could also describe it as being biased towards ending war as a scourge against humankind while still seeking to mitigate the effects of war until this can be accomplished.

What can you contribute?

Having seen a few examples of the work of non-state actors, consider what you might be able to do to help ensure respect for IHL during an armed conflict.

Some might be able to work for the ICRC or one of the other NGOs that have well established systems for reporting or providing assistance to victims of war.

Some might seek to start your own initiatives by seeking funding from philanthropic donors who are moved by the plight of others affected by war.

Some might be able to contribute by going to regions affected by wars and volunteering to assist the people affected. While this might put a strain on already scarce resources among vulnerable populations such as refugees, in cases where the vulnerable population is a whole country including its government such as is the case in Afghanistan or Iraq, assisting those affected most by the war might be welcome despite the additional stress on resources. If you do attempt this more dangerous path you will also often see that there is often a willingness of the parties to an armed conflict to adhere to IHL and a willingness, even in the mist of an armed conflict, to learn more about how this law protects them.

Getting caught up in an armed conflict is not something that is wise for novices and when there are also many other ways to contribute to promoting respect for IHL from the relative safety of your own home. Merely by observing media reports—including the often insightful reports posted to the internet—or communicating with people in a place of armed conflict you can see actions that at least raise questions about their legitimacy under IHL. Where others are not reporting on these events or only reporting them as unchecked facts, your reports can evaluate these facts for their consistency with IHL.

Finally, merely disseminating information about IHL in your community can be a valuable contribution to raising others awareness about the law. To this end the ICRC provides a wealth of materials that one could use, but you might also wish to create you own unique materials that are best suited to communicate to the group of people around you. Although neither you nor your audience may be embroiled in an armed conflict, your creating awareness of the rules of law applying to an armed conflict as well as the horrors of armed conflict, might be a significant step towards preventing future armed conflicts and ending ongoing armed conflicts.

Activity

Discuss and then write a draft plan of action for your NGO in a currently ongoing armed conflict. This draft plan should include (1) a general or overall goal, (2) a description of specific activities, (3) a timetable for the implementation of these activities, (4) a list of personnel needed to implement these activities, and (5) a summary budget.

Conclusion

While few would deny the value of international humanitarian law, its future is uncertain.

On the positive side, the development of the law has continued as we have seen though the creation of forums for punishing individuals who violate the most fundamental laws of war. The International Criminal Court is one such forum. Although some states attempt to remain aloft from the newly created forums of international justice, an increasing number of states are willing to participate in these forums.

There is a slowed but continuing trend towards specifying with even greater detail the rules of international humanitarian law through additional treaties, like the Ottawa Convention on the Prohibition of the Use, Stockpiling, Production and Transfer of Anti-Personnel Mines and on their Destruction adopted on 18 September 1997.

The development of international humanitarian law is not a foregone conclusion. Areas of law frequently fall into disuse and sometimes even digress to the state that the international community no longer respect the law.

Evidence of such digressions abounds in the international community. The former deputy Secretary of Defense of the United States and a professor of law, for example, have argued that the Geneva Conventions could be suspended at will by one country. His views were not only shared by many of his colleagues, but even became the prevailing view of the United States government, which instructed its soldiers that the Geneva Conventions do not apply in instances when the executive decides to suspend them. While such views did not gain currency in most of the world, the fact that they are often heard in the most militarily and economically powerful country in the world is cause for concern.

These views indicate that there are some who seek to undermine international humanitarian law and replace it with power politics. Such views were the norm hundreds of years ago as we have seen in Chapter One, but is such a digression valuable today? Have we not learned from our mistakes of the past? Does not IHL reflect progress in ensuring human dignity?

These are questions that students and policy makers alike must grapple with today. Moreover, today's students can play a role in influencing these trends. As future lawyers and political leaders in our increasingly interconnected society it will be your responsibility to decide if you will defend international humanitarian law or whether you will allow the short-sightedness of naked power based on the possession of greater military.

Once again the future policy makers of our societies are confronted by the same choice Henri Dunant once faced as he tried to reconcile the mitigation of the horrors with his efforts to eliminate war. He choose to stand by his commitment to law that achieved the ideal of peace and was consequently ostracized by his contemporaries. The wisdom of his decision, however, was perhaps ultimately acknowledged by his being awarded the first Noble Peace Prize. Who will be the next champion of international humanitarian law to show such foresight based on a real commitment to ensuring respect for the law?

Selected Further Readings

Peter Walker and Daniel G. Maxwell, *Shaping the humanitarian world*, Routledge: Abingdon, UK & New York, NY, USA (2008).

Avril McDonald, Jann K. Kleffner, and Brigit C. A. Toebes, (eds.), *Depleted Uranium Weapons and International Law: A Precautionary Approach*, Cambridge University Press: Cambridge, UK (2009).

Robert Kolb, Gabriele Porretto and Sylvain Vité, *L'application du droit international humanitaire et des droits de l'homme aux organisations internationals*, Bruylant: Geneva (2005).

Jean-Marie Henckaerts and Louise Doswald-Beck, *Customary International Humanitarian Law*, four vols., ICRC: Geneva & Cambridge University Press: Geneva & Cambridge, UK (2005).

Fritz Kalshoven and Liesbeth Zegveld, *Constraints on the waging of war: an introduction to international humanitarian law*, ICRC: Geneva (3rd ed. 2001).

Liesbeth Zegveld, *Armed Opposition Groups in International Law: The Quest for Accountability*, Cambridge University Press: Cambridge, UK (2001).

Adam Roberts and Richard Guelff, (eds.), *Documents on the Laws of War*, Oxford University Press: Oxford, UK (Oxford, 2000).

L.C. Green, *The Contemporary Law of Armed Conflict*, Longmann Press: Manchester, U.S.A. (2000)

Marco Sassòli and Antoine A. Bouvier, *How does law protect in war? Cases, documents and teaching materials on contemporary practice in international humanitarian law*, ICRC: Geneva (1999).

David Fleck, (ed.), *The Handbook of Humanitarian Law*, Oxford University Press: Oxford (1999).

Yves Sandoz, Christophe Swinarski, Bruno Zimmermann, (eds.), *Commentary on the Additional Protocols*, ICRC: Geneva (1987).

Jean S. Pictet, Jean de Preux, et al, (eds.), *Commentaries on the Four Geneva Conventions*, 4 vols., ICRC: Geneva (1952-1960).

Henri Dunant, *A Memory of Solferino* (1862).

Additional Resources

Internet sites

www.icrc.int or www.icrc.org: the International Committee of the Red Cross, the best site for information on IHL.

www.un.org: the United Nations, where UN General Assembly Resolutions can be found and information from the UN Secretary-General's Special Representative for Children and Armed Conflict.

www.crimesofwar.org: a project based at the Washington College of Law in the United States that provides commentaries on the application of IHL to ongoing armed conflicts.

www.warchild.ca: the NGO War Child Canada, a site for information on the effects of war on children.

Courses

International Institute of Humantarian Law in San Remo, Italy (www.iihl.org) offers IHL courses throughout the year.

Lancaster University in Lancaster in the United Kingdom offers an LL.M. in International Human Rights and Humanitarian Law.

Summer Courses

Every year the ICRC (icrc-cicr.org) hosts summer courses on IHL in Warsaw, Poland in English and in Brussels, Belgium in French. Contact your local ICRC Delegate for more information.

An-Najah National University (najah.edu) offers a Summer Session in June or July of each year that includes a course in international humanitarian law.

Annexes containing
complete or excerpted texts

Fourth Hague Convention and Regulations from 1907

* * *

Fourth Geneva Convention relative to the Protection
of Civilians in Time of War, 12 August 1949,

* * *

Third Geneva Convention relative to the Treatment
of Prisoners of War, 12 August 1949,

* * *

First Protocol Additional to the Geneva Conventions
of 12 August 1949, and Relating to the Protection
of Victims of International Armed Conflicts

* * *

Convention on the Prevention and
Punishment of the Crime of Genocide

Hague Convention (IV) respecting the Laws and Customs of War on Land and its Annex: Regulations concerning the Laws and Customs of War on Land.

Done in The Hague, The Netherlands on 18 October 1907.

Preamble

Seeing that while seeking means to preserve peace and prevent armed conflicts between nations, it is likewise necessary to bear in mind the case where the appeal to arms has been brought about by events which their care was unable to avert;

Animated by the desire to serve, even in this extreme case, the interests of humanity and the ever progressive needs of civilization;

Thinking it important, with this object, to revise the general laws and customs of war, either with a view to defining them with greater precision or to confining them within such limits as would mitigate their severity as far as possible;

Have deemed it necessary to complete and explain in certain particulars the work of the First Peace Conference, which, following on the Brussels Conference of 1874, and inspired by the ideas dictated by a wise and generous forethought, adopted provisions intended to define land govern the usages of war on land.

According to the views of the High Contracting Parties, these provisions, the wording of which has been inspired by the desire to diminish the evils of war, as far as military requirements permit, are intended to serve as a general rule of conduct for the belligerents in their mutual relations and in their relations with the inhabitants.

It has not, however, been found possible at present to concert regulations covering all the circumstances which arise in practice;

On the other hand, the High Contracting Parties clearly do not intend that unforeseen cases should, in the absence of a written undertaking, be left to the arbitrary judgment of military commanders.

Until a more complete code of the laws of war has been issued, the High Contracting Parties deem it expedient to declare that, in cases not included in the Regulations adopted by them, the inhabitants and the belligerents remain under the protection and the rule of the principles of the law of nations, as they result from the usages established among civilized peoples,

from the laws of humanity, and the dictates of the public conscience.

They declare that it is in this sense especially that Articles I and 2 of the Regulations adopted must be understood.

The High Contracting Parties, wishing to conclude a fresh Convention to this effect, have appointed the following as their Plenipotentiaries:

[The names of Plenipotentiaries have been omitted.]

Who, after having deposited their full powers, found in good and due form, have agreed upon the following:

Article 1

The Contracting Powers shall issue instructions to their armed land forces, which shall be in conformity with the Regulations respecting the laws and customs of war on land, annexed to the present Convention.

Article 2

The provisions contained in the Regulations referred to in Article 1, as well as in the present Convention, do not apply except between Contracting powers, and then only if all the belligerents are parties to the Convention.

Article 3

A belligerent party which violates the provisions of the said Regulations shall, if the case demands, be liable to pay compensation. It shall be responsible for all acts committed by persons forming part of its armed forces.

Article 4

The present Convention, duly ratified, shall as between the Contracting Powers, be substituted for the Convention of 29 July 1899, respecting the laws land customs of war on land.

The Convention of 1899 remains in force as between the Powers which signed it, and which do not also ratify the present Convention.

Article 5

The present Convention shall be ratified as soon as possible.

The ratifications shall be deposited at The Hague.

The first deposit of ratifications shall be recorded in a process verbal signed by the Representatives of the Powers, which take part therein and, by the Netherlands Minister for Foreign Affairs.

The subsequent deposits of ratifications shall be made by means of a written notification, addressed to the Netherlands Government and accompanied by the instrument of ratification.

A duly certified copy of the proces-verbal relative to the first deposit of ratifications, of the notifications mentioned in the preceding paragraph, as well as of the instruments of ratification, shall be immediately sent by the Netherlands Government, through the diplomatic channel, to the powers invited to the Second Peace Conference, as well as to the other Powers which have adhered to the Convention. In the cases contemplated in the preceding paragraph the said Government shall at the same time inform them of the date on which it received the notification.

Article 6

Non-Signatory Powers may adhere to the present Convention.

The Power, which desires to adhere, notifies in writing its intention to the Netherlands Government, forwarding to it the act of adhesion, which shall be deposited in the archives of the said Government.

This Government shall at once transmit to all the other Powers a duly certified copy of the notification as well as of the act of adhesion, mentioning the date on which it received the notification.

Article 7

The present Convention shall come into force, in the case of the Powers which were a party to the first deposit of ratifications, sixty days after the date of the process-verbal of this deposit, and, in the case of the Powers which ratify subsequently or which adhere, sixty days after the notification of their ratification or of their adhesion has been received by the Netherlands Government.

Article 8

In the event of one of the Contracting Powers wishing to denounce the present Convention, the denunciation shall be notified in writing to the Netherlands Government, which shall at once communicate a duly certified copy of the notification to all the other Powers, informing them of the date on which it was received.

The denunciation shall only have effect in regard to the notifying Power, land one year after the notification has reached the Netherlands Government.

Article 9

A register kept by the Netherlands Ministry for Foreign Affairs shall give the date of the deposit of ratifications made in virtue of Article 5, paragraphs 3 land 4, as well as the date on which the notifications of adhesion (Article 6, paragraph 2), or of denunciation (Article 8, paragraph 1) were received.

Each Contracting Power is entitled to have access to this register and to be supplied with duly certified extracts.

In faith whereof the Plenipotentiaries have appended their signatures to the present Convention.

Done at The Hague 18 October 1907, in a single copy, which shall remain deposited in the archives of the Netherlands Government, and duly certified copies of which shall be sent, through the diplomatic channel to the Powers which have been invited to the Second Peace Conference.

[Signatures omitted.]

ANNEX TO THE CONVENTION

REGULATIONS RESPECTING THE LAWS AND CUSTOMS OF WAR ON LAND

SECTION I

ON BELLIGERENTS

CHAPTER I

The qualifications of belligerents

Article 1

The laws, rights, and duties of war apply not only to armies, but also to militia and volunteer corps fulfilling the following conditions:

1. To be commanded by a person responsible for his subordinates;

2. To have a fixed distinctive emblem recognizable at a distance;

3. To carry arms openly; and

4. To conduct their operations in accordance with the laws and customs of war.

In countries where militia or volunteer corps constitute the army, or form part of it, they are included under the denomination "army."

Article 2

The inhabitants of a territory, which has not been occupied, who, on the approach of the enemy, spontaneously take up arms to resist the invading troops without having had time to organize themselves in accordance with Article 1, shall be regarded as belligerents if they carry arms openly and if they respect the laws and customs of war.

Article 3

The armed forces of the belligerent parties may consist of combatants and noncombatants.

In the case of capture by the enemy, both have a right to be treated as prisoners of war.

CHAPTER II

Prisoners of war

Article 4

Prisoners of war are in the power of the hostile Government, but not of the individuals or corps who capture them.

They must be humanely treated.

All their personal belongings, except arms, horses, and military papers, remain their property.

Article 5

Prisoners of war may be interned in a town, fortress, camp, or other place, and bound not to go beyond certain fixed limits; but they cannot be confined except as in indispensable measure of safety land only while the circumstances which necessitate the measure continue to exist.

Article 6

The State may utilize the labor of prisoners of war according to their rank and aptitude, officers excepted. The tasks shall not be excessive and shall have no connection with the operations of the war.

Prisoners may be authorized to work for the public service, for private persons, or on their own account.

Work done for the State is paid for at the rates in force for work of a similar kind done by soldiers of the national army, or, if there are none in force, at a rate according to the work executed.

When the work is for other branches of the public service or for private persons the conditions are settled in agreement with the military authorities.

The wages of the prisoners shall go towards improving their position, and the balance shall be paid them on their release, after deducting the cost of their maintenance.

Article 7

The Government into whose hands prisoners of war have fallen is charged with their maintenance.

In the absence of a special agreement between the belligerents, prisoners of war shall be treated as regards board, lodging, and clothing on the same footing as the troops of the Government who captured them.

Article 8

Prisoners of war shall be subject to the laws, regulations, and orders in force in the army of the State in whose power they are. Any act of insubordination justifies the adoption towards them of such measures of severity as may be considered necessary.

Escaped prisoners who are retaken before being able to rejoin their own army or before leaving the territory occupied by the army which captured them are liable to disciplinary punishment. Prisoners, who, after succeeding in escaping, are again taken prisoners, are not liable to any punishment on account of the previous flight.

Article 9

Every prisoner of war is bound to give, if he is questioned on the subject, his true name and rank, and if he infringes this rule, he is liable to have the advantages given to prisoners of his class curtailed.

Article 10

Prisoners of war may be set at liberty on parole if the laws of their country allow, and, in such cases, they are bound, on their personal honor, scrupulously to fulfill, both towards their own Government and the Government by whom they were made prisoners, the engagements they have contracted.

In such cases their own Government is bound neither to require of nor accept from them any service incompatible with the parole given.

Article 11

A prisoner of war cannot be compelled to accept his liberty on parole; similarly the hostile Government is not obliged to accede to the request of the prisoner to be set at liberty on parole.

Article 12

Prisoners of war liberated on parole and recaptured bearing arms against the Government to whom they had pledged their honor, or against the allies of that Government, forfeit their right to be treated as prisoners of war, and can be brought before the courts.

Article 13

Individuals who follow an army without directly belonging to it, such as newspaper correspondents and reporters, sutlers and contractors, who fall into the enemy's hands and whom the latter thinks expedient to detain, are entitled to be treated as prisoners of war, provided they are in possession of a certificate from the military authorities of the army which they were accompanying.

Article 14

An inquiry office for prisoners of war is instituted on the commencement of hostilities in each of the belligerent States, and, when necessary, in neutral countries which have received belligerents in their territory. It is the function of this office to reply to all inquiries about the prisoners it receives from the various services concerned full information respecting internments arid transfers, releases on parole, exchanges, escapes, admissions into hospital, deaths, as well as other information necessary to enable it to make out land keep up to date an individual return for each prisoner of war. The office must state in this return the regimental number, name and surname, age, place of origin, rank, unit, wounds, date and place of capture, internment, wounding, and death, as well as any observations of a special character. The individual return shall be sent to the Government of the other belligerent after the conclusion of peace.

It is likewise the function of the inquiry office to receive and collect all objects of personal use, valuables, letters, etc., found on the field of battle or left by prisoners who have been released on parole, or exchanged, or who have escaped, or died in hospitals or ambulances, and to forward them to those concerned.

Article 15

Relief societies for prisoners of war, which are properly constituted in accordance with the laws of their country and with the object of serving as the channel for charitable effort shall receive from the belligerents, for themselves and their duly accredited agents every facility for the efficient performance of their humane task within the bounds imposed by military necessities and administrative regulations. Agents of these societies may be admitted to the places of internment for the purpose of distributing relief, as also to the halting places of repatriated prisoners, if furnished with a personal permit by the military authorities, and on giving an undertaking in writing to comply with all measures of order and police which the latter may issue.

Article 16

Inquiry offices enjoy the privilege of free postage. Letters, money orders, and valuables, as well as parcels by post, intended for prisoners of war, or dispatched by them, shall be exempt from all postal duties in the countries of origin and destination, as well as in the countries they pass through.

Presents and relief in kind for prisoners of war shall be admitted free of all import or other duties, as well as of payments for carriage by the State railways.

Article 17

Officers taken prisoners shall receive the same rate of pay as officers of corresponding rank in the country where they are detained, the amount to be ultimately refunded by their own Government.

Article 18

Prisoners of war shall enjoy complete liberty in the exercise of their religion, including attendance at the services of whatever church they may belong to, on the sole condition that they comply with the measures of order and police issued by the military authorities.

Article 19

The wills of prisoners of war are received or drawn up in the same way as for soldiers of the national army.

The same rules shall be observed regarding death certificates as well as for the burial of prisoners of war, due regard being paid to their grade and rank.

Article 20

After the conclusion of peace, the repatriation of prisoners of war shall be carried out as quickly as possible.

CHAPTER III

The sick and wounded:

Article 21

The obligations of belligerents with regard to the sick and wounded are governed by the Geneva Convention.

SECTION II

HOSTILITIES

CHAPTER I

Means of injuring the enemy, sieges, and bombardments

Article 22

The right of belligerents to adopt means of injuring the enemy is not unlimited.

Article 23

In addition to the prohibitions provided by special Conventions, it is especially forbidden

(a) To employ poison or poisoned weapons;

(b) To kill or wound treacherously individuals belonging to the hostile nation or army;

(c) To kill or wound an enemy who, having laid down his arms, or having no longer means of defense, has surrendered at discretion;

(d) To declare that no quarter will be given;

(e) To employ arms, projectiles, or material calculated to cause unnecessary suffering;

(f) To make improper use of a flag of truce, of the national flag or of the military insignia and uniform of the enemy, as well as the distinctive badges of the Geneva Convention;

(g) To destroy or seize the enemy's property, unless such destruction or seizure be imperatively demanded by the necessities of war;

(h) To declare abolished, suspended, or inadmissible in a court of law the rights and actions of the nationals of the hostile party. A belligerent is likewise forbidden to compel the nationals of the hostile party to take part in the operations of war directed against their own country, even if they were in the belligerent's service before the commencement of the war.

Article 24

Ruses of war and the employment of measures necessary for obtaining information about the enemy and the country are considered permissible.

Article 25

The attack or bombardment, by whatever means, of towns, villages, dwellings, or buildings which are undefended is prohibited.

Article 26

The officer in command of an attacking force must, before commencing a bombardment, except in cases of assault, do all in his power to warn the authorities.

Article 27

In sieges and bombardments all necessary steps must be taken to spare, as far as possible, buildings dedicated to religion, art, science, or charitable purposes, historic monuments, hospitals, and places where the sick and wounded are collected, provided they are not being used at the time for military purposes.

It is the duty of the besieged to indicate the presence of such buildings or places by distinctive and visible signs, which shall be notified to the enemy beforehand.

Article 28

The pillage of a town or place, even when taken by assault, is prohibited.

CHAPTER II

Spies

Article 29

A person can only be considered a spy when, acting clandestinely or on false pretenses, he obtains or endeavors to obtain information in the zone of operations of a belligerent, with the intention of communicating it to the hostile party.

Thus, soldiers not wearing a disguise who have penetrated into the zone of operations of the hostile army, for the purpose of obtaining information, are not considered spies. Similarly, the following are not considered spies: Soldiers and civilians, carrying out their mission openly, entrusted with the delivery of dispatches intended either for their own army or for the enemy's army. To this class belong likewise persons sent in balloons for the purpose of carrying dispatches and, generally, of maintaining communications between the different parts of an army or a territory.

Article 30

A spy taken in the act shall not be punished without previous trial.

Article 31

A spy who, after rejoining the army to which he belongs, is subsequently captured by the enemy, is treated as a prisoner of war, and incurs no responsibility for his previous acts of espionage.

CHAPTER III

Flags of truce

Article 32

A person is regarded as a parlementaire who has been authorized by one of the belligerents to enter into communication with the other, and who advances bearing a white flag. He has a right to inviolability, as well as the trumpeter, bugler or drummer, the flagbearer and interpreter who may accompany him.

Article 33

The commander to whom a parlementaire is sent is not in all cases obliged to receive him.

He may take all the necessary steps to prevent the parlementaire taking advantage of his mission to obtain information.

In case of abuse, he has the right to detain the parlementaire temporarily.

Article 34

The parlementaire loses his rights of inviolability if it is proved in a clear and incontestable manner that he has taken advantage of his privileged position to provoke or commit an act of treason.

CHAPTER IV

Capitulations

Article 35

Capitulations agreed upon between the Contracting Parties must take into account the rules of military honor.

Once settled, they must be scrupulously observed by both parties.

CHAPTER V

Armistices

Article 36

An armistice suspends military operations by mutual agreement between the belligerent parties. If its duration is not defined, the belligerent parties may resume operations at any time, provided always that the enemy is warned within the time agreed upon, in accordance with the terms of the armistice.

Article 37

An armistice may be general or local. The first suspends the military operations of the belligerent States everywhere; the second only between certain fractions of the belligerent armies and within a fixed radius.

Article 38

An armistice must be notified officially and in good time to the competent authorities and to the troops. Hostilities are suspended immediately after the notification, or on the date fixed.

Article 39

It rests with the Contracting Parties to settle, in the terms of the armistice, what communications may be held in the theatre of war with the inhabitants and between the inhabitants of one belligerent State and those of the other.

Article 40

Any serious violation of the armistice by one of the parties gives the other party the right of denouncing it, and even, in cases of urgency, of recommencing hostilities immediately.

Article 41

A violation of the terms of the armistice by private persons acting on their own initiative only entitles the injured party to demand the punishment of the offenders or, if necessary, compensation for the losses sustained.

SECTION III

MILITARY AUTHORITY OVER THE TERRITORY OF THE HOSTILE STATE

Article 42

Territory is considered occupied when it is actually placed under the authority of the hostile army.

The occupation extends only to the territory where such authority has been established and can be exercised.

Article 43

The authority of the legitimate power having in fact passed into the hands of the occupant, the latter shall take all the measures in his power to restore, and ensure, as far as possible, public order and safety, while respecting, unless absolutely prevented, the laws in force in the country.

Article 44

A belligerent is forbidden to force the inhabitants of territory occupied by it to furnish information about the army of the other belligerent, or about its means of defense.

Article 45

It is forbidden to compel the inhabitants of occupied territory to swear allegiance to the hostile Power.

Article 46

Family honor and rights, the lives of persons, and private property, as well as religious convictions and practice, must be respected.

Private property cannot be confiscated.

Article 47

Pillage is formally forbidden.

Article 48

If, in the territory occupied, the occupant collects the taxes, dues, and tolls imposed for the benefit of the State, he shall do so, as far as is possible, in accordance with the rules of assessment and incidence in force, and shall in consequence be bound to defray the expenses of the administration of the occupied territory to the same extent as the legitimate Government was so bound.

Article 49

If, in addition to the taxes mentioned in the above article, the occupant levies other money contributions in the occupied territory, this shall only be for the needs of the army or of the administration of the territory in question.

Article 50

No general penalty, pecuniary or otherwise, shall be inflicted upon the population on account of the acts of individuals for which they cannot be regarded as jointly and severally responsible.

Article 51

No contribution shall be collected except under a written order, and on the responsibility of a commander-in-chief.

The collection of the said contribution shall only be effected as far as possible in accordance with the rules of assessment and incidence of the taxes in force.

For every contribution a receipt shall be given to the contributors.

Article 52

Requisitions in kind and services shall not be demanded from municipalities or inhabitants except for the needs of the army of occupation. They shall be in proportion to the resources of the country, and of such a nature as not to involve the inhabitants in the obligation of taking part in military operations against their own country.

Such requisitions and services shall only be demanded on the authority of the commander in the locality occupied.

Contributions in kind shall as far is possible be paid for in cash; if not, a receipt shall be given land the payment of the amount due shall be made as soon as possible.

Article 53

An army of occupation can only take possession of cash, funds, and realizable securities which are strictly the property of the State, depots of arms, means of transport, stores and supplies, and, generally, all movable property belonging to the State which may be used for military operations.

All appliances, whether on land, at sea, or in the air, adapted for the transmission of news, or for the transport of persons or things, exclusive of cases governed by naval law, depots of arms, and, generally, all kinds of munitions of war, may be seized, even if they belong to private individuals, but must be restored and compensation fixed when peace is made.

Article 54

Submarine cables connecting an occupied territory with a neutral territory shall not be seized or destroyed except in the case of absolute necessity. They must likewise be restored land compensation fixed when peace is made.

Article 55

The occupying State shall be regarded only as administrator and usufructuary of public buildings, real estate, forests, and agricultural estates belonging to the hostile State, and situated in the occupied country. It must safeguard the capital of these properties, and administer them in accordance with the rules of usufruct.

Article 56

The property of municipalities, that of institutions dedicated to religion, charity and education, the arts and sciences, even when State property, shall be treated as private property.

All seizure of, destruction or willful damage done to institutions of this character, historic monuments, works of art and science, is forbidden, and should be made the subject of legal proceedings.

Geneva Convention relative to the Treatment of Prisoners of War

75 U.N.T.S. 135, entered into force 21 October 1950.

PART I: GENERAL PROVISIONS

Article 1

The High Contracting Parties undertake to respect and to ensure respect for the present Convention in all circumstances.

Article 2

In addition to the provisions which shall be implemented in peace time, the present Convention shall apply to all cases of declared war or of any other armed conflict which may arise between two or more of the High Contracting Parties, even if the state of war is not recognized by one of them.

The Convention shall also apply to all cases of partial or total occupation of the territory of a High Contracting Party, even if the said occupation meets with no armed resistance.

Although one of the Powers in conflict may not be a party to the present Convention, the Powers who are parties thereto shall remain bound by it in their mutual relations. They shall furthermore be bound by the Convention in relation to the said Power, if the latter accepts and applies the provisions thereof.

Article 3

In the case of armed conflict not of an international character occurring in the territory of one of the High Contracting Parties, each Party to the conflict shall be bound to apply, as a minimum, the following provisions:

(1) Persons taking no active part in the hostilities, including members of armed forces who have laid down their arms and those placed hors de combat by sickness, wounds, detention, or any other cause, shall in all circumstances be treated humanely, without any adverse distinction founded on race, colour, religion or faith, sex, birth or wealth, or any other similar criteria. To this end the following acts are and shall remain prohibited at any time and in any place whatsoever with respect to the above-mentioned persons:

(a) violence to life and person, in particular murder of all kinds, mutilation, cruel treatment and torture;

(b) taking of hostages;

(c) outrages upon personal dignity, in particular, humiliating and degrading treatment;

(d) the passing of sentences and the carrying out of executions without previous judgment pronounced by a regularly constituted court affording all the judicial guarantees which are recognized as indispensable by civilized peoples.

(2) The wounded and sick shall be collected and cared for.

An impartial humanitarian body, such as the International Committee of the Red Cross, may offer its services to the Parties to the conflict.

The Parties to the conflict should further endeavour to bring into force, by means of special agreements, all or part of the other provisions of the present Convention.

The application of the preceding provisions shall not affect the legal status of the Parties to the conflict.

Article 4

A. Prisoners of war, in the sense of the present Convention, are persons belonging to one of the following categories, who have fallen into the power of the enemy:

(1) Members of the armed forces of a Party to the conflict, as well as members of militias or volunteer corps forming part of such armed forces.

(2) Members of other militias and members of other volunteer corps, including those of organized resistance movements, belonging to a Party to the conflict and operating in or outside their own territory, even if this territory is occupied, provided that such militias or volunteer corps, including such organized resistance movements, fulfil the following conditions:

(a) that of being commanded by a person responsible for his subordinates;

(b) that of having a fixed distinctive sign recognizable at a distance;

(c) that of carrying arms openly;

(d) that of conducting their operations in accordance with the laws and customs of war.

(3) Members of regular armed forces who profess allegiance to a government or an authority not recognized by the Detaining Power.

(4) Persons who accompany the armed forces without actually being members thereof, such as civilian members of military aircraft crews, war correspondents, supply contractors, members of labour units or of services responsible for the welfare of the armed forces, provided that they have received authorization, from the armed forces which they accompany, who shall provide them for that purpose with an identity card similar to the annexed model.

(5) Members of crews, including masters, pilots and apprentices, of the merchant marine and the crews of civil aircraft of the Parties to the conflict, who do not benefit by more favourable treatment under any other provisions of international law.

(6) Inhabitants of a non-occupied territory, who on the approach of the enemy spontaneously take up arms to resist the invading forces, without having had time to form themselves into regular armed units, provided they carry arms openly and respect the laws and customs of war.

B. The following shall likewise be treated as prisoners of war under the present Convention:

(1) Persons belonging, or having belonged, to the armed forces of the occupied country, if the occupying Power considers it necessary by reason of such allegiance to intern them, even though it has originally liberated them while hostilities were going on outside the territory it occupies, in particular where such persons have made an unsuccessful

attempt to rejoin the armed forces to which they belong and which are engaged in combat, or where they fail to comply with a summons made to them with a view to internment.

(2) The persons belonging to one of the categories enumerated in the present Article, who have been received by neutral or non-belligerent Powers on their territory and whom these Powers are required to intern under international law, without prejudice to any more favourable treatment which these Powers may choose to give and with the exception of Articles 8, 10, 15, 30, fifth paragraph, 58-67, 92, 126 and, where diplomatic relations exist between the Parties to the conflict and the neutral or non-belligerent Power concerned, those Articles concerning the Protecting Power. Where such diplomatic relations exist, the Parties to a conflict on whom these persons depend shall be allowed to perform towards them the functions of a Protecting Power as provided in the present Convention, without prejudice to the functions which these Parties normally exercise in conformity with diplomatic and consular usage and treaties.

C. This Article shall in no way affect the status of medical personnel and chaplains as provided for in Article 33 of the present Convention.

Article 5

The present Convention shall apply to the persons referred to in Article 4 from the time they fall into the power of the enemy and until their final release and repatriation.

Should any doubt arise as to whether persons, having committed a belligerent act and having fallen into the hands of the enemy, belong to any of the categories enumerated in Article 4, such persons shall enjoy the protection of the present Convention until such time as their status has been determined by a competent tribunal.

Article 6

In addition to the agreements expressly provided for in Articles 10, 23, 28, 33, 60, 65, 66, 67, 72, 73, 75, 109, 110, 118, 119, 122 and 132, the High Contracting Parties may conclude other special agreements for all matters concerning which they may deem it suitable to make separate provision. No special agreement shall adversely affect the situation of prisoners of war, as defined by the present Convention, nor restrict the rights which it confers upon them.

Prisoners of war shall continue to have the benefit of such agreements as long as the Convention is applicable to them, except where express provisions to the contrary are contained in the aforesaid or in subsequent agreements, or where more favourable measures have been taken with regard to them by one or other of the Parties to the conflict.

Article 7

Prisoners of war may in no circumstances renounce in part or in entirety the rights secured to them by the present Convention, and by the special agreements referred to in the foregoing Article, if such there be.

Article 8

The present Convention shall be applied with the cooperation and under the scrutiny of the Protecting Powers whose duty it is to safeguard the interests of the Parties to the conflict. For this purpose, the Protecting Powers may appoint, apart from their diplomatic or consular staff, delegates from amongst their own nationals or the nationals of other neutral Powers. The said delegates shall be subject to the approval of the Power with which they are to carry out their duties.

The Parties to the conflict shall facilitate to the greatest extent possible the task of the representatives or delegates of the Protecting Powers.

The representatives or delegates of the Protecting Powers shall not in any case exceed their mission under the present Convention. They shall, in particular, take account of the imperative necessities of security of the State wherein they carry out their duties.

Article 9

The provisions of the present Convention constitute no obstacle to the humanitarian activities which the International Committee of the Red Cross or any other impartial humanitarian organization may, subject to the consent of the Parties to the conflict concerned, undertake for the protection of prisoners of war and for their relief.

Article 10

The High Contracting Parties may at any time agree to entrust to an organization which offers all guarantees of impartiality and efficacy the duties incumbent on the Protecting Powers by virtue of the present Convention.

When prisoners of war do not benefit or cease to benefit, no matter for what reason, by the activities of a Protecting Power or of an organization provided for in the first paragraph above, the Detaining Power shall request a neutral State, or such an organization, to undertake the functions performed under the present Convention by a Protecting Power designated by the Parties to a conflict.

If protection cannot be arranged accordingly, the Detaining Power shall request or shall accept, subject to the provisions of this Article, the offer of the services of a humanitarian organization, such as the International Committee of the Red Cross to assume the humanitarian functions performed by Protecting Powers under the present Convention.

Any neutral Power or any organization invited by the Power concerned or offering itself for these purposes, shall be required to act with a sense of responsibility towards the Party to the conflict on which persons protected by the present Convention depend, and shall be required to furnish sufficient assurances that it is in a position to undertake the appropriate functions and to discharge them impartially.

No derogation from the preceding provisions shall be made by special agreements between Powers one of which is restricted, even temporarily, in its freedom to negotiate with the other Power or its allies by reason of military events, more particularly where the whole, or a substantial part, of the territory of the said Power is occupied.

Whenever in the present Convention mention is made of a Protecting Power, such mention applies to substitute organizations in the sense of the present Article.

Article 11

In cases where they deem it advisable in the interest of protected persons, particularly in cases of disagreement between the Parties to the conflict as to the application or interpretation of the provisions of the present Convention, the Protecting Powers shall lend their good offices with a view to settling the disagreement.

For this purpose, each of the Protecting Powers may, either at the invitation of one Party or on its own initiative, propose to the Parties to the conflict a meeting of their representatives, and in particular of the authorities responsible for prisoners of war, possibly on neutral territory suitably chosen. The Parties to the conflict shall be bound to give effect to the proposals made to them for this purpose. The Protecting Powers may, if necessary, propose for approval by the Parties to the conflict a person belonging to a neutral Power, or delegated by the International Committee of the Red Cross, who shall be invited to take part in such a meeting.

Part II

General Protection of Prisoners of War

Article 12

Prisoners of war are in the hands of the enemy Power, but not of the individuals or military units who have captured them. Irrespective of the individual responsibilities that may exist, the Detaining Power is responsible for the treatment given them.

Prisoners of war may only be transferred by the Detaining Power to a Power which is a party to the Convention and after the Detaining Power has satisfied itself of the willingness and ability of such transferee Power to apply the Convention. When prisoners of war are transferred under such circumstances, responsibility for the application of the Convention rests on the Power accepting them while they are in its custody.

Nevertheless, if that Power fails to carry out the provisions of the Convention in any important respect, the Power by whom the prisoners of war were transferred shall, upon being notified by the Protecting Power, take effective measures to correct the situation or shall request the return of the prisoners of war. Such requests must be complied with.

Article 13

Prisoners of war must at all times be humanely treated. Any unlawful act or omission by the Detaining Power causing death or seriously endangering the health of a prisoner of war in its custody is prohibited, and will be regarded as a serious breach of the present Convention. In particular, no prisoner of war may be subjected to physical mutilation or to medical or scientific experiments of any kind which are not justified by the medical, dental or hospital treatment of the prisoner concerned and carried out in his interest.

Likewise, prisoners of war must at all times be protected, particularly against acts of violence or intimidation and against insults and public curiosity.

Measures of reprisal against prisoners of war are prohibited.

Article 14

Prisoners of war are entitled in all circumstances to respect for their persons and their honour.

Women shall be treated with all the regard due to their sex and shall in all cases benefit by treatment as favourable as that granted to men.

Prisoners of war shall retain the full civil capacity which they enjoyed at the time of their capture. The Detaining Power may not restrict the exercise, either within or without its own territory, of the rights such capacity confers except in so far as the captivity requires.

Article 15

The Power detaining prisoners of war shall be bound to provide free of charge for their maintenance and for the medical attention required by their state of health.

Article 16

Taking into consideration the provisions of the present Convention relating to rank and sex, and subject to any privileged treatment which may be accorded to them by reason of their state of health, age or professional qualifications, all prisoners of war shall be treated alike by the Detaining Power, without any adverse distinction based on race, nationality, religious belief or political opinions, or any other distinction founded on similar criteria.

Part III

Captivity

Section 1

Beginning of Captivity

Article 17

Every prisoner of war, when questioned on the subject, is bound to give only his surname, first names and rank, date of birth, and army, regimental, personal or serial number, or failing this, equivalent information.

If he wilfully infringes this rule, he may render himself liable to a restriction of the privileges accorded to his rank or status.

Each Party to a conflict is required to furnish the persons under its jurisdiction who are liable to become prisoners of war, with an identity card showing the owner's surname, first names, rank, army, regimental, personal or serial number or equivalent information, and date of birth. The identity card may, furthermore, bear the signature or the fingerprints, or both, of the owner, and may bear, as well, any other information the Party to the conflict may wish to add concerning persons belonging to its armed forces. As far as possible the card shall measure 6.5 x 10 cm. and shall be issued in duplicate. The identity card shall be shown by the prisoner of war upon demand, but may in no case be taken away from him.

No physical or mental torture, nor any other form of coercion, may be inflicted on prisoners of war to secure from them information of any kind whatever. Prisoners of war who refuse to answer may not be threatened, insulted, or exposed to unpleasant or disadvantageous treatment of any kind.

Prisoners of war who, owing to their physical or mental condition, are unable to state their identity, shall be handed over to the medical service. The identity of such prisoners shall be established by all possible means, subject to the provisions of the preceding paragraph.

The questioning of prisoners of war shall be carried out in a language which they understand.

Article 18

All effects and articles of personal use, except arms, horses, military equipment and military documents, shall remain in the possession of prisoners of war, likewise their metal helmets and gas masks and like articles issued for personal protection. Effects and articles used for their clothing or feeding shall likewise remain in their possession, even if such effects and articles belong to their regulation military equipment.

At no time should prisoners of war be without identity documents. The Detaining Power shall supply such documents to prisoners of war who possess none.

Badges of rank and nationality, decorations and articles having above all a personal or sentimental value may not be taken from prisoners of war.

Sums of money carried by prisoners of war may not be taken away from them except by order of an officer, and after the amount and particulars of the owner have been recorded in a special register and an itemized receipt has been given, legibly inscribed with the name, rank and unit of the person issuing the said receipt. Sums in the currency of the Detaining Power, or which are changed into such currency at the prisoner's request, shall be placed to the credit of the prisoner's account as provided in Article 64.

The Detaining Power may withdraw articles of value from prisoners of war only for reasons of security; when such articles are withdrawn, the procedure laid down for sums of money impounded shall apply.

Such objects, likewise sums taken away in any currency other than that of the Detaining Power and the conversion of which has not been asked for by the owners, shall be kept in the custody of the Detaining Power and shall be returned in their initial shape to prisoners of war at the end of their captivity.

Article 19

Prisoners of war shall be evacuated, as soon as possible after their capture, to camps situated in an area far enough from the combat zone for them to be out of danger.

Only those prisoners of war who, owing to wounds or sickness, would run greater risks by being evacuated than by remaining where they are, may be temporarily kept back in a danger zone.

Prisoners of war shall not be unnecessarily exposed to danger while awaiting evacuation from a fighting zone.

Article 20

The evacuation of prisoners of war shall always be effected humanely and in conditions similar to those for the forces of the Detaining Power in their changes of station.

The Detaining Power shall supply prisoners of war who are being evacuated with sufficient food and potable water, and with the necessary clothing and medical attention. The Detaining Power shall take all suitable precautions to ensure their safety during evacuation, and shall establish as soon as possible a list of the prisoners of war who are evacuated.

If prisoners of war must, during evacuation, pass through transit camps, their stay in such camps shall be as brief as possible.

Section II

Internment of Prisoners of War

Chapter I

General Observations

Article 21

The Detaining Power may subject prisoners of war to internment. It may impose on them the obligation of not leaving, beyond certain limits, the camp where they are interned, or if the said camp is fenced in, of not going outside its perimeter. Subject to the provisions of the present Convention relative to penal and disciplinary sanctions, prisoners of war may not be held in close confinement except where necessary to safeguard their health and then only during the continuation of the circumstances which make such confinement necessary.

Prisoners of war may be partially or wholly released on parole or promise, in so far as is allowed by the laws of the Power on which they depend. Such measures shall be taken particularly in cases where this may contribute to the improvement of their state of health. No prisoner of war shall be compelled to accept liberty on parole or promise.

Upon the outbreak of hostilities, each Party to the conflict shall notify the adverse Party of the laws and regulations allowing or forbidding its own nationals to accept liberty on parole or promise. Prisoners of war who are paroled or who have given their promise in conformity with the laws and regulations so notified, are bound on their personal honour scrupulously to fulfil, both towards the Power on which they depend and towards the Power which has captured them, the engagements of their paroles or promises. In such cases, the Power on which they depend is bound neither to require nor to accept from them any service incompatible with the parole or promise given.

Article 22

Prisoners of war may be interned only in premises located on land and affording every guarantee of hygiene and healthfulness. Except in particular cases which are justified by the interest of the prisoners themselves, they shall not be interned in penitentiaries.

Prisoners of war interned in unhealthy areas, or where the climate is injurious for them, shall be removed as soon as possible to a more favourable climate.

The Detaining Power shall assemble prisoners of war in camps or camp compounds according to their nationality, language and customs, provided that such prisoners shall not be separated from prisoners of war belonging to the armed forces with which they were serving at the time of their capture, except with their consent.

Article 23

No prisoner of war may at any time be sent to, or detained in areas where he may be exposed to the fire of the combat zone, nor may his presence be used to render certain points or areas immune from military operations.

Prisoners of war shall have shelters against air bombardment and other hazards of war, to the same extent as the local civilian population. With the exception of those engaged in the protection of their quarters against the aforesaid hazards, they may enter such shelters as soon as possible after the giving of the alarm. Any other protective measure taken in favour of the population shall also apply to them.

Detaining Powers shall give the Powers concerned, through the intermediary of the Protecting Powers, all useful information regarding the geographical location of prisoner of war camps.

Whenever military considerations permit, prisoner of war camps shall be indicated in the day-time by the letters PW or PG, placed so as to be clearly visible from the air. The Powers concerned may, however, agree upon any other system of marking. Only prisoner of war camps shall be marked as such.

Article 24

Transit or screening camps of a permanent kind shall be fitted out under conditions similar to those described in the present Section, and the prisoners therein shall have the same treatment as in other camps.

Chapter II

Quarters, Food and Clothing of Prisoners of War

Article 25

Prisoners of war shall be quartered under conditions as favourable as those for the forces of the Detaining Power who are billeted in the same area. The said conditions shall make allowance for the habits and customs of the prisoners and shall in no case be prejudicial to their health.

The foregoing provisions shall apply in particular to the dormitories of prisoners of war as regards both total surface and minimum cubic space, and the general installations, bedding and blankets.

The premises provided for the use of prisoners of war individually or collectively, shall be entirely protected from dampness and adequately heated and lighted, in particular between dusk and lights out. All precautions must be taken against the danger of fire.

In any camps in which women prisoners of war, as well as men, are accommodated, separate dormitories shall be provided for them.

Article 26

The basic daily food rations shall be sufficient in quantity, quality and variety to keep prisoners of war in good health and to prevent loss of weight or the development of nutritional deficiencies. Account shall also be taken of the habitual diet of the prisoners.

The Detaining Power shall supply prisoners of war who work with such additional rations as are necessary for the labour on which they are employed.

Sufficient drinking water shall be supplied to prisoners of war. The use of tobacco shall be permitted.

Prisoners of war shall, as far as possible, be associated with the preparation of their meals; they may be employed for that purpose in the kitchens. Furthermore, they shall be given the means of preparing, themselves, the additional food in their possession.

Adequate premises shall be provided for messing.

Collective disciplinary measures affecting food are prohibited.

Article 27

Clothing, underwear and footwear shall be supplied to prisoners of war in sufficient quantities by the Detaining Power, which shall make allowance for the climate of the region where the prisoners are detained. Uniforms of enemy armed forces captured by the Detaining Power should, if suitable for the climate, be made available to clothe prisoners of war.

The regular replacement and repair of the above articles shall be assured by the Detaining Power. In addition, prisoners of war who work shall receive appropriate clothing, wherever the nature of the work demands.

Article 28

Canteens shall be installed in all camps, where prisoners of war may procure foodstuffs, soap and tobacco and ordinary articles in daily use. The tariff shall never be in excess of local market prices.

The profits made by camp canteens shall be used for the benefit of the prisoners; a special fund shall be created for this purpose. The prisoners' representative shall have the right to collaborate in the management of the canteen and of this fund.

When a camp is closed down, the credit balance of the special fund shall be handed to an international welfare organization, to be employed for the benefit of prisoners of war of the same nationality as those who have contributed to the fund. In case of a general repatriation, such profits shall be kept by the Detaining Power, subject to any agreement to the contrary between the Powers concerned.

Chapter III

Hygiene and Medical Attention

Article 29

The Detaining Power shall be bound to take all sanitary measures necessary to ensure the cleanliness and healthfulness of camps and to prevent epidemics.

Prisoners of war shall have for their use, day and night, conveniences which conform to the rules of hygiene and are maintained in a constant state of cleanliness. In any camps in which women prisoners of war are accommodated, separate conveniences shall be provided for them.

Also, apart from the baths and showers with which the camps shall be furnished prisoners of war shall be provided with sufficient water and soap for their personal toilet and for washing their personal laundry; the necessary installations, facilities and time shall be granted them for that purpose.

Article 30

Every camp shall have an adequate infirmary where prisoners of war may have the attention they require, as well as appropriate diet. Isolation wards shall, if necessary, be set aside for cases of contagious or mental disease.

Prisoners of war suffering from serious disease, or whose condition necessitates special treatment, a surgical operation or hospital care, must be admitted to any military or civilian medical unit where such treatment can be given, even if their repatriation is contemplated in the near future. Special facilities shall be afforded for the care to be given to the disabled, in particular to the blind, and for their rehabilitation, pending repatriation.

Prisoners of war shall have the attention, preferably, of medical personnel of the Power on which they depend and, if possible, of their nationality.

Prisoners of war may not be prevented from presenting themselves to the medical authorities for examination. The detaining authorities shall, upon request, issue to every prisoner who has undergone treatment, an official certificate indicating the nature of his illness or injury, and the duration and kind of treatment received. A duplicate of this certificate shall be forwarded to the Central Prisoners of War Agency.

The costs of treatment, including those of any apparatus necessary for the maintenance of prisoners of war in good health, particularly dentures and other artificial appliances, and spectacles, shall be borne by the Detaining Power.

Article 31

Medical inspections of prisoners of war shall be held at least once a month. They shall include the checking and the recording of the weight of each prisoner of war.

Their purpose shall be, in particular, to supervise the general state of health, nutrition and cleanliness of prisoners and to detect contagious diseases, especially tuberculosis, malaria and venereal disease. For this purpose the most efficient methods available shall be employed, e.g. periodic mass miniature radiography for the early detection of tuberculosis.

Article 32

Prisoners of war who, though not attached to the medical service of their armed forces, are physicians, surgeons, dentists, nurses or medical orderlies, may be required by the Detaining Power to exercise their medical functions in the interests of prisoners of war dependent on the same Power. In that case they shall continue to be prisoners of war, but shall receive the same treatment as corresponding medical personnel retained by the Detaining Power. They shall be exempted from any other work under Article 49.

Chapter IV

Medical Personnel and Chaplains Retained to Assist Prisoners of War

Article 33

Members of the medical personnel and chaplains while retained by the Detaining Power with a view to assisting prisoners of war, shall not be considered as prisoners of war. They shall, however, receive as a minimum the benefits and protection of the present Convention, and shall also be granted all facilities necessary to provide for the medical care of, and religious ministration to prisoners of war.

They shall continue to exercise their medical and spiritual functions for the benefit of prisoners of war, preferably those belonging to the armed forces upon which they depend, within the scope of the military laws and regulations of the Detaining Power and under the control of its competent services, in accordance with their professional etiquette. They shall also benefit by the following facilities in the exercise of their medical or spiritual functions:

(a) They shall be authorized to visit periodically prisoners of war situated in working detachments or in hospitals outside the camp. For this purpose, the Detaining Power shall place at their disposal the necessary means of transport.

(b) The senior medical officer in each camp shall be responsible to the camp military authorities for everything connected with the activities of retained medical personnel. For this purpose, Parties to the conflict shall agree at the outbreak of hostilities on the subject of the corresponding ranks of the medical personnel, including that of societies mentioned in Article 26 of the Geneva Convention for the Amelioration of the Condition of the Wounded and Sick in Armed Forces in the Field of August 12, 1949. This senior medical officer, as well as chaplains, shall have the right to deal with the competent authorities of the camp on all questions relating to their duties. Such authorities shall afford them all necessary facilities for correspondence relating to these questions.

(c) Although they shall be subject to the internal discipline of the camp in which they are retained, such personnel may not be compelled to carry out any work other than that concerned with their medical or religious duties.

During hostilities, the Parties to the conflict shall agree concerning the possible relief of retained personnel and shall settle the procedure to be followed.

None of the preceding provisions shall relieve the Detaining Power of its obligations with regard to prisoners of war from the medical or spiritual point of view.

Chapter V

Religious, Intellectual and Physical Activities

Article 34

Prisoners of war shall enjoy complete latitude in the exercise of their religious duties, including attendance at the service of their faith, on condition that they comply with the disciplinary routine prescribed by the military authorities.

Adequate premises shall be provided where religious services may be held.

Article 35

Chaplains who fall into the hands of the enemy Power and who remain or are retained with a view to assisting prisoners of war, shall be allowed to minister to them and to exercise freely their ministry amongst prisoners of war of the same religion, in accordance with their religious conscience. They shall be allocated among the various camps and labour detachments containing prisoners of war belonging to the same forces, speaking the same language or practising the same religion. They shall enjoy the necessary facilities, including the means of transport provided for in Article 33, for visiting the prisoners of war outside their camp. They shall be free to correspond, subject to censorship, on matters concerning their religious duties with the ecclesiastical authorities in the country of detention and with international religious organizations. Letters and cards which they may send for this purpose shall be in addition to the quota provided for in Article 71.

Article 36

Prisoners of war who are ministers of religion, without having officiated as chaplains to their own forces, shall be at liberty, whatever their denomination, to minister freely to the members of their community. For this purpose, they shall receive the same treatment as the chaplains retained by the Detaining Power. They shall not be obliged to do any other work.

Article 37

When prisoners of war have not the assistance of a retained chaplain or of a prisoner of war minister of their faith, a minister belonging to the prisoners' or a similar denomination, or in his absence a qualified layman, if such a course is feasible from a confessional point of view, shall be appointed, at the request of the prisoners concerned, to fill this office. This appointment, subject to the approval of the Detaining Power, shall take place with the agreement of the community of prisoners concerned and, wherever necessary, with the approval of the local religious authorities of the same faith. The person thus appointed shall comply with all regulations established by the Detaining Power in the interests of discipline and military security.

Article 38

While respecting the individual preferences of every prisoner, the Detaining Power shall encourage the practice of intellectual, educational, and recreational pursuits, sports and games amongst prisoners, and shall take the measures necessary to ensure the exercise thereof by providing them with adequate premises and necessary equipment.

Prisoners shall have opportunities for taking physical exercise, including sports and games, and for being out of doors. Sufficient open spaces shall be provided for this purpose in all camps.

Chapter VI

Discipline

Article 39

Every prisoner of war camp shall be put under the immediate authority of a responsible commissioned officer belonging to the regular armed forces of the Detaining Power. Such officer shall have in his possession a copy of the present Convention; he shall ensure that its provisions are known to the camp staff and the guard and shall be responsible, under the direction of his government, for its application.

Prisoners of war, with the exception of officers, must salute and show to all officers of the Detaining Power the external marks of respect provided for by the regulations applying in their own forces.

Officer prisoners of war are bound to salute only officers of a higher rank of the Detaining Power; they must, however, salute the camp commander regardless of his rank.

Article 40

The wearing of badges of rank and nationality, as well as of decorations, shall be permitted.

Article 41

In every camp the text of the present Convention and its Annexes and the contents of any special agreement provided for in Article 6, shall be posted, in the prisoners' own language, in places where all may read them. Copies shall be supplied, on request, to the prisoners who cannot have access to the copy which has been posted.

Regulations, orders, notices and publications of every kind relating to the conduct of prisoners of war shall be issued to them in a language which they understand. Such regulations, orders and publications shall be posted in the manner described above and copies shall be handed to the prisoners' representative. Every order and command addressed to prisoners of war individually must likewise be given in a language which they understand.

Article 42

The use of weapons against prisoners of war, especially against those who are escaping or attempting to escape, shall constitute an extreme measure, which shall always be preceded by warnings appropriate to the circumstances.

Chapter VII

Rank of Prisoners of War

Article 43.

Upon the outbreak of hostilities, the Parties to the conflict shall communicate to one another the titles and ranks of all the persons mentioned in Article 4 of the present Convention, in order to ensure equality of treatment between prisoners of equivalent rank. Titles and ranks which are subsequently created shall form the subject of similar communications.

The Detaining Power shall recognize promotions in rank which have been accorded to prisoners of war and which have been duly notified by the Power on which these prisoners depend.

Article 44

Officers and prisoners of equivalent status shall be treated with the regard due to their rank and age.

In order to ensure service in officers' camps, other ranks of the same armed forces who, as far as possible, speak the same language, shall be assigned in sufficient numbers, account being taken of the rank of officers and prisoners of equivalent status. Such orderlies shall not be required to perform any other work.

Supervision of the mess by the officers themselves shall be facilitated in every way.

Article 45

Prisoners of war other than officers and prisoners of equivalent status shall be treated with the regard due to their rank and age.

Supervision of the mess by the prisoners themselves shall be facilitated in every way.

Chapter VIII

Transfer of Prisoners of War after their Arrival in Camp

Article 46

The Detaining Power, when deciding upon the transfer of prisoners of war, shall take into account the interests of the prisoners themselves, more especially so as not to increase the difficulty of their repatriation.

The transfer of prisoners of war shall always be effected humanely and in conditions not less favourable than those under which the forces of the Detaining Power are transferred. Account shall always be taken of the climatic conditions to which the prisoners of war are accustomed and the conditions of transfer shall in no case be prejudicial to their health.

The Detaining Power shall supply prisoners of war during transfer with sufficient food and drinking water to keep them in good health, likewise with the necessary clothing, shelter and medical attention. The Detaining Power shall take adequate precautions especially in case of transport by sea or by air, to ensure their safety during transfer, and shall draw up a complete list of all transferred prisoners before their departure.

Article 47

Sick or wounded prisoners of war shall not be transferred as long as their recovery may be endangered by the journey, unless their safety imperatively demands it.

If the combat zone draws closer to a camp, the prisoners of war in the said camp shall not be transferred unless their transfer can be carried out in adequate conditions of safety, or unless they are exposed to greater risks by remaining on the spot than by being transferred.

Article 48

In the event of transfer, prisoners of war shall be officially advised of their departure and of their new postal address. Such notifications shall be given in time for them to pack their luggage and inform their next of kin.

They shall be allowed to take with them their personal effects, and the correspondence and parcels which have arrived for them. The weight of such baggage may be limited, if the conditions of transfer so require, to what each prisoner can reasonably carry, which shall in no case be more than twenty-five kilograms per head.

Mail and parcels addressed to their former camp shall be forwarded to them without delay. The camp commander shall take, in agreement with the prisoners' representative, any measures needed to ensure the transport of the prisoners' community property and of the luggage they are unable to take with them in consequence of restrictions imposed by virtue of the second paragraph of this Article.

The costs of transfers shall be borne by the Detaining Power.

Section III

Labour of Prisoners of War

Article 49

The Detaining Power may utilize the labour of prisoners of war who are physically fit, taking into account their age, sex, rank and physical aptitude, and with a view particularly to maintaining them in a good state of physical and mental health.

Non-commissioned officers who are prisoners of war shall only be required to do supervisory work. Those not so required may ask for other suitable work which shall, so far as possible, be found for them.

If officers or persons of equivalent status ask for suitable work, it shall be found for them, so far as possible, but they may in no circumstances be compelled to work.

Article 50

Besides work connected with camp administration, installation or maintenance, prisoners of war may be compelled to do only such work as is included in the following classes:

(a) agriculture;

(b) industries connected with the production or the extraction of raw materials, and manufacturing industries, with the exception of metallurgical, machinery and chemical industries; public works and building operations which have no military character or purpose;

(c) transport and handling of stores which are not military in character or purpose;

(d) commercial business, and arts and crafts;

(e) domestic service;

(f) public utility services having no military character or purpose.

Should the above provisions be infringed, prisoners of war shall be allowed to exercise their right of complaint, in conformity with Article 78.

Article 51

Prisoners of war must be granted suitable working conditions, especially as regards accommodation, food, clothing and equipment; such conditions shall not be inferior to those enjoyed by nationals of the Detaining Power employed in similar work; account shall also be taken of climatic conditions.

The Detaining Power, in utilizing the labour of prisoners of war, shall ensure that in areas in which such prisoners are employed, the national legislation concerning the protection of labour, and, more particularly, the regulations for the safety of workers, are duly applied.

Prisoners of war shall receive training and be provided with the means of protection suitable to the work they will have to do and similar to those accorded to the nationals of the Detaining Power. Subject to the provisions of Article 52, prisoners may be submitted to the normal risks run by these civilian workers.

Conditions of labour shall in no case be rendered more arduous by disciplinary measures.

Article 52

Unless he be a volunteer, no prisoner of war may be employed on labour which is of an unhealthy or dangerous nature.

No prisoner of war shall be assigned to labour which would be looked upon as humiliating for a member of the Detaining Power's own forces.

The removal of mines or similar devices shall be considered as dangerous labour.

Article 53

The duration of the daily labour of prisoners of war, including the time of the journey to and fro, shall not be excessive, and must in no case exceed that permitted for civilian workers in the district, who are nationals of the Detaining Power and employed on the same work.

Prisoners of war must be allowed, in the middle of the day's work, a rest of not less than one hour. This rest will be the same as that to which workers of the Detaining Power are entitled, if the latter is of longer duration. They shall be allowed in addition a rest of twenty-four consecutive hours every week, preferably on Sunday or the day of rest in their country of origin. Furthermore, every prisoner who has worked for one year shall be granted a rest of eight consecutive days, during which his working pay shall be paid him.

If methods of labour such as piece work are employed, the length of the working period shall not be rendered excessive thereby.

Article 54

The working pay due to prisoners of war shall be fixed in accordance with the provisions of Article 62 of the present Convention.

Prisoners of war who sustain accidents in connection with work, or who contract a disease in the course, or in consequence of their work, shall receive all the care their condition may require. The Detaining Power shall furthermore deliver to such prisoners of war a medical certificate enabling them to submit their claims to the Power on which they depend, and shall send a duplicate to the Central Prisoners of War Agency provided for in Article 123.

Article 55

The fitness of prisoners of war for work shall be periodically verified by medical examinations at least once a month. The examinations shall have particular regard to the nature of the work which prisoners of war are required to do.

If any prisoner of war considers himself incapable of working, he shall be permitted to appear before the medical authorities of his camp. Physicians or surgeons may recommend that the prisoners who are, in their opinion, unfit for work, be exempted therefrom.

Article 56

The organization and administration of labour detachments shall be similar to those of prisoner of war camps.

Every labour detachment shall remain under the control of and administratively part of a prisoner of war camp. The military authorities and the commander of the said camp shall be responsible, under the direction of their government, for the observance of the provisions of the present Convention in labour detachments.

The camp commander shall keep an up-to-date record of the labour detachments dependent on his camp, and shall communicate it to the delegates of the Protecting Power, of the International Committee of the Red Cross, or of other agencies giving relief to prisoners of war, who may visit the camp.

Article 57

The treatment of prisoners of war who work for private persons, even if the latter are responsible for guarding and protecting them, shall not be inferior to that which is provided for by the present Convention. The Detaining Power, the military authorities and the commander of the camp to which such prisoners belong shall be entirely responsible for the maintenance, care, treatment, and payment of the working pay of such prisoners of war.

Such prisoners of war shall have the right to remain in communication with the prisoners' representatives in the camps on which they depend.

Section IV

Financial Resources of Prisoners of War

Article 58

Upon the outbreak of hostilities, and pending an arrangement on this matter with the Protecting Power, the Detaining Power may determine the maximum amount of money in cash or in any similar form, that prisoners may have in their possession. Any amount in excess, which was properly in their possession and which has been taken or withheld from them, shall be placed to their account, together with any monies deposited by them, and shall not be converted into any other currency without their consent.

If prisoners of war are permitted to purchase services or commodities outside the camp against payment in cash, such payments shall be made by the prisoner himself or by the camp administration who will charge them to the accounts of the prisoners concerned. The Detaining Power will establish the necessary rules in this respect.

Article 59

Cash which was taken from prisoners of war, in accordance with Article 18, at the time of their capture, and which is in the currency of the Detaining Power, shall be placed to their separate accounts, in accordance with the provisions of Article 64 of the present Section.

The amounts, in the currency of the Detaining Power, due to the conversion of sums in other currencies that are taken from the prisoners of war at the same time, shall also be credited to their separate accounts.

Article 60.

The Detaining Power shall grant all prisoners of war a monthly advance of pay, the amount of which shall be fixed by conversion, into the currency of the said Power, of the following amounts:

Category I : Prisoners ranking below sergeants: eight Swiss francs.

Category II : Sergeants and other non-commissioned officers, or prisoners of equivalent rank: twelve Swiss francs.

Category III: Warrant officers and commissioned officers below the rank of major or prisoners of equivalent rank: fifty Swiss francs.

Category IV: Majors, lieutenant-colonels, colonels or prisoners of equivalent rank: sixty Swiss francs.

Category V: General officers or prisoners of war of equivalent rank: seventy-five Swiss francs.

However, the Parties to the conflict concerned may by special agreement modify the amount of advances of pay due to prisoners of the preceding categories.

Furthermore, if the amounts indicated in the first paragraph above would be unduly high compared with the pay of the Detaining Power's armed forces or would, for any reason, seriously embarrass the Detaining Power, then, pending the conclusion of a special agreement with the Power on which the prisoners depend to vary the amounts indicated above, the Detaining Power:

(a) shall continue to credit the accounts of the prisoners with the amounts indicated in the first paragraph above;

(b) may temporarily limit the amount made available from these advances of pay to prisoners of war for their own use, to sums which are reasonable, but which, for Category I, shall never be inferior to the amount that the Detaining Power gives to the members of its own armed forces.

The reasons for any limitations will be given without delay to the Protecting Power.

Article 61

The Detaining Power shall accept for distribution as supplementary pay to prisoners of war sums which the Power on which the prisoners depend may forward to them, on condition that the sums to be paid shall be the same for each prisoner of the same category, shall be payable to all prisoners of that category depending on that Power, and shall be placed in their separate accounts, at the earliest opportunity, in accordance with the provisions of Article 64. Such supplementary pay shall not relieve the Detaining Power of any obligation under this Convention.

Article 62

Prisoners of war shall be paid a fair working rate of pay by the detaining authorities direct. The rate shall be fixed by the said authorities, but shall at no time be less than one-fourth of one Swiss franc for a full working day. The Detaining Power shall inform prisoners of war, as well as the Power on which they depend, through the intermediary of the Protecting Power, of the rate of daily working pay that it has fixed.

Working pay shall likewise be paid by the detaining authorities to prisoners of war permanently detailed to duties or to a skilled or semi-skilled occupation in connection with the administration, installation or maintenance of camps, and to the prisoners who are required to carry out spiritual or medical duties on behalf of their comrades.

The working pay of the prisoners' representative, of his advisers, if any, and of his assistants, shall be paid out of the fund maintained by canteen profits. The scale of this working pay shall be fixed by the prisoners' representative and approved by the camp commander. If there is no such fund, the detaining authorities shall pay these prisoners a fair working rate of pay.

Article 63

Prisoners of war shall be permitted to receive remittances of money addressed to them individually or collectively.

Every prisoner of war shall have at his disposal the credit balance of his account as provided for in the following Article, within the limits fixed by the Detaining Power, which shall make such payments as are requested. Subject to financial or monetary restrictions which the Detaining Power regards as essential, prisoners of war may also have payments made abroad. In this case payments addressed by prisoners of war to dependents shall be given priority.

In any event, and subject to the consent of the Power on which they depend, prisoners may have payments made in their own country, as follows: the Detaining Power shall send to the aforesaid Power through the Protecting Power, a notification giving all the necessary particulars concerning the prisoners of war, the beneficiaries of the payments, and the amount of the sums to be paid, expressed in the Detaining Power's currency. The said notification shall be signed by the prisoners and countersigned by the camp commander. The Detaining Power shall debit the prisoners' account by a corresponding amount; the sums thus debited shall be placed by it to the credit of the Power on which the prisoners depend.

To apply the foregoing provisions, the Detaining Power may usefully consult the Model Regulations in Annex V of the present Convention.

Article 64

The Detaining Power shall hold an account for each prisoner of war, showing at least the following:

(1) The amounts due to the prisoner or received by him as advances of pay, as working pay or derived from any other source; the sums in the currency of the Detaining Power which were taken from him; the sums taken from him and converted at his request into the currency of the said Power.

(2) The payments made to the prisoner in cash, or in any other similar form; the payments made on his behalf and at his request; the sums transferred under Article 63, third paragraph.

Article 65

Every item entered in the account of a prisoner of war shall be countersigned or initialled by him, or by the prisoners' representative acting on his behalf.

Prisoners of war shall at all times be afforded reasonable facilities for consulting and obtaining copies of their accounts, which may likewise be inspected by the representatives of the Protecting Powers at the time of visits to the camp.

When prisoners of war are transferred from one camp to another, their personal accounts will follow them. In case of transfer from one Detaining Power to another, the monies which are their property and are not in the currency of the Detaining Power will follow them. They shall be given certificates for any other monies standing to the credit of their accounts.

The Parties to the conflict concerned may agree to notify to each other at specific intervals through the Protecting Power, the amount of the accounts of the prisoners of war.

Article 66

On the termination of captivity, through the release of a prisoner of war or his repatriation, the Detaining Power shall give him a statement, signed by an authorized officer of that Power, showing the credit balance then due to him. The Detaining Power shall also send through the Protecting Power to the government upon which the prisoner of war depends, lists giving all appropriate particulars of all prisoners of war whose captivity has been terminated by repatriation, release, escape, death or any other means, and showing the amount of their credit balances. Such lists shall be certified on each sheet by an authorized representative of the Detaining Power.

Any of the above provisions of this Article may be varied by mutual agreement between any two Parties to the conflict.

The Power on which the prisoner of war depends shall be responsible for settling with him any credit balance due to him from the Detaining Power on the termination of his captivity.

Article 67

Advances of pay, issued to prisoners of war in conformity with Article 60, shall be considered as made on behalf of the Power on which they depend. Such advances of pay, as well as all payments made by the said Power under Article 63, third paragraph, and Article 68, shall form the subject of arrangements between the Powers concerned, at the close of hostilities.

Article 68

Any claim by a prisoner of war for compensation in respect of any injury or other disability arising out of work shall be referred to the Power on which he depends, through the Protecting Power. In accordance with Article 54, the Detaining Power will, in all cases, provide the prisoner of war concerned with a statement showing the nature of the injury or disability, the circumstances in which it arose and particulars of medical or hospital treatment given for it. This statement will be signed by a responsible officer of the Detaining Power and the medical particulars certified by a medical officer.

Any claim by a prisoner of war for compensation in respect of personal effects monies or valuables impounded by the Detaining Power under Article 18 and not forthcoming on his repatriation, or in respect of loss alleged to be due to the fault of the Detaining Power or any of its servants, shall likewise be referred to the Power on which he depends. Nevertheless, any such personal effects required for use by the prisoners of war whilst in captivity shall be replaced at the expense of the Detaining Power. The Detaining Power will, in all cases, provide the prisoner of war with a statement, signed by a responsible officer, showing all available information regarding the reasons why such effects, monies or valuables have not been restored to him. A copy of this statement will be forwarded to the Power on which he depends through the Central Prisoners of War Agency provided for in Article 123.

Section V

Relations of Prisoners of War With the Exterior

Article 69

Immediately upon prisoners of war falling into its power, the Detaining Power shall inform them and the Powers on which they depend, through the Protecting Power, of the measures taken to carry out the provisions of the present Section. They shall likewise inform the parties concerned of any subsequent modifications of such measures.

Article 70

Immediately upon capture, or not more than one week after arrival at a camp, even if it is a transit camp, likewise in case of sickness or transfer to hospital or to another camp, every prisoner of war shall be enabled to write direct to his family, on the one hand, and to the Central Prisoners of War Agency provided for in Article 123, on the other hand, a card similar, if possible, to the model annexed to the present Convention, informing his relatives of his capture, address and state of health. The said cards shall be forwarded as rapidly as possible and may not be delayed in any manner.

Article 71

Prisoners of war shall be allowed to send and receive letters and cards. If the Detaining Power deems it necessary to limit the number of letters and cards sent by each prisoner of war, the said number shall not be less than two letters and four cards monthly, exclusive of the capture cards provided for in Article 70, and conforming as closely as possible to the models annexed to the present Convention. Further limitations may be imposed only if the Protecting Power is satisfied that it would be in the interests of the prisoners of war concerned to do so owing to difficulties of translation caused by the Detaining Power's inability to find sufficient qualified linguists to carry out the necessary censorship. If limitations must be placed on the correspondence addressed to prisoners of war, they may be ordered only by the Power on which the prisoners depend, possibly at the request of the Detaining Power. Such letters and cards must be conveyed by the most rapid method at the disposal of the Detaining Power; they may not be delayed or retained for disciplinary reasons.

Prisoners of war who have been without news for a long period, or who are unable to receive news from their next of kin or to give them news by the ordinary postal route, as well as those who are at a great distance from their homes, shall be permitted to send telegrams, the fees being charged against the prisoners of war's accounts with the Detaining Power or paid in the currency at their disposal. They shall likewise benefit by this measure in cases of urgency.

As a general rule, the correspondence of prisoners of war shall be written in their native language. The Parties to the conflict may allow correspondence in other languages.

Sacks containing prisoner of war mail must be securely sealed and labelled so as clearly to indicate their contents, and must be addressed to offices of destination.

Article 72

Prisoners of war shall be allowed to receive by post or by any other means individual parcels or collective shipments containing, in particular, foodstuffs, clothing, medical supplies and articles of a religious, educational or recreational character which may meet their needs, including books, devotional articles, scientific equipment, examination papers, musical instruments, sports outfits and materials allowing prisoners of war to pursue their studies or their cultural activities.

Such shipments shall in no way free the Detaining Power from the obligations imposed upon it by virtue of the present Convention.

The only limits which may be placed on these shipments shall be those proposed by the Protecting Power in the interest of the prisoners themselves, or by the International Committee of the Red Cross or any other organization giving assistance to the prisoners, in respect of their own shipments only, on account of exceptional strain on transport or communications.

The conditions for the sending of individual parcels and collective relief shall, if necessary, be the subject of special agreements between the Powers concerned, which may in no case delay the receipt by the prisoners of relief supplies. Books may not be included in parcels of clothing and foodstuffs. Medical supplies shall, as a rule, be sent in collective parcels.

Article 73

In the absence of special agreements between the Powers concerned on the conditions for the receipt and distribution of collective relief shipments, the rules and regulations concerning collective shipments, which are annexed to the present Convention, shall be applied.

The special agreements referred to above shall in no case restrict the right of prisoners' representatives to take possession of collective relief shipments intended for prisoners of war, to proceed to their distribution or to dispose of them in the interest of the prisoners.

Nor shall such agreements restrict the right of representatives of the Protecting Power, the International Committee of the Red Cross or any other organization giving assistance to prisoners of war and responsible for the forwarding of collective shipments, to supervise their distribution to the recipients.

Article 74

All relief shipments for prisoners of war shall be exempt from import, customs and other dues.

Correspondence, relief shipments and authorized remittances of money addressed to prisoners of war or despatched by them through the post office, either direct or through the Information Bureaux provided for in Article 122 and the Central Prisoners of War Agency provided for in Article 123, shall be exempt from any postal dues, both in the countries of origin and destination, and in intermediate countries.

If relief shipments intended for prisoners of war cannot be sent through the post office by reason of weight or for any other cause, the cost of transportation shall be borne by the Detaining Power in all the territories under its control. The other Powers party to the Convention shall bear the cost of transport in their respective territories. In the absence of special agreements between the Parties concerned, the costs connected with transport of such shipments, other than costs covered by the above exemption, shall be charged to the senders.

The High Contracting Parties shall endeavour to reduce, so far as possible, the rates charged for telegrams sent by prisoners of war, or addressed to them.

Article 75

Should military operations prevent the Powers concerned from fulfilling their obligation to assure the transport of the shipments referred to in Articles 70, 71, 72 and 77, the Protecting Powers concerned, the International Committee of the Red Cross or any other organization duly approved by the Parties to the conflict may undertake to ensure the conveyance of such shipments by suitable means (railway wagons, motor vehicles, vessels or aircraft, etc.). For this purpose, the High Contracting Parties shall endeavour to supply them with such transport and to allow its circulation, especially by granting the necessary safe-conducts.

Such transport may also be used to convey:

(a) correspondence, lists and reports exchanged between the Central Information Agency referred to in Article 123 and the National Bureaux referred to in Article 122;

(b) correspondence and reports relating to prisoners of war which the Protecting Powers, the International Committee of the Red Cross or any other body assisting the prisoners, exchange either with their own delegates or with the Parties to the conflict.

These provisions in no way detract from the right of any Party to the conflict to arrange other means of transport, if it should so prefer, nor preclude the granting of safe-conducts, under mutually agreed conditions, to such means of transport.

In the absence of special agreements, the costs occasioned by the use of such means of transport shall be borne proportionally by the Parties to the conflict whose nationals are benefited thereby.

Article 76

The censoring of correspondence addressed to prisoners of war or despatched by them shall be done as quickly as possible. Mail shall be censored only by the despatching State and the receiving State, and once only by each.

The examination of consignments intended for prisoners of war shall not be carried out under conditions that will expose the goods contained in them to deterioration; except in the case of written or printed matter, it shall be done in the presence of the addressee, or of a fellow-prisoner duly delegated by him. The delivery to prisoners of individual or collective consignments shall not be delayed under the pretext of difficulties of censorship.

Any prohibition of correspondence ordered by Parties to the conflict, either for military or political reasons, shall be only temporary and its duration shall be as short as possible.

Article 77

The Detaining Powers shall provide all facilities for the transmission, through the Protecting Power or the Central Prisoners of War Agency provided for in Article 123 of instruments, papers or documents intended for prisoners of war or despatched by them, especially powers of attorney and wills.

In all cases they shall facilitate the preparation and execution of such documents on behalf of prisoners of war; in particular, they shall allow them to consult a lawyer and shall take what measures are necessary for the authentication of their signatures.

Section VI

Relations Between Prisoners of War and the Authorities

Chapter I

Complaints of Prisoners of War Respecting the Conditions of Captivity

Article 78

Prisoners of war shall have the right to make known to the military authorities in whose power they are, their requests regarding the conditions of captivity to which they are subjected.

They shall also have the unrestricted right to apply to the representatives of the Protecting Powers either through their prisoners' representative or, if they consider it necessary, direct, in order to draw their attention to any points on which they may have complaints to make regarding their conditions of captivity.

These requests and complaints shall not be limited nor considered to be a part of the correspondence quota referred to in Article 71. They must be transmitted immediately. Even if they are recognized to be unfounded, they may not give rise to any punishment.

Prisoners' representatives may send periodic reports on the situation in the camps and the needs of the prisoners of war to the representatives of the Protecting Powers.

Chapter II

Prisoner of War Representatives

Article 79

In all places where there are prisoners of war, except in those where there are officers, the prisoners shall freely elect by secret ballot, every six months, and also in case of vacancies, prisoners' representatives entrusted with representing them before the military authorities, the Protecting Powers, the International Committee of the Red Cross and any other organization which may assist them. These prisoners' representatives shall be eligible for re-election.

In camps for officers and persons of equivalent status or in mixed camps, the senior officer among the prisoners of war shall be recognized as the camp prisoners' representative. In camps for officers, he shall be assisted by one or more advisers chosen by the officers; in mixed camps, his assistants shall be chosen from among the prisoners of war who are not officers and shall be elected by them.

Officer prisoners of war of the same nationality shall be stationed in labour camps for prisoners of war, for the purpose of carrying out the camp administration duties for which the prisoners of war are responsible. These officers may be elected as prisoners' representatives under the first paragraph of this Article. In such a case the assistants to the prisoners' representatives shall be chosen from among those prisoners of war who are not officers.

Every representative elected must be approved by the Detaining Power before he has the right to commence his duties. Where the Detaining Power refuses to approve a prisoner of war elected by his fellow prisoners of war, it must inform the Protecting Power of the reason for such refusal.

In all cases the prisoners' representative must have the same nationality, language and customs as the prisoners of war whom he represents. Thus, prisoners of war distributed in different sections of a camp, according to their nationality, language or customs, shall have for each section their own prisoners' representative, in accordance with the foregoing paragraphs.

Article 80

Prisoners' representatives shall further the physical, spiritual and intellectual well-being of prisoners of war.

In particular, where the prisoners decide to organize amongst themselves a system of mutual assistance, this organization will be within the province of the prisoners' representative, in addition to the special duties entrusted to him by other provisions of the present Convention.

Prisoners' representatives shall not be held responsible, simply by reason of their duties, for any offences committed by prisoners of war.

Article 81

Prisoners' representatives shall not be required to perform any other work, if the accomplishment of their duties is thereby made more difficult.

Prisoners' representatives may appoint from amongst the prisoners such assistants as they may require. All material facilities shall be granted them, particularly a certain freedom of movement necessary for the accomplishment of their duties (inspection of labour detachments, receipt of supplies, etc.).

Prisoners' representatives shall be permitted to visit premises where prisoners of war are detained, and every prisoner of war shall have the right to consult freely his prisoners' representative.

All facilities shall likewise be accorded to the prisoners' representatives for communication by post and telegraph with the detaining authorities, the Protecting Powers, the International Committee of the Red Cross and their delegates, the Mixed Medical Commissions and the bodies which give assistance to prisoners of war. Prisoners' representatives of labour detachments shall enjoy the same facilities for communication with the prisoners' representatives of the principal camp. Such communications shall not be restricted, nor considered as forming a part of the quota mentioned in Article 71.

Prisoners' representatives who are transferred shall be allowed a reasonable time to acquaint their successors with current affairs.

In case of dismissal, the reasons therefor shall be communicated to the Protecting Power.

Chapter III

Penal and Disciplinary Sanctions

I. General Provisions

Article 82

A prisoner of war shall be subject to the laws, regulations and orders in force in the armed forces of the Detaining Power; the Detaining Power shall be justified in taking judicial or disciplinary measures in respect of any offence committed by a prisoner of war against such laws, regulations or orders. However, no proceedings or punishments contrary to the provisions of this Chapter shall be allowed.

If any law, regulation or order of the Detaining Power shall declare acts committed by a prisoner of war to be punishable, whereas the same acts would not be punishable if committed by a member of the forces of the Detaining Power, such acts shall entail disciplinary punishments only.

Article 83

In deciding whether proceedings in respect of an offence alleged to have been committed by a prisoner of war shall be judicial or disciplinary, the Detaining Power shall ensure that the competent authorities exercise the greatest leniency and adopt, wherever possible, disciplinary rather than judicial measures.

Article 84

A prisoner of war shall be tried only by a military court, unless the existing laws of the Detaining Power expressly permit the civil courts to try a member of the armed forces of the Detaining Power in respect of the particular offence alleged to have been committed by the prisoner of war.

In no circumstances whatever shall a prisoner of war be tried by a court of any kind which does not offer the essential guarantees of independence and impartiality as generally recognized, and, in particular, the procedure of which does not afford the accused the rights and means of defence provided for in Article 105.

Article 85

Prisoners of war prosecuted under the laws of the Detaining Power for acts committed prior to capture shall retain, even if convicted, the benefits of the present Convention.

Article 86

No prisoner of war may be punished more than once for the same act or on the same charge.

Article 87

Prisoners of war may not be sentenced by the military authorities and courts of the Detaining Power to any penalties except those provided for in respect of members of the armed forces of the said Power who have committed the same acts.

When fixing the penalty, the courts or authorities of the Detaining Power shall take into consideration, to the widest extent possible, the fact that the accused, not being a national of the Detaining Power, is not bound to it by any duty of allegiance, and that he is in its power as the result of circumstances independent of his own will. The said courts or authorities shall be at liberty to reduce the penalty provided for the violation of which the prisoner of war is accused, and shall therefore not be bound to apply the minimum penalty prescribed.

Collective punishment for individual acts, corporal punishment, imprisonment in premises without daylight and, in general, any form of torture or cruelty, are forbidden.

No prisoner of war may be deprived of his rank by the Detaining Power, or prevented from wearing his badges.

Article 88

Officers, non-commissioned officers and men who are prisoners of war undergoing a disciplinary or judicial punishment, shall not be subjected to more severe treatment than that applied in respect of the same punishment to members of the armed forces of the Detaining Power of equivalent rank.

A woman prisoner of war shall not be awarded or sentenced to a punishment more severe, or treated whilst undergoing punishment more severely, than a woman member of the armed forces of the Detaining Power dealt with for a similar offence.

In no case may a woman prisoner of war be awarded or sentenced to a punishment more severe, or treated whilst undergoing punishment more severely, than a male member of the armed forces of the Detaining Power dealt with for a similar offence.

Prisoners of war who have served disciplinary or judicial sentences may not be treated differently from other prisoners of war.

II. Disciplinary Sanctions

Article 88

The disciplinary punishments applicable to prisoners of war are the following:

(1) A fine which shall not exceed 50 per cent of the advances of pay and working pay which the prisoner of war would otherwise receive under the provisions of Articles 60 and 62 during a period of not more than thirty days.

(2) Discontinuance of privileges granted over and above the treatment provided for by the present Convention.

(3) Fatigue duties not exceeding two hours daily.

(4) Confinement.

The punishment referred to under (3) shall not be applied to officers.

In no case shall disciplinary punishments be inhuman, brutal or dangerous to the health of prisoners of war.

Article 90

The duration of any single punishment shall in no case exceed thirty days. Any period of confinement awaiting the hearing of a disciplinary offence or the award of disciplinary punishment shall be deducted from an award pronounced against a prisoner of war.

The maximum of thirty days provided above may not be exceeded, even if the prisoner of war is answerable for several acts at the same time when he is awarded punishment, whether such acts are related or not.

The period between the pronouncing of an award of disciplinary punishment and its execution shall not exceed one month.

When a prisoner of war is awarded a further disciplinary punishment, a period of at least three days shall elapse between the execution of any two of the punishments, if the duration of one of these is ten days or more.

Article 91

The escape of a prisoner of war shall be deemed to have succeeded when:

(1) he has joined the armed forces of the Power on which he depends, or those of an allied Power;

(2) he has left the territory under the control of the Detaining Power, or of an ally of the said Power;

(3) he has joined a ship flying the flag of the Power on which he depends, or of an allied Power, in the territorial waters of the Detaining Power, the said ship not being under the control of the last named Power.

Prisoners of war who have made good their escape in the sense of this Article and who are recaptured, shall not be liable to any punishment in respect of their previous escape.

Article 92

A prisoner of war who attempts to escape and is recaptured before having made good his escape in the sense of Article 91 shall be liable only to a disciplinary punishment in respect of this act, even if it is a repeated offence.

A prisoner of war who is recaptured shall be handed over without delay to the competent military authority.

Article 88, fourth paragraph, notwithstanding, prisoners of war punished as a result of an unsuccessful escape may be subjected to special surveillance. Such surveillance must not affect the state of their health, must be undergone in a prisoner of war camp, and must not entail the suppression of any of the safeguards granted them by the present Convention.

Article 93

Escape or attempt to escape, even if it is a repeated offence, shall not be deemed an aggravating circumstance if the prisoner of war is subjected to trial by judicial proceedings in respect of an offence committed during his escape or attempt to escape.

In conformity with the principle stated in Article 83, offences committed by prisoners of war with the sole intention of facilitating their escape and which do not entail any violence against life or limb, such as offences against public property, theft without intention of self-enrichment, the drawing up or use of false papers, or the wearing of civilian clothing, shall occasion disciplinary punishment only.

Prisoners of war who aid or abet an escape or an attempt to escape shall be liable on this count to disciplinary punishment only.

Article 94

If an escaped prisoner of war is recaptured, the Power on which he depends shall be notified thereof in the manner defined in Article 122, provided notification of his escape has been made.

Article 95

A prisoner of war accused of an offence against discipline shall not be kept in confinement pending the hearing unless a member of the armed forces of the Detaining Power would be so kept if he were accused of a similar offence, or if it is essential in the interests of camp order and discipline.

Any period spent by a prisoner of war in confinement awaiting the disposal of an offence against discipline shall be reduced to an absolute minimum and shall not exceed fourteen days.

The provisions of Articles 97 and 98 of this Chapter shall apply to prisoners of war who are in confinement awaiting the disposal of offences against discipline.

Article 96

Acts which constitute offences against discipline shall be investigated immediately.

Without prejudice to the competence of courts and superior military authorities, disciplinary punishment may be ordered only by an officer having disciplinary powers in his capacity as camp commander, or by a responsible officer who replaces him or to whom he has delegated his disciplinary powers.

In no case may such powers be delegated to a prisoner of war or be exercised by a prisoner of war.

Before any disciplinary award is pronounced, the accused shall be given precise information regarding the offences of which he is accused, and given an opportunity of explaining his conduct and of defending himself. He shall be permitted, in particular, to call witnesses and to have recourse, if necessary, to the services of a qualified interpreter. The decision shall be announced to the accused prisoner of war and to the prisoners' representative.

A record of disciplinary punishments shall be maintained by the camp commander and shall be open to inspection by representatives of the Protecting Power.

Article 97

Prisoners of war shall not in any case be transferred to penitentiary establishments (prisons, penitentiaries, convict prisons, etc.) to undergo disciplinary punishment therein.

All premises in which disciplinary punishments are undergone shall conform to the sanitary requirements set forth in Article 25. A prisoner of war undergoing punishment shall be enabled to keep himself in a state of cleanliness, in conformity with Article 29.

Officers and persons of equivalent status shall not be lodged in the same quarters as non-commissioned officers or men.

Women prisoners of war undergoing disciplinary punishment shall be confined in separate quarters from male prisoners of war and shall be under the immediate supervision of women.

Article 98

A prisoner of war undergoing confinement as a disciplinary punishment, shall continue to enjoy the benefits of the provisions of this Convention except in so far as these are necessarily rendered inapplicable by the mere fact that he is confined. In no case may he be deprived of the benefits of the provisions of Articles 78 and 126.

A prisoner of war awarded disciplinary punishment may not be deprived of the prerogatives attached to his rank.

Prisoners of war awarded disciplinary punishment shall be allowed to exercise and to stay in the open air at least two hours daily.

They shall be allowed, on their request, to be present at the daily medical inspections. They shall receive the attention which their state of health requires and, if necessary, shall be removed to the camp infirmary or to a hospital.

They shall have permission to read and write, likewise to send and receive letters. Parcels and remittances of money however, may be withheld from them until the completion of the punishment; they shall meanwhile be entrusted to the prisoners' representative, who will hand over to the infirmary the perishable goods contained in such parcels.

III. Juridical Proceedings

Article 99

No prisoner of war may be tried or sentenced for an act which is not forbidden by the law of the Detaining Power or by international law, in force at the time the said act was committed.

No moral or physical coercion may be exerted on a prisoner of war in order to induce him to admit himself guilty of the act of which he is accused.

No prisoner of war may be convicted without having had an opportunity to present his defence and the assistance of a qualified advocate or counsel.

Article 100

Prisoners of war and the Protecting Powers shall be informed as soon as possible of the offences which are punishable by the death sentence under the laws of the Detaining Power.

Other offences shall not thereafter be made punishable by the death penalty without the concurrence of the Power on which the prisoners of war depend.

The death sentence cannot be pronounced on a prisoner of war unless the attention of the court has, in accordance with Article 87, second paragraph, been particularly called to the fact that since the accused is not a national of the Detaining Power, he is not bound to it by any duty of allegiance, and that he is in its power as the result of circumstances independent of his own will.

Article 101

If the death penalty is pronounced on a prisoner of war, the sentence shall not be executed before the expiration of a period of at least six months from the date when the Protecting Power receives, at an indicated address, the detailed communication provided for in Article 107.

Article 102

A prisoner of war can be validly sentenced only if the sentence has been pronounced by the same courts according to the same procedure as in the case of members of the armed forces of the Detaining Power, and if, furthermore, the provisions of the present Chapter have been observed.

Article 103

Judicial investigations relating to a prisoner of war shall be conducted as rapidly as circumstances permit and so that his trial shall take place as soon as possible. A prisoner of war shall not be confined while awaiting trial unless a member of the armed forces of the Detaining Power would be so confined if he were accused of a similar offence, or if it is essential to do so in the interests of national security. In no circumstances shall this confinement exceed three months.

Any period spent by a prisoner of war in confinement awaiting trial shall be deducted from any sentence of imprisonment passed upon him and taken into account in fixing any penalty.

The provisions of Articles 97 and 98 of this Chapter shall apply to a prisoner of war whilst in confinement awaiting trial.

Article 104

In any case in which the Detaining Power has decided to institute judicial proceedings against a prisoner of war, it shall notify the Protecting Power as soon as possible and at least three weeks before the opening of the trial. This period of three weeks shall run as from the day on which such notification reaches the Protecting Power at the address previously indicated by the latter to the Detaining Power.

The said notification shall contain the following information:

(1) Surname and first names of the prisoner of war, his rank, his army, regimental, personal or serial number, his date of birth, and his profession or trade, if any;

(2) Place of internment or confinement;

(3) Specification of the charge or charges on which the prisoner of war is to be arraigned, giving the legal provisions applicable;

(4) Designation of the court which will try the case, likewise the date and place fixed for the opening of the trial.

The same communication shall be made by the Detaining Power to the prisoners' representative.

If no evidence is submitted, at the opening of a trial, that the notification referred to above was received by the Protecting Power, by the prisoner of war and by the prisoners' representative concerned, at least three weeks before the opening of the trial, then the latter cannot take place and must be adjourned.

Article 105

The prisoner of war shall be entitled to assistance by one of his prisoner comrades, to defence by a qualified advocate or counsel of his own choice, to the calling of witnesses and, if he deems necessary, to the services of a competent interpreter. He shall be advised of these rights by the Detaining Power in due time before the trial.

Failing a choice by the prisoner of war, the Protecting Power shall find him an advocate or counsel, and shall have at least one week at its disposal for the purpose. The Detaining Power shall deliver to the said Power, on request, a list of persons qualified to present the defence. Failing a choice of an advocate or counsel by the prisoner of war or the Protecting Power, the Detaining Power shall appoint a competent advocate or counsel to conduct the defence.

The advocate or counsel conducting the defence on behalf of the prisoner of war shall have at his disposal a period of two weeks at least before the opening of the trial, as well as the necessary facilities to prepare the defence of the accused. He may, in particular, freely visit the accused and interview him in private. He may also confer with any witnesses for the defence, including prisoners of war. He shall have the benefit of these facilities until the term of appeal or petition has expired.

Particulars of the charge or charges on which the prisoner of war is to be arraigned, as well as the documents which are generally communicated to the accused by virtue of the laws in force in the armed forces of the Detaining Power, shall be communicated to the accused prisoner of war in a language which he understands, and in good time before the opening of the trial. The same communication in the same circumstances shall be made to the advocate or counsel conducting the defence on behalf of the prisoner of war.

The representatives of the Protecting Power shall be entitled to attend the trial of the case, unless, exceptionally, this is held in camera in the interest of State security. In such a case the Detaining Power shall advise the Protecting Power accordingly.

Article 106

Every prisoner of war shall have, in the same manner as the members of the armed forces of the Detaining Power, the right of appeal or petition from any sentence pronounced upon him, with a view to the quashing or revising of the sentence or the reopening of the trial. He shall be fully informed of his right to appeal or petition and of the time limit within which he may do so.

Article 107

Any judgment and sentence pronounced upon a prisoner of war shall be immediately reported to the Protecting Power in the form of a summary communication, which shall also indicate whether he has the right of appeal with a view to the quashing of the sentence or the reopening of the trial. This communication shall likewise be sent to the prisoners' representative concerned. It shall also be sent to the accused prisoner of war in a language he understands, if the sentence was not pronounced in his presence. The Detaining Power shall also immediately communicate to the Protecting Power the decision of the prisoner of war to use or to waive his right of appeal.

Furthermore, if a prisoner of war is finally convicted or if a sentence pronounced on a prisoner of war in the first instance is a death sentence, the Detaining Power shall as soon as possible address to the Protecting Power a detailed communication containing:

(1) the precise wording of the finding and sentence;

(2) a summarized report of any preliminary investigation and of the trial, emphasizing in particular the elements of the prosecution and the defence;

(3) notification, where applicable, of the establishment where the sentence will be served.

The communications provided for in the foregoing sub-paragraphs shall be sent to the Protecting Power at the address previously made known to the Detaining Power.

Article 108

Sentences pronounced on prisoners of war after a conviction has become duly enforceable, shall be served in the same establishments and under the same conditions as in the case of members of the armed forces of the Detaining Power. These conditions shall in all cases conform to the requirements of health and humanity.

A woman prisoner of war on whom such a sentence has been pronounced shall be confined in separate quarters and shall be under the supervision of women.

In any case, prisoners of war sentenced to a penalty depriving them of their liberty shall retain the benefit of the provisions of Articles 78 and 126 of the present Convention. Furthermore, they shall be entitled to receive and despatch correspondence, to receive at least one relief parcel monthly, to take regular exercise in the open air, to have the medical care required by their state of health, and the spiritual assistance they may desire. Penalties to which they may be subjected shall be in accordance with the provisions of Article 87, third paragraph.

Part IV

Termination of Captivity

Section I

Direct Repatriation and Accommodation in Neutral Countries

Article 109

Subject to the provisions of the third paragraph of this Article, Parties to the conflict are bound to send back to their own country, regardless of number or rank, seriously wounded and seriously sick prisoners of war, after having cared for them until they are fit to travel, in accordance with the first paragraph of the following Article.

Throughout the duration of hostilities, Parties to the conflict shall endeavour, with the cooperation of the neutral Powers concerned, to make arrangements for the accommodation in neutral countries of the sick and wounded prisoners of war referred to in the second paragraph of the following Article. They may, in addition, conclude agreements with a view to the direct repatriation or internment in a neutral country of able-bodied prisoners of war who have undergone a long period of captivity.

No sick or injured prisoner of war who is eligible for repatriation under the first paragraph of this Article, may be repatriated against his will during hostilities.

Article 110

The following shall be repatriated direct:

(1) Incurably wounded and sick whose mental or physical fitness seems to have been gravely diminished.

(2) Wounded and sick who, according to medical opinion, are not likely to recover within one year, whose condition requires treatment and whose mental or physical fitness seems to have been gravely diminished.

(3) Wounded and sick who have recovered, but whose mental or physical fitness seems to have been gravely and permanently diminished.

The following may be accommodated in a neutral country:

(1) Wounded and sick whose recovery may be expected within one year of the date of the wound or the beginning of the illness, if treatment in a neutral country might increase the prospects of a more certain and speedy recovery.

(2) Prisoners of war whose mental or physical health, according to medical opinion, is seriously threatened by continued captivity, but whose accommodation in a neutral country might remove such a threat.

The conditions which prisoners of war accommodated in a neutral country must fulfil in order to permit their repatriation shall be fixed, as shall likewise their status, by agreement between the Powers concerned. In general, prisoners of war who have been accommodated in a neutral country, and who belong to the following categories, should be repatriated:

(1) Those whose state of health has deteriorated so as to fulfil the condition laid down for direct repatriation;

(2) Those whose mental or physical powers remain, even after treatment, considerably impaired.

If no special agreements are concluded between the Parties to the conflict concerned, to determine the cases of disablement or sickness entailing direct repatriation or accommodation in a neutral country, such cases shall be settled in accordance with the principles laid down in the Model Agreement concerning direct repatriation and accommodation in neutral countries of wounded and sick prisoners of war and in the Regulations concerning Mixed Medical Commissions annexed to the present Convention.

Article 111

The Detaining Power, the Power on which the prisoners of war depend, and a neutral Power agreed upon by these two Powers, shall endeavour to conclude agreements which will enable prisoners of war to be interned in the territory of the said neutral Power until the close of hostilities.

Article 112

Upon the outbreak of hostilities, Mixed Medical Commissions shall be appointed to examine sick and wounded prisoners of war, and to make all appropriate decisions regarding them. The appointment, duties and functioning of these Commissions shall be in conformity with the provisions of the Regulations annexed to the present Convention.

However, prisoners of war who, in the opinion of the medical authorities of the Detaining Power, are manifestly seriously injured or seriously sick, may be repatriated without having to be examined by a Mixed Medical Commission.

Article 113

Besides those who are designated by the medical authorities of the Detaining Power, wounded or sick prisoners of war belonging to the categories listed below shall be entitled to present themselves for examination by the Mixed Medical Commissions provided for in the foregoing Article:

(1) Wounded and sick proposed by a physician or surgeon who is of the same nationality, or a national of a Party to the conflict allied with the Power on which the said prisoners depend, and who exercises his functions in the camp.

(2) Wounded and sick proposed by their prisoners' representative.

(3) Wounded and sick proposed by the Power on which they depend, or by an organization duly recognized by the said Power and giving assistance to the prisoners.

Prisoners of war who do not belong to one of the three foregoing categories may nevertheless present themselves for examination by Mixed Medical Commissions, but shall be examined only after those belonging to the said categories.

The physician or surgeon of the same nationality as the prisoners who present themselves for examination by the Mixed Medical Commission, likewise the prisoners' representative of the said prisoners, shall have permission to be present at the examination.

Article 114

Prisoners of war who meet with accidents shall, unless the injury is self-inflicted, have the benefit of the provisions of this Convention as regards repatriation or accommodation in a neutral country.

Article 115

No prisoner of war on whom a disciplinary punishment has been imposed and who is eligible for repatriation or for accommodation in a neutral country, may be kept back on the plea that he has not undergone his punishment.

Prisoners of war detained in connection with a judicial prosecution or conviction, and who are designated for repatriation or accommodation in a neutral country, may benefit by such measures before the end of the proceedings or the completion of the punishment, if the Detaining Power consents.

Parties to the conflict shall communicate to each other the names of those who will be detained until the end of the proceedings or the completion of the punishment.

Article 116

The cost of repatriating prisoners of war or of transporting them to a neutral country shall be borne, from the frontiers of the Detaining Power, by the Power on which the said prisoners depend.

Article 117

No repatriated person may be employed on active military service.

Section II

Release and Repatriation of Prisoners of War at the Close of Hostilities

Article 118

Prisoners of war shall be released and repatriated without delay after the cessation of active hostilities.

In the absence of stipulations to the above effect in any agreement concluded between the Parties to the conflict with a view to the cessation of hostilities, or failing any such agreement, each of the Detaining Powers shall itself establish and execute without delay a plan of repatriation in conformity with the principle laid down in the foregoing paragraph.

In either case, the measures adopted shall be brought to the knowledge of the prisoners of war.

The costs of repatriation of prisoners of war shall in all cases be equitably apportioned between the Detaining Power and the Power on which the prisoners depend. This apportionment shall be carried out on the following basis:

(a) If the two Powers are contiguous, the Power on which the prisoners of war depend shall bear the costs of repatriation from the frontiers of the Detaining Power.

(b) If the two Powers are not contiguous, the Detaining Power shall bear the costs of transport of prisoners of war over its own territory as far as its frontier or its port of embarkation nearest to the territory of the Power on which the prisoners of war depend. The Parties concerned shall agree between themselves as to the equitable apportionment of the remaining costs of the repatriation. The conclusion of this agreement shall in no circumstances justify any delay in the repatriation of the prisoners of war.

Article 119

Repatriation shall be effected in conditions similar to those laid down in Articles 46 to 48 inclusive of the present Convention for the transfer of prisoners of war, having regard to the provisions of Article 118 and to those of the following paragraphs.

On repatriation, any articles of value impounded from prisoners of war under Article 18, and any foreign currency which has not been converted into the currency of the Detaining Power, shall be restored to them. Articles of value and foreign currency which, for any reason whatever, are not restored to prisoners of war on repatriation, shall be despatched to the Information Bureau set up under Article 122.

Prisoners of war shall be allowed to take with them their personal effects, and any correspondence and parcels which have arrived for them. The weight of such baggage may be limited, if the conditions of repatriation so require, to what each prisoner can reasonably carry. Each prisoner shall in all cases be authorized to carry at least twenty-five kilograms.

The other personal effects of the repatriated prisoner shall be left in the charge of the Detaining Power which shall have them forwarded to him as soon as it has concluded an agreement to this effect, regulating the conditions of transport and the payment of the costs involved, with the Power on which the prisoner depends.

Prisoners of war against whom criminal proceedings for an indictable offence are pending may be detained until the end of such proceedings, and, if necessary, until the completion of the punishment. The same shall apply to prisoners of war already convicted for an indictable offence.

Parties to the conflict shall communicate to each other the names of any prisoners of war who are detained until the end of the proceedings or until punishment has been completed.

By agreement between the Parties to the conflict, commissions shall be established for the purpose of searching for dispersed prisoners of war and of assuring their repatriation with the least possible delay.

Section III

Death of Prisoners of War

Article 120

Wills of prisoners of war shall be drawn up so as to satisfy the conditions of validity required by the legislation of their country of origin, which will take steps to inform the Detaining Power of its requirements in this respect. At the request of the prisoner of war and, in all cases, after death, the will shall be transmitted without delay to the Protecting Power; a certified copy shall be sent to the Central Agency.

Death certificates, in the form annexed to the present Convention, or lists certified by a responsible officer, of all persons who die as prisoners of war shall be forwarded as rapidly as possible to the Prisoner of War Information Bureau established in accordance with Article 122. The death certificates or certified lists shall show particulars of identity as set out in the third paragraph of Article 17, and also the date and place of death, the cause of death, the date and place of burial and all particulars necessary to identify the graves.

The burial or cremation of a prisoner of war shall be preceded by a medical examination of the body with a view to confirming death and enabling a report to be made and, where necessary, establishing identity.

The detaining authorities shall ensure that prisoners of war who have died in captivity are honourably buried, if possible according to the rites of the religion to which they belonged, and that their graves are respected, suitably maintained and marked so as to be found at any time. Wherever possible, deceased prisoners of war who depended on the same Power shall be interred in the same place.

Deceased prisoners of war shall be buried in individual graves unless unavoidable circumstances require the use of collective graves. Bodies may be cremated only for imperative reasons of hygiene, on account of the religion of the deceased or in accordance with his express wish to this effect. In case of cremation, the fact shall be stated and the reasons given in the death certificate of the deceased.

In order that graves may always be found, all particulars of burials and graves shall be recorded with a Graves Registration Service established by the Detaining Power. Lists of graves and particulars of the prisoners of war interred in cemeteries and elsewhere shall be transmitted to the Power on which such prisoners of war depended. Responsibility for the care of these graves and for records of any subsequent moves of the bodies shall rest on the Power controlling the territory, if a Party to the present Convention. These provisions shall also apply to the ashes, which shall be kept by the Graves Registration Service until proper disposal thereof in accordance with the wishes of the home country.

Article 121

Every death or serious injury of a prisoner of war caused or suspected to have been caused by a sentry, another prisoner of war, or any other person, as well as any death the cause of which is unknown, shall be immediately followed by an official enquiry by the Detaining Power.

A communication on this subject shall be sent immediately to the Protecting Power. Statements shall be taken from witnesses, especially from those who are prisoners of war, and a report including such statements shall be forwarded to the Protecting Power.

If the enquiry indicates the guilt of one or more persons, the Detaining Power shall take all measures for the prosecution of the person or persons responsible.

PART V

Information Bureaux and Relief Societies for Prisoners of War

Article 122

Upon the outbreak of a conflict and in all cases of occupation, each of the Parties to the conflict shall institute an official Information Bureau for prisoners of war who are in its power. Neutral or non-belligerent Powers who may have received within their territory persons belonging to one of the categories referred to in Article 4, shall take the same action with respect to such persons. The Power concerned shall ensure that the Prisoners of War Information Bureau is provided with the necessary accommodation, equipment and staff to ensure its efficient working. It shall be at liberty to employ prisoners of war in such a Bureau under the conditions laid down in the Section of the present Convention dealing with work by prisoners of war.

Within the shortest possible period, each of the Parties to the conflict shall give its Bureau the information referred to in the fourth, fifth and sixth paragraphs of this Article regarding any enemy person belonging to one of the categories referred to in Article 4, who has fallen into its power. Neutral or non-belligerent Powers shall take the same action with regard to persons belonging to such categories whom they have received within their territory.

The Bureau shall immediately forward such information by the most rapid means to the Powers concerned, through the intermediary of the Protecting Powers and likewise of the Central Agency provided for in Article 123.

This information shall make it possible quickly to advise the next of kin concerned. Subject to the provisions of Article 17, the information shall include, in so far as available to the Information Bureau, in respect of each prisoner of war, his surname, first names, rank, army, regimental, personal or serial number, place and full date of birth, indication of the Power on which he depends, first name of the father and maiden name of the mother, name and address of the person to be informed and the address to which correspondence for the prisoner may be sent.

The Information Bureau shall receive from the various departments concerned information regarding transfers, releases, repatriations, escapes, admissions to hospital, and deaths, and shall transmit such information in the manner described in the third paragraph above.

Likewise, information regarding the state of health of prisoners of war who are seriously ill or seriously wounded shall be supplied regularly, every week if possible.

The Information Bureau shall also be responsible for replying to all enquiries sent to it concerning prisoners of war, including those who have died in captivity; it will make any enquiries necessary to obtain the information which is asked for if this is not in its possession.

All written communications made by the Bureau shall be authenticated by a signature or a seal.

The Information Bureau shall furthermore be charged with collecting all personal valuables, including sums in currencies other than that of the Detaining Power and documents of importance to the next of kin, left by prisoners of war who have been repatriated or released, or who have escaped or died, and shall forward the said valuables to the Powers concerned. Such articles shall be sent by the Bureau in sealed packets which shall be accompanied by statements giving clear and full particulars of the identity of the person to whom the articles belonged, and by a complete list of the contents of the parcel. Other personal effects of such prisoners of war shall be transmitted under arrangements agreed upon between the Parties to the conflict concerned.

Article 123

A Central Prisoners of War Information Agency shall be created in a neutral country. The International Committee of the Red Cross shall, if it deems necessary, propose to the Powers concerned the organization of such an Agency.

The function of the Agency shall be to collect all the information it may obtain through official or private channels respecting prisoners of war, and to transmit it as rapidly as possible to the country of origin of the prisoners of war or to the Power on which they depend. It shall receive from the Parties to the conflict all facilities for effecting such transmissions.

The High Contracting Parties, and in particular those whose nationals benefit by the services of the Central Agency, are requested to give the said Agency the financial aid it may require.

The foregoing provisions shall in no way be interpreted as restricting the humanitarian activities of the International Committee of the Red Cross, or of the relief societies provided for in Article 125.

Article 124

The national Information Bureaux and the Central Information Agency shall enjoy free postage for mail, likewise all the exemptions provided for in Article 74, and further, so far as possible, exemption from telegraphic charges or, at least, greatly reduced rates.

Article 125

Subject to the measures which the Detaining Powers may consider essential to ensure their security or to meet any other reasonable need, the representatives of religious organizations, relief societies, or any other organization assisting prisoners of war, shall receive from the said Powers, for themselves and their duly accredited agents, all necessary facilities for visiting the prisoners, for distributing relief supplies and material, from any source, intended for religious, educational or recreative purposes, and for assisting them in organizing their leisure time within the camps. Such societies or organizations may be constituted in the territory of the Detaining Power or in any other country, or they may have an international character.

The Detaining Power may limit the number of societies and organizations whose delegates are allowed to carry out their activities in its territory and under its supervision, on condition, however, that such limitation shall not hinder the effective operation of adequate relief to all prisoners of war.

The special position of the International Committee of the Red Cross in this field shall be recognized and respected at all times.

As soon as relief supplies or material intended for the above-mentioned purposes are handed over to prisoners of war, or very shortly afterwards, receipts for each consignment, signed by the prisoners' representative, shall be forwarded to the relief society or organization making the shipment. At the same time, receipts for these consignments shall be supplied by the administrative authorities responsible for guarding the prisoners.

Part VI

Execution of the Convention

Section I

General Provisions

Article 126

Representatives or delegates of the Protecting Powers shall have permission to go to all places where prisoners of war may be, particularly to places of internment, imprisonment and labour, and shall have access to all premises occupied by prisoners of war; they shall also be allowed to go to the places of departure, passage and arrival of prisoners who are being transferred. They shall be able to interview the prisoners, and in particular the prisoners' representatives, without witnesses, either personally or through an interpreter.

Representatives and delegates of the Protecting Powers shall have full liberty to select the places they wish to visit. The duration and frequency of these visits shall not be restricted. Visits may not be prohibited except for reasons of imperative military necessity, and then only as an exceptional and temporary measure.

The Detaining Power and the Power on which the said prisoners of war depend may agree, if necessary, that compatriots of these prisoners of war be permitted to participate in the visits.

The delegates of the International Committee of the Red Cross shall enjoy the same prerogatives. The appointment of such delegates shall be submitted to the approval of the Power detaining the prisoners of war to be visited.

Article 127

The High Contracting Parties undertake, in time of peace as in time of war, to disseminate the text of the present Convention as widely as possible in their respective countries, and, in particular, to include the study thereof in their programmes of military and, if possible, civil instruction, so that the principles thereof may become known to all their armed forces and to the entire population.

Any military or other authorities, who in time of war assume responsibilities in respect of prisoners of war, must possess the text of the Convention and be specially instructed as to its provisions.

Article 128

The High Contracting Parties shall communicate to one another through the Swiss Federal Council and, during hostilities, through the Protecting Powers, the official translations of the present Convention, as well as the laws and regulations which they may adopt to ensure the application thereof.

Article 129

The High Contracting Parties undertake to enact any legislation necessary to provide effective penal sanctions for persons committing, or ordering to be committed, any of the grave breaches of the present Convention defined in the following Article.

Each High Contracting Party shall be under the obligation to search for persons alleged to have committed or to have ordered to be committed, such grave breaches, and shall bring such persons, regardless of their nationality, before its own courts. It may also, if it prefers, and in accordance with the provisions of its own legislation, hand such persons over for trial to another High Contracting Party concerned, provided such High Contracting Party has made out a prima facie case.

Each High Contracting Party shall take measures necessary for the suppression of all acts contrary to the provisions of the present Convention other than the grave breaches defined in the following Article.

In all circumstances, the accused persons shall benefit by safeguards of proper trial and defence, which shall not be less favourable than those provided by Article 105 and those following of the present Convention.

Article 130

Grave breaches to which the preceding Article relates shall be those involving any of the following acts, if committed against persons or property protected by the Convention:

wilful killing, torture or inhuman treatment, including biological experiments, wilfully causing great suffering or serious injury to body or health, compelling a prisoner of war to serve in the forces of the hostile Power, or wilfully depriving a prisoner of war of the rights of fair and regular trial prescribed in this Convention.

Article 131

No High Contracting Party shall be allowed to absolve itself or any other High Contracting Party of any liability incurred by itself or by another High Contracting Party in respect of breaches referred to in the preceding Article.

Article 132

At the request of a Party to the conflict, an enquiry shall be instituted, in a manner to be decided between the interested Parties, concerning any alleged violation of the Convention.

If agreement has not been reached concerning the procedure for the enquiry, the Parties should agree on the choice of an umpire who will decide upon the procedure to be followed.

Once the violation has been established, the Parties to the conflict shall put an end to it and shall repress it with the least possible delay.

Section II.
Final Provisions

Article 133

The present Convention is established in English and in French. Both texts are equally authentic.

The Swiss Federal Council shall arrange for official translations of the Convention to be made in the Russian and Spanish languages.

Article 134

The present Convention replaces the Convention of July 27, 1929, in relations between the High Contracting Parties.

Article 135

In the relations between the Powers which are bound by the Hague Convention respecting the Laws and Customs of War on Land, whether that of July 29, 1899, or that of October 18, 1907, and which are parties to the present Convention, this last Convention shall be complementary to Chapter II of the Regulations annexed to the above-mentioned Conventions of the Hague. ...

Article 142

Each of the High Contracting Parties shall be at liberty to denounce the present Convention.

The denunciation shall be notified in writing to the Swiss Federal Council, which shall transmit it to the Governments of all the High Contracting Parties.

The denunciation shall take effect one year after the notification thereof has been made to the Swiss Federal Council. However, a denunciation of which notification has been made at a time when the denouncing Power is involved in a conflict shall not take effect until peace has been concluded, and until after operations connected with release and repatriation of the persons protected by the present Convention have been terminated.

The denunciation shall have effect only in respect of the denouncing Power. It shall in no way impair the obligations which the Parties to the conflict shall remain bound to fulfil by virtue of the principles of the law of nations, as they result from the usages established among civilized peoples, from the laws of humanity and the dictates of the public conscience.

Geneva Convention relative to the Protection of Civilian Persons in Time of War

75 U.N.T.S. 287, entered into force 21 October 1950.

PART I: GENERAL PROVISIONS

Article 1

The High Contracting Parties undertake to respect and to ensure respect for the present Convention in all circumstances.

Article 2

In addition to the provisions which shall be implemented in peacetime, the present Convention shall apply to all cases of declared war or of any other armed conflict which may arise between two or more of the High Contracting Parties, even if the state of war is not recognized by one of them.

The Convention shall also apply to all cases of partial or total occupation of the territory of a High Contracting Party, even if the said occupation meets with no armed resistance. Although one of the Powers in conflict may not be a party to the present Convention, the Powers who are parties thereto shall remain bound by it in their mutual relations.

They shall furthermore be bound by the Convention in relation to the said Power, if the latter accepts and applies the provisions thereof.

Article 3

In the case of armed conflict not of an international character occurring in the territory of one of the High Contracting Parties, each Party to the conflict shall be bound to apply, as a minimum, the following provisions:

1. Persons taking no active part in the hostilities, including members of armed forces who have laid down their arms and those placed hors de combat by sickness, wounds, detention, or any other cause, shall in all circumstances be treated humanely, without any adverse distinction founded on race, color, religion or faith, sex, birth or wealth, or any other similar criteria.

To this end, the following acts are and shall remain prohibited at any time and in any place whatsoever with respect to the above-mentioned persons:

(a) Violence to life and person, in particular murder of all kinds, mutilation, cruel treatment and torture;

(b) Taking of hostages;

(c) Outrages upon personal dignity, in particular humiliating and degrading treatment;

(d) The passing of sentences and the carrying out of executions without previous judgment pronounced by a regularly constituted court, affording all the judicial guarantees which are recognized as indispensable by civilized peoples.

2. The wounded and sick shall be collected and cared for.

An impartial humanitarian body, such as the International Committee of the Red Cross, may offer its services to the Parties to the conflict. The Parties to the conflict should further endeavor to bring into force, by means of special agreements, all or part of the other provisions of the present Convention.

The application of the preceding provisions shall not affect the legal status of the Parties to the conflict.

Article 4

Persons protected by the Convention are those who, at a given moment and in any manner whatsoever, find themselves, in case of a conflict or occupation, in the hands of a Party to the conflict or Occupying Power of which they are not nationals.

Nationals of a State which is not bound by the Convention are not protected by it. Nationals of a neutral State, who find themselves in the territory of a belligerent State, and nationals of a co-belligerent State, shall not be regarded as protected persons while the State of which they are nationals has normal diplomatic representation in the State in whose hands they are.

The provisions of Part II are, however, wider in application, as defined in Article 13.

Persons protected by the Geneva Convention for the Amelioration of the Condition of the Wounded and Sick in Armed Forces in the Field of August 12, 1949, or by the Geneva Convention for the Amelioration of the Condition of Wounded, Sick and Shipwrecked Members of Armed Forces at Sea of August 12, 1949, or by the Geneva Convention relative to the Treatment of Prisoners of War of August 12, 1949, shall not be considered as protected persons within the meaning of the present Convention.

Article 5

Where, in the territory of a Party to the conflict, the latter is satisfied that an individual protected person is definitely suspected of or engaged in activities hostile to the security of the State, such individual person shall not be entitled to claim such rights and privileges under the present Convention as would, if exercised in the favor of such individual person, be prejudicial to the security of such State.

Where in occupied territory an individual protected person is detained as a spy or saboteur, or as a person under definite suspicion of activity hostile to the security of the Occupying Power, such person shall, in those cases where absolute military security so requires, be regarded as having forfeited rights of communication under the present Convention.

In each case, such persons shall nevertheless be treated with humanity, and in case of trial, shall not be deprived of the rights of fair and regular trial prescribed by the present Convention. They shall also be granted the full rights and privileges of a protected person under the present Convention at the earliest date consistent with the security of the State or Occupying Power, as the case may be.

Article 6

The present Convention shall apply from the outset of any conflict or occupation mentioned in Article 2. In the territory of Parties to the conflict, the application of the present Convention shall cease on the general close of military operations.

In the case of occupied territory, the application of the present Convention shall cease one year after the general close of military operations; however, the Occupying Power shall be bound, for the duration of the occupation, to the extent that such Power exercises the functions of government in such territory, by the provisions of the following Articles of the present Convention: I to 12, 27, 29 to 34, 47, 49, 51, 52, 53, 59, 61 to 77, and 143.

Protected persons whose release, repatriation or re-establishment may take place after such dates shall meanwhile continue to benefit by the present Convention.

Article 7

In addition to the agreements expressly provided for in Articles 11, 14, 15, 17, 36, 108, 109, 132, 133 and 149, the High Contracting Parties may conclude other special agreements for all matters concerning which they may deem it suitable to make separate provision.

No special agreement shall adversely affect the situation of protected persons, as defined by the present Convention, nor restrict the rights which it confers upon them.

Protected persons shall continue to have the benefit of such agreements as long as the Convention is applicable to them, except where express provisions to the contrary are contained in the aforesaid or in subsequent agreements, or where more favorable measures have been taken with regard to them by one or other of the Parties to the conflict.

Article 8

Protected persons may in no circumstances renounce in part or in entirety the rights secured to them by the present Convention, and by the special agreements referred to in the foregoing Article, if such there be.

Article 9

The present Convention shall be applied with the cooperation and under the scrutiny of the Protecting Powers whose duty it is to safeguard the interests of the Parties to the conflict. For this purpose, the Protecting Powers may appoint, apart from their diplomatic or consular staff, delegates from amongst their own nationals or the nationals of other neutral Powers. The said delegates shall be subject to the approval of the Power with which they are to carry out their duties. The Parties to the conflict shall facilitate to the greatest extent possible the task of the representatives or delegates of the Protecting Powers. The representatives or delegates of the Protecting Powers shall not in any case exceed their mission under the present Convention. They shall, in particular, take account of the imperative necessities of security of the State wherein they carry out their duties.

Article 10

The provisions of the present Convention constitute no obstacle to the humanitarian activities which the International Committee of the Red Cross or any other impartial humanitarian organization may, subject to the consent of the Parties to the conflict concerned, undertake for the protection of civilian persons and for their relief.

Article 11

The High Contracting Parties may at any time agree to entrust to an organization which offers all guarantees of impartiality and efficacy the duties incumbent on the Protecting Powers by virtue of the present Convention.

When persons protected by the present Convention do not benefit or cease to benefit, no matter for what reason, by the activities of a Protecting Power or of an organization provided for in the first paragraph above, the Detaining Power shall request a neutral State, or such an organization, to undertake the functions performed under the present Convention by a Protecting Power designated by the Parties to a conflict.

If protection cannot be arranged accordingly, the Detaining Power shall request or shall accept, subject to the provisions of this Article, the offer of the services of a humanitarian organization, such as the International Committee of the Red Cross, to assume the humanitarian functions performed by Protecting Powers under the present Convention. Any neutral Power, or any organization invited by the Power concerned or offering itself for these purposes, shall be required to act with a sense of responsibility towards the Party to the conflict on which persons protected by the present Convention depend, and shall be required to furnish sufficient assurances that it is in a position to undertake the appropriate functions and to discharge them impartially.

No derogation from the preceding provisions shall be made by special agreements between Powers one of which is restricted, even temporarily, in its freedom to negotiate with the other Power or its allies by reason of military events, more particularly where the whole, or a substantial part, of the territory of the said Power is occupied.

Whenever in the present Convention mention is made of a Protecting Power, such mention applies to substitute organizations in the sense of the present Article. The provisions of this Article shall extend and be adapted to cases of nationals of a neutral State who are in occupied territory or who find themselves in the territory of a belligerent State with which the State of which they are nationals has not normal diplomatic representation.

Article 12

In cases where they deem it advisable in the interest of protected persons, particularly in cases of disagreement between the Parties to the conflict as to the application or interpretation of the provisions of the present Convention, the Protecting Powers shall lend their good offices with a view to settling the disagreement. For this purpose, each of the Protecting Powers may, either at the invitation of one Party or on its own initiative, propose to the Parties to the conflict a meeting of their representatives, and in particular of the authorities responsible for protected person, possibly on neutral territory suitably chosen. The Parties to the conflict shall be bound to give effect to the proposals made to them for this purpose. The Protecting Powers may, if necessary, propose for approval by the Parties to the conflict, a person belonging to a neutral Power or delegated by the International Committee of the Red Cross who shall be invited to take part in such a meeting.

PART II

GENERAL PROTECTION OF POPULATIONS AGAINST CERTAIN CONSEQUENCES OF WAR

Article 13

The provisions of Part II cover the whole of the populations of the countries in conflict, without any adverse distinction based, in particular, on race, nationality, religion or political opinion, and are intended to alleviate the sufferings caused by war.

Article 14

In time of peace, the High Contracting Parties and, after the outbreak of hostilities, the Parties thereto, may establish in their own territory and, if the need arises, in occupied areas, hospital and safety zones and localities so organized as to protect from the effects of war, wounded, sick and aged persons, children under fifteen, expectant mothers and mothers of children under seven.

Upon the outbreak and during the course of hostilities, the Parties concerned may conclude agreements on mutual recognition of the zones and localities they have created.

They may for this purpose implement the provisions of the Draft Agreement annexed to the present Convention, with such amendments as they may consider necessary. The Protecting Powers and the International Committee of the Red Cross are invited to lend their good offices in order to facilitate the institution and recognition of these hospital and safety zones and localities.

Article 15

Any Party to the conflict may, either directly or through a neutral State or some humanitarian organization, propose to the adverse Party to establish, in the regions where fighting is taking place, neutralized zones intended to shelter from the effects of war the following persons, without distinction:

(a) Wounded and sick combatants or non-combatants;

(b) Civilian persons who take no part in hostilities, and who, while they reside in the zones, perform no work of a military character.

When the Parties concerned have agreed upon the geographical position, administration, food supply and supervision of the proposed neutralized zone, a written agreement shall be concluded and signed by the representatives of the Parties to the conflict. The agreement shall fix the beginning and the duration of the neutralization of the zone.

Article 16

The wounded and sick, as well as the infirm, and expectant mothers, shall be the object of particular protection and respect. As far as military considerations allow, each Party to the conflict shall facilitate the steps taken to search for the killed and wounded, to assist the shipwrecked and other persons exposed to grave danger, and to protect them against pillage and ill-treatment.

Article 17

The Parties to the conflict shall endeavor to conclude local agreements for the removal from besieged or encircled areas, of wounded, sick, infirm, and aged persons, children and maternity cases, and for the passage of ministers of all religions, medical personnel and medical equipment on their way to such areas.

Article 18

Civilian hospitals organized to give care to the wounded and sick, the infirm and maternity cases, may in no circumstances be the object of attack, but shall at all times be respected and protected by the Parties to the conflict....

Article 19

The protection to which civilian hospitals are entitled shall not cease unless they are used to commit, outside their humanitarian duties, acts harmful to the enemy. Protection may, however, cease only after due warning has been given, naming, in all appropriate cases, a reasonable time limit, and after such warning has remained unheeded.

The fact that sick or wounded members of the armed forces are nursed in these hospitals, or the presence of small arms and ammunition taken from such combatants which have not yet been handed to the proper service, shall not be considered to be acts harmful to the enemy.

Article 20

Persons regularly and solely engaged in the operation and administration of civilian hospitals, including the personnel engaged in the search for, removal and transporting of and caring for wounded and sick civilians, the infirm and maternity cases, shall be respected and protected....

Article 21

Convoys of vehicles or hospital trains on land or specially provided vessels on sea, conveying wounded and sick civilians, the infirm and maternity cases, shall be respected and protected in the same manner as the hospitals provided for in Article 18, and shall be marked, with the consent of the State, by the display of the distinctive emblem provided for in Article 38 of the Geneva Convention for the Amelioration of the Condition of the Wounded and Sick in Armed Forces in the Field of August 12, 1949.

Article 22

Aircraft exclusively employed for the removal of wounded and sick civilians, the infirm and maternity cases, or for the transport of medical personnel and equipment, shall not be attacked, but shall be respected while flying at heights, times and on routes specifically agreed upon between all the Parties to the conflict concerned.

They may be marked with the distinctive emblem provided for in Article 38 of the Geneva Convention for the Amelioration of the Condition of the Wounded and Sick in Armed Forces in the Field of August 12, 1949. Unless agreed otherwise, flights over enemy or enemy-occupied territory are prohibited. Such aircraft shall obey every summons to land. In the event of a landing thus imposed, the aircraft with its occupants may continue its flight after examination, if any.

Article 23

Each High Contracting Party shall allow the free passage of all consignments of medical and hospital stores and objects necessary for religious worship intended only for civilians of another High Contracting Party, even if the latter is its adversary.

It shall likewise permit the free passage of all consignments of essential foodstuffs, clothing and tonics intended for children under fifteen, expectant mothers and maternity cases.

The obligation of a High Contracting Party to allow the free passage of the consignments indicated in the preceding paragraph is subject to the condition that this Party is satisfied that there are no serious reasons for fearing:

(a) That the consignments may be diverted from their destination;

(b) That the control may not be effective; or

(c) That a definite advantage may accrue to the military efforts or economy of the enemy through the substitution of the above-mentioned consignments for goods which would otherwise be provided or produced by the enemy or through the release of such material, services or facilities as would otherwise be required for the production of such goods.

The Power which allows the passage of the consignments indicated in the first paragraph of this Article may make such permission conditional on the distribution to the persons benefited there by being made under the local supervision of the Protecting Powers.

Such consignments shall be forwarded as rapidly as possible, and the Power which permits their free passage shall have the right to prescribe the technical arrangements under which such passage is allowed.

Article 24

The Parties to the conflict shall take the necessary measures to ensure that children under fifteen, who are orphaned or are separated from their families as a result of the war, are not left to their own resources, and that their maintenance, the exercise of their religion and their education are facilitated in all circumstances. Their education shall, as far as possible, be entrusted to persons of a similar cultural tradition.

The Parties to the conflict shall facilitate the reception of such children in a neutral country for the duration of the conflict with the consent of the Protecting Power, if any, and under due safeguards for the observance of the principles stated in the first paragraph. They shall, furthermore, endeavor to arrange for all children under twelve to be identified by the wearing of identity discs, or by some other means.

Article 25

All persons in the territory of a Party to the conflict, or in a territory occupied by it, shall be enabled to give news of a strictly personal nature to members of their families, wherever they may be, and to receive news from them....

PART III

STATUS AND TREATMENT OF PROTECTED PERSONS SECTION I PROVISIONS COMMON TO THE TERRITORIES OF THE PARTIES TO THE CONFLICT AND TO OCCUPIED TERRITORIES

Article 27

Protected persons are entitled, in all circumstances, to respect for their persons, their honor, their family rights, their religious convictions and practices, and their manners and customs.

They shall at all times be humanely treated, and shall be protected especially against all acts of violence or threats thereof and against insults and public curiosity.

Women shall be especially protected against any attack on their honor, in particular against rape, enforced prostitution, or any form of indecent assault.

Without prejudice to the provisions relating to their state of health, age and sex, all protected persons shall be treated with the same consideration by the Party to the conflict in whose power they are, without any adverse distinction based, in particular, on race, religion or political opinion.

However, the Parties to the conflict may take such measures of control and security in regard to protected persons as may be necessary as a result of the war.

Article 28

The presence of a protected person may not be used to render certain points or areas immune from military operations.

Article 29

The Party to the conflict in whose hands protected persons may be is responsible for the treatment accorded to them by its agents, irrespective of any individual responsibility which may be incurred.

Article 30

Protected persons shall have every facility for making application to the Protecting Powers, the International Committee of the Red Cross, the National Red Cross (Red Crescent, Red Lion and Sun) Society of the country where they may be, as well as to any organization that might assist them.

These several organizations shall be granted all facilities for that purpose by the authorities, within the bounds set by military or security considerations.

Apart from the visits of the delegates of the Protecting Powers and of the International Committee of the Red Cross, provided for by Article 143, the Detaining or Occupying Powers shall facilitate as much as possible visits to protected persons by the representatives of other organizations whose object is to give spiritual aid or material relief to such persons.

Article 31

No physical or moral coercion shall be exercised against protected persons, in particular to obtain information from them or from third parties.

Article 32

The High Contracting Parties specifically agree that each of them is prohibited from taking any measure of such a character as to cause the physical suffering or extermination of protected persons in their hands. This prohibition applies not only to murder, torture, corporal punishment, mutilation and medical or scientific experiments not necessitated by the medical treatment of a protected person but also to any other measures of brutality whether applied by civilian or military agents.

Article 33

No protected person may be punished for an offence he or she has not personally committed.

Collective penalties and likewise all measures of intimidation or of terrorism are prohibited.

Pillage is prohibited.

Reprisals against protected persons and their property are prohibited.

Article 34

The taking of hostages is prohibited.

SECTION II

ALIENS IN THE TERRITORY OF A PARTY TO THE CONFLICT

Article 35

All protected persons who may desire to leave the territory at the outset of, or during a conflict, shall be entitled to do so, unless their departure is contrary to the national interests of the State. The applications of such persons to leave shall be decided in accordance with regularly established procedures and the decision shall be taken as rapidly as possible. Those persons permitted to leave may provide themselves with the necessary funds for their journey and take with them a reasonable amount of their effects and articles of personal use.

If any such person is refused permission to leave the territory, he shall be entitled to have refusal reconsidered, as soon as possible by an appropriate court or administrative board designated by the Detaining Power for that purpose.

Upon request, representatives of the Protecting Power shall, unless reasons of security prevent it, or the persons concerned object, be furnished with the reasons for refusal of any request for permission to leave the territory and be given, as expeditiously as possible, the names of all persons who have been denied permission to leave.

Article 36

Departures permitted under the foregoing Article shall be carried out in satisfactory conditions as regards safety, hygiene, sanitation and food. All costs in connection therewith, from the point of exit in the territory of the Detaining Power, shall be borne by the country of destination, or, in the case of accommodation in a neutral country, by the Power whose nationals are benefited. The practical details of such movements may, if necessary, be settled by special agreements between the Powers concerned.

The foregoing shall not prejudice such special agreements as may be concluded between Parties to the conflict concerning the exchange and repatriation of their nationals in enemy hands.

Article 37

Protected persons who are confined pending proceedings or serving a sentence involving loss of liberty, shall during their confinement be humanely treated.

As soon as they are released, they may ask to leave the territory in conformity with the foregoing Articles.

Article 38

With the exception of special measures authorized by the present Convention, in particularly by Article 27 and 41 thereof, the situation of protected persons shall continue to be regulated, in principle, by the provisions concerning aliens in time of peace. In any case, the following rights shall be granted to them:

(1) they shall be enabled to receive the individual or collective relief that may be sent to them.

(2) they shall, if their state of health so requires, receive medical attention and hospital treatment to the same extent as the nationals of the State concerned.

(3) they shall be allowed to practise their religion and to receive spiritual assistance from ministers of their faith.

(4) if they reside in an area particularly exposed to the dangers of war, they shall be authorized to move from that area to the same extent as the nationals of the State concerned.

(5) children under fifteen years, pregnant women and mothers of children under seven years shall benefit by any preferential treatment to the same extent as the nationals of the State concerned.

Article 39

Protected persons who, as a result of the war, have lost their gainful employment, shall be granted the opportunity to find paid employment. That opportunity shall, subject to security considerations and to the provisions of Article 40, be equal to that enjoyed by the nationals of the Power in whose territory they are.

Where a Party to the conflict applies to a protected person methods of control which result in his being unable to support himself, and especially if such a person is prevented for reasons of security from finding paid employment on reasonable conditions, the said Party shall ensure his support and that of his dependents.

Protected persons may in any case receive allowances from their home country, the Protecting Power, or the relief societies referred to in Article 30.

Article 40

Protected persons may be compelled to work only to the same extent as nationals of the Party to the conflict in whose territory they are.

If protected persons are of enemy nationality, they may only be compelled to do work which is normally necessary to ensure the feeding, sheltering, clothing, transport and health of human beings and which is not directly related to the conduct of military operations.

In the cases mentioned in the two preceding paragraphs, protected persons compelled to work shall have the benefit of the same working conditions and of the same safeguards as national workers in particular as regards wages, hours of labour, clothing and equipment, previous training and compensation for occupational accidents and diseases.

If the above provisions are infringed, protected persons shall be allowed to exercise their right of complaint in accordance with Article 30.

Article 41

Should the Power, in whose hands protected persons may be, consider the measures of control mentioned in the present Convention to be inadequate, it may not have recourse to any other measure of control more severe than that of assigned residence or internment, in accordance with the provisions of Articles 42 and 43.

In applying the provisions of Article 39, second paragraph, to the cases of persons required to leave their usual places of residence by virtue of a decision placing them in assigned residence elsewhere, the Detaining Power shall be guided as closely as possible by the standards of welfare set forth in Part III, Section IV of this Convention.

Article 42

The internment or placing in assigned residence of protected persons may be ordered only if the security of the Detaining Power makes it absolutely necessary.

If any person, acting through the representatives of the Protecting Power, voluntarily demands internment, and if his situation renders this step necessary, he shall be interned by the Power in whose hands he may be.

Article 43

Any protected person who has been interned or placed in assigned residence shall be entitled to have such action reconsidered as soon as possible by an appropriate court or administrative board designated by the Detaining Power for that purpose. If the internment or placing in assigned residence is maintained, the court or administrative board shall periodically, and at least twice yearly, give consideration to his or her case, with a view to the favourable amendment of the initial decision, if circumstances permit.

Unless the protected persons concerned object, the Detaining Power shall, as rapidly as possible, give the Protecting Power the names of any protected persons who have been interned or subjected to assigned residence, or who have been released from internment or assigned residence. The decisions of the courts or boards mentioned in the first paragraph of the present Article shall also, subject to the same conditions, be notified as rapidly as possible to the Protecting Power.

Article 44

In applying the measures of control mentioned in the present Convention, the Detaining Power shall not treat as enemy aliens exclusively on the basis of their nationality de jure of an enemy State, refugees who do not, in fact, enjoy the protection of any government.

Article 45

Protected persons shall not be transferred to a Power which is not a party to the Convention.

This provision shall in no way constitute an obstacle to the repatriation of protected persons, or to their return to their country of residence after the cessation of hostilities.

Protected persons may be transferred by the Detaining Power only to a Power which is a party to the present Convention and after the Detaining Power has satisfied itself of the willingness and ability of such transferee Power to apply the present Convention. If protected persons are transferred under such circumstances, responsibility for the application of the present Convention rests on the Power accepting them, while they are in its custody. Nevertheless, if that Power fails to carry out the provisions of the present Convention in any important respect, the Power by which the protected persons were transferred shall, upon being so notified by the Protecting Power, take effective measures to correct the situation or shall request the return of the protected persons. Such request must be complied with.

In no circumstances shall a protected person be transferred to a country where he or she may have reason to fear persecution for his or her political opinions or religious beliefs.

The provisions of this Article do not constitute an obstacle to the extradition, in pursuance of extradition treaties concluded before the outbreak of hostilities, of protected persons accused of offences against ordinary criminal law.

Article 46

In so far as they have not been previously withdrawn, restrictive measures taken regarding protected persons shall be cancelled as soon as possible after the close of hostilities.

Restrictive measures affecting their property shall be cancelled, in accordance with the law of the Detaining Power, as soon as possible after the close of hostilities.

SECTION III

OCCUPIED TERRITORIES

Article 47

Protected persons who are in occupied territory shall not be deprived, in any case or in any manner whatsoever, of the benefits of the present Convention by any change introduced, as the result of the occupation of a territory, into the institutions or government of the said territory, nor by any agreement concluded between the authorities of the occupied territories and the Occupying Power, nor by any annexation by the latter of the whole or part of the occupied territory.

Article 48

Protected persons who are not nationals of the Power whose territory is occupied may avail themselves of the right to leave the territory subject to the provisions of Article 35, and decisions thereon shall be taken according to the procedure which the Occupying Power shall establish in accordance with the said Article.

Article 49

Individual or mass forcible transfers, as well as deportations of protected persons from occupied territory to the territory of the Occupying Power or to that of any other country, occupied or not, are prohibited, regardless of their motive.

Nevertheless, the Occupying Power may undertake total or partial evacuation of a given area if the security of the population or imperative military reasons do demand.

Such evacuations may not involve the displacement of protected persons outside the bounds of the occupied territory except when for material reasons it is impossible to avoid such displacement.

Persons thus evacuated shall be transferred back to their homes as soon as hostilities in the area in question have ceased.

The Occupying Power undertaking such transfers or evacuations shall ensure, to the greatest practicable extent, that proper accommodation is provided to receive the protected persons, that the removals are effected in satisfactory conditions of hygiene, health, safety and nutrition, and that members of the same family are not separated.

The Protecting Power shall be informed of any transfers and evacuations as soon as they have taken place.

The Occupying Power shall not detain protected persons in an area particularly exposed to the dangers of war unless the security of the population or imperative military reasons so demand.

The Occupying Power shall not deport or transfer parts of its own civilian population into the territory it occupies.

Article 50

The Occupying Power shall, with the cooperation of the national and local authorities, facilitate the proper working of all institutions devoted to the care and education of children.

The Occupying Power shall take all necessary steps to facilitate the identification of children and the registration of their parentage.

It may not, in any case, change their personal status, nor enlist them in formations or organizations subordinate to it.

Should the local institutions be inadequate for the purpose, the Occupying Power shall make arrangements for the maintenance and education, if possible by persons of their own nationality, language and religion, of children who are orphaned or separated from their parents as a result of the war and who cannot be adequately cared for by a near relative or friend.

A special section of the Bureau set up in accordance with Article 136 shall be responsible for taking all necessary steps to identify children whose identity is in doubt.

Particulars of their parents or other near relatives should always be recorded if available.

The Occupying Power shall not hinder the application of any preferential measures in regard to food, medical care and protection against the effects of war, which may have been adopted prior to the occupation in favor of children under fifteen years, expectant mothers, and mothers of children under seven years.

Article 51

The Occupying Power may not compel protected persons to serve in its armed or auxiliary forces.

No pressure or propaganda which aims at securing voluntary enlistment is permitted.

The Occupying Power may not compel protected persons to work unless they are over eighteen years of age, and then only on work which is necessary either for the needs of the army of occupation, or for the public utility services, or for the feeding, sheltering, clothing, transportation or health of the population of the occupied country.

Protected persons may not be compelled to undertake any work which would involve them in the obligation of taking part in military operations.

The Occupying Power may not compel protected persons to employ forcible means to ensure the security of the installations where they are performing compulsory labor. The work shall be carried out only in the occupied territory where the persons whose services have been requisitioned are.

Every such person shall, so far as possible, be kept in his usual place of employment. Workers shall be paid a fair wage and the work shall be proportionate to their physical and intellectual capacities.

The legislation in force in the occupied country concerning working conditions, and safeguards as regards, in particular, such matters as wages, hours of work, equipment, preliminary training and compensation for occupational accidents and diseases, shall be applicable to the protected persons assigned to the work referred to in this Article.

In no case shall requisition of labor lead to a mobilization of workers in an organization of a military or semi-military character.

Article 52

No contract, agreement or regulation shall impair the right of any worker, whether voluntary or not and wherever he may be, to apply to the representatives of the Protecting Power in order to request the said Power's intervention.

All measures aiming at creating unemployment or at restricting the opportunities offered to workers in an occupied territory, in order to induce them to work for the Occupying Power, are prohibited.

Article 53

Any destruction by the Occupying Power of real or personal property belonging individually or collectively to private persons, or to the State, or to other public authorities, or to social or cooperative organizations, is prohibited, except where such destruction is rendered absolutely necessary by military operations.

Article 54

The Occupying Power may not alter the status of public officials or judges in the occupied territories or in any way apply sanctions to or take any measures of coercion or discrimination against them, should they abstain from fulfilling their functions for reasons of conscience.

This prohibition does not prejudice the application of the second paragraph of Article 51. It does not affect the right of the Occupying Power to remove public officials from their posts.

Article 55

To the fullest extent of the means available to it the Occupying Power has the duty of ensuring the food and medical supplies of the population; it should, in particular, bring in the necessary foodstuffs, medical stores and other articles if the resources of the occupied territory are inadequate.

The Occupying Power may not requisition foodstuffs, articles or medical supplies available in the occupied territory, except for use by the occupation forces and administration personnel, and then only if the requirements of the civilian population have been taken into account.

Subject to the provisions of other international Conventions, the Occupying Power shall make arrangements to ensure that fair value is paid for any requisitioned goods.

The Protecting Power shall, at any time, be at liberty to verify the state of the food and medical supplies in occupied territories, except where temporary restrictions are made necessary by imperative military requirements.

Article 56

To the fullest extent of the means available to it, the Occupying Power has the duty of ensuring and maintaining, with the cooperation of national and local authorities, the medical and hospital establishments and services, public health and hygiene in the occupied territory, with particular reference to the adoption and application of the prophylactic and preventive measures necessary to combat the spread of contagious diseases and epidemics.

Medical personnel of all categories shall be allowed to carry out their duties.

If new hospitals are set up in occupied territory and if the competent organs of the occupied State are not operating there, the occupying authorities shall, if necessary, grant them the recognition provided for in Article 18. In similar circumstances, the occupying authorities shall also grant recognition to hospital personnel and transport vehicles under the provisions of Articles 20 and 21.

In adopting measures of health and hygiene and in their implementation, the Occupying Power shall take into consideration the moral and ethical susceptibilities of the population of the occupied territory.

Article 57

The Occupying Power may requisition civilian hospitals only temporarily and only in cases of urgent necessity for the care of military wounded and sick, and then on condition that suitable arrangements are made in due time for the care and treatment of the patients and for the needs of the civilian population for hospital accommodation.

The material and stores of civilian hospitals cannot be requisitioned so long as they are necessary for the needs of the civilian population.

Article 58

The Occupying Power shall permit ministers of religion to give spiritual assistance to the members of their religious communities.

The Occupying Power shall also accept consignments of books and articles required for religious needs and shall facilitate their distribution in occupied territory.

Article 59

If the whole or part of the population of an occupied territory is inadequately supplied, the Occupying Power shall agree to relief schemes on behalf of the said population, and shall facilitate them by all the means at its disposal. Such schemes, which may be undertaken either by States or by impartial humanitarian organizations such as the International Committee of the Red Cross, shall consist, in particular, of the provision of consignments of foodstuffs, medical supplies and clothing. All Contracting Parties shall permit the free passage of these consignments and shall guarantee their protection.

A Power granting free passage to consignments on their way to territory occupied by an adverse Party to the conflict shall, however, have the right to search the consignments, to regulate their passage according to prescribed times and routes, and to be reasonably satisfied through the Protecting Power that these consignments are to be used for the relief of the needy population and are not to be used for the benefit of the Occupying Power.

Article 60

Relief consignments shall in no way relieve the Occupying Power of any of its responsibilities under Articles 55, 56 and 59.

The Occupying Power shall in no way whatsoever divert relief consignments from the purpose for which they are intended, except in cases of urgent necessity, in the interests of the population of the occupied territory and with the consent of the Protecting Power.

Article 61

The distribution of the relief consignments referred to in the foregoing Articles shall be carried out with the cooperation and under the supervision of the Protecting Power. This duty may also be delegated, by agreement between the Occupying Power and the Protecting Power, to a neutral Power, to the International Committee of the Red Cross or to any other impartial humanitarian body. Such consignments shall be exempt in occupied territory from all charges, taxes or customs duties unless these are necessary in the interests of the economy of the territory.

The Occupying Power shall facilitate the rapid distribution of these consignments.

All Contracting Parties shall endeavor to permit the transit and transport, free of charge, of such relief consignments on their way to occupied territories.

Article 62

Subject to imperative reasons of security, protected persons in occupied territories shall be permitted to receive the individual relief consignments sent to them.

Article 63

Subject to temporary and exceptional measures imposed for urgent reasons of security by the Occupying Power:

(a) Recognized National Red Cross (Red Crescent, Red Lion and Sun) Societies shall be able to pursue their activities in accordance with Red Cross principles, as defined by the International Red Cross Conferences. Other relief societies shall be permitted to continue their humanitarian activities under similar conditions;

(b) The Occupying Power may not require any changes in the personnel or structure of these societies, which would prejudice the aforesaid activities.

The same principles shall apply to the activities and personnel of special organizations of a non-military character, which already exist or which may be established, for the purpose of ensuring the living conditions of the civilian population by the maintenance of the essential public utility services, by the distribution of relief and by the organization of rescues.

Article 64

The penal laws of the occupied territory shall remain in force, with the exception that they may be repealed or suspended by the Occupying Power in cases where they constitute a threat to its security or an obstacle to the application of the present Convention.

Subject to the latter consideration and to the necessity for ensuring the effective administration of justice, the tribunals of the occupied territory shall continue to function in respect of all offences covered by the said laws.

The Occupying Power may, however, subject the population of the occupied territory to provisions which are essential to enable the Occupying Power to fulfill its obligations under the present Convention, to maintain the orderly government of the territory, and to ensure the security of the Occupying Power, of the members and property of the occupying forces or administration, and likewise of the establishments and lines of communication used by them.

Article 65

The penal provisions enacted by the Occupying Power shall not come into force before they have been published and brought to the knowledge of the inhabitants in their own language.

The effect of these penal provisions shall not be retroactive.

Article 66

In case of a breach of the penal provisions promulgated by it by virtue of the second paragraph of Article 64, the Occupying Power may hand over the accused to its properly constituted, non-political military courts, on condition that the said courts sit in the occupied country. Courts of appeal shall preferably sit in the occupied country.

Article 67

The courts shall apply only those provisions of law which were applicable prior to the offence, and which are in accordance with general principles of law, in particular the principle that the penalty shall be proportioned to the offence. They shall take into consideration the fact that the accused is not a national of the Occupying Power.

Article 68

Protected persons who commit an offence which is solely intended to harm the Occupying Power, but which does not constitute an attempt on the life or limb of members of the occupying forces or administration, nor a grave collective danger, nor seriously damage the property of the occupying forces or administration or the installations used by them, shall be liable to internment or simple imprisonment, provided the duration of such internment or imprisonment is proportionate to the offence committed.

Furthermore, internment or imprisonment shall, for such offences, be the only measure adopted for depriving protected persons of liberty. The courts provided for under Article 66 of the present Convention may at their discretion convert a sentence of imprisonment to one of internment for the same period.

The penal provisions promulgated by the Occupying Power in accordance with Articles 64 and 65 may impose the death penalty on a protected person only in cases where the person is guilty of espionage, of serious acts of sabotage against the military installations of the Occupying Power or of intentional offences which have caused the death of one or more persons, provided that such offences were punishable by death under the law of the occupied territory in force before the occupation began.

The death penalty may not be pronounced against a protected person unless the attention of the court has been particularly called to the fact that, since the accused is not a national of the Occupying Power, he is not bound to it by any duty of allegiance.

In any case, the death penalty may not be pronounced against a protected person who was under eighteen years of age at the time of the offence.

Article 69

In all cases, the duration of the period during which a protected person accused of an offence is under arrest awaiting trial or punishment shall be deducted from any period of imprisonment awarded.

Article 70

Protected persons shall not be arrested, prosecuted or convicted by the Occupying Power for acts committed or for opinions expressed before the occupation, or during a temporary interruption thereof, with the exception of breaches of the laws and customs of war.

Nationals of the Occupying Power who, before the outbreak of hostilities, have sought refuge in the territory of the occupied State, shall not be arrested, prosecuted, convicted or deported from the occupied territory, except for offences committed after the outbreak of hostilities, or for offences under common law committed before the outbreak of hostilities which, according to the law of the occupied State, would have justified extradition in time of peace.

Article 71

No sentence shall be pronounced by the competent courts of the Occupying Power except after a regular trial.

Accused persons who are prosecuted by the Occupying Power shall be promptly informed, in writing, in a language which they understand, of the particulars of the charges preferred against them, and shall be brought to trial as rapidly as possible.

The Protecting Power shall be informed of all proceedings instituted by the Occupying Power against protected persons in respect of charges involving the death penalty or imprisonment for two years or more; it shall be enabled, at any time, to obtain information regarding the state of such proceedings.

Furthermore, the Protecting Power shall be entitled, on request, to be furnished with all particulars of these and of any other proceedings instituted by the Occupying Power against protected persons.

The notification to the Protecting Power, as provided for in the second paragraph above, shall be sent immediately, and shall in any case reach the Protecting Power three weeks before the date of the first hearing.

Unless, at the opening of the trial, evidence is submitted that the provisions of this Article are fully complied with, the trial shall not proceed.

The notification shall include the following particulars:

(a) Description of the accused;

(b) Place of residence or detention;

(c) Specification of the charge or charges (with mention of the penal provisions under which it is brought);

(d) Designation of the court which will hear the case;

(e) Place and date of the first hearing.

Article 72

Accused persons shall have the right to present evidence necessary to their defense and may, in particular, call witnesses.

They shall have the right to be assisted by a qualified advocate or counsel of their own choice, who shall be able to visit them freely and shall enjoy the necessary facilities for preparing the defense.

Failing a choice by the accused, the Protecting Power may provide him with an advocate or counsel.

When an accused person has to meet a serious charge and the Protecting Power is not functioning, the Occupying Power, subject to the consent of the accused, shall provide an advocate or counsel.

Accused persons shall, unless they freely waive such assistance, be aided by an interpreter, both during preliminary investigation and during the hearing in court.

They shall have the right at any time to object to the interpreter and to ask for his replacement.

Article 73

A convicted person shall have the right of appeal provided for by the laws applied by the court.

He shall be fully informed of his right to appeal or petition and of the time limit within which he may do so.

The penal procedure provided in the present Section shall apply, as far as it is applicable, to appeals.

Where the laws applied by the Court make no provision for appeals, the convicted person shall have the right to petition against the finding and sentence to the competent authority of the Occupying Power.

Article 74

Representatives of the Protecting Power shall have the right to attend the trial of any protected person, unless the hearing has, as an exceptional measure, to be held in camera in the interests of the security of the Occupying Power, which shall then notify the Protecting Power.

A notification in respect of the date and place of trial shall be sent to the Protecting Power. Any judgment involving a sentence of death, or imprisonment for two years or more shall be communicated, with the relevant grounds, as rapidly as possible to the Protecting Power. The notification shall contain a reference to the notification made under Article 71, and in the case of sentences of imprisonment, the name of the place where the sentence is to be served.

A record of judgments other than those referred to above shall be kept by the court and shall be open to inspection by representatives of the Protecting Power.

Any period allowed for appeal in the case of sentences involving the death penalty, or imprisonment for two years or more, shall not run until notification of judgment has been received by the Protecting Power.

Article 75

In no case shall persons condemned to death be deprived of the right of petition for pardon or reprieve.

No death sentence shall be carried out before the expiration of a period of at least six months from the date of receipt by the Protecting Power of the notification of the final judgment confirming such death sentence, or of an order denying pardon or reprieve.

The six months period of suspension of the death sentence herein prescribed may be reduced in individual cases in circumstances of grave emergency involving an organized threat to the security of the Occupying Power or its forces, provided always that the Protecting Power is notified of such reduction and is given reasonable time and opportunity to make representations to the competent occupying authorities in respect of such death sentences.

Article 76

Protected persons accused of offences shall be detained in the occupied country, and if convicted they shall serve their sentences therein.

They shall, if possible, be separated from other detainees and shall enjoy conditions of food and hygiene which will be sufficient to keep them in good health, and which will be at least equal to those obtaining in prisons in the occupied country.

They shall receive the medical attention required by their state of health.

They shall also have the right to receive any spiritual assistance which they may require.

Women shall be confined in separate quarters and shall be under the direct supervision of women.

Proper regard shall be paid to the special treatment due to minors. Protected persons who are detained shall have the right to be visited by delegates of the Protecting Power and of the International Committee of the Red Cross, in accordance with the provisions of Article 143.

Such persons shall have the right to receive at least one relief parcel monthly.

Article 77

Protected persons who have been accused of offences or convicted by the courts in occupied territory shall be handed over at the close of occupation, with the relevant records, to the authorities of the liberated territory.

Article 78

If the Occupying Power considers it necessary, for imperative reasons of security, to take safety measures concerning protected persons, it may, at the most, subject them to assigned residence or to internment.

Decisions regarding such assigned residence or internment shall be made according to a regular procedure to be prescribed by the Occupying Power in accordance with the provisions of the present Convention.

This procedure shall include the right of appeal for the parties concerned.

Appeals shall be decided with the least possible delay.

In the event of the decision being upheld, it shall be subject to periodical review, if possible every six months, by a competent body set up by the said Power. Protected persons made subject to assigned residence and thus required to leave their homes shall enjoy the full benefit of Article 39 of the present Convention.

SECTION IV

REGULATIONS FOR THE TREATMENT OF INTERNEES

Chapter I

GENERAL PROVISIONS

Article 79

The Parties to the conflict shall not intern protected persons, except in accordance with the provisions of Articles 41, 42, 43, 68 and 78.

Article 80

Internees shall retain their full civil capacity and shall exercise such attendant rights as may be compatible with their status.

Article 81

Parties to the conflict who intern protected persons shall be bound to provide free of charge for their maintenance, and to grant them also the medical attention required by their state of health.

No deduction from the allowances, salaries or credits due to the internees shall be made for the repayment of these costs.

The Detaining Power shall provide for the support of those dependent on the internees, if such dependants are without adequate means of support or are unable to earn a living.

Article 82

The Detaining Power shall, as far as possible, accommodate the internees according to their nationality, language and customs.

Internees who are nationals of the same country shall not be separated merely because they have different languages.

Throughout the duration of their internment, members of the same family, and in particular parents and children, shall be lodged together in the same place of internment, except when separation of a temporary nature is necessitated for reasons of employment or health or for the purposes of enforcement of the provisions of Chapter IX of the present Section.

Internees may request that their children who are left at liberty without parental care shall be interned with them.

Wherever possible, interned members of the same family shall be housed in the same premises and given separate accommodation from other internees, together with facilities for leading a proper family life.

Chapter II

PLACES OF INTERNMENT

Article 83

The Detaining Power shall not set up places of internment in areas particularly exposed to the dangers of war.

The Detaining Power shall give the enemy Powers, through the intermediary of the Protecting Powers, all useful information regarding the geographical location of places of internment.

Whenever military considerations permit, internment camps shall be indicated by the letters IC, placed so as to be clearly visible in the daytime from the air. The Powers concerned may, however, agree upon any other system of marking.

No place other than an internment camp shall be marked as such.

Article 84

Internees shall be accommodated and administered separately from prisoners of war and from persons deprived of liberty for any other reason.

Article 85

The Detaining Power is bound to take all necessary and possible measures to ensure that protected persons shall, from the outset of their internment, be accommodated in buildings or quarters which afford every possible safeguard as regards hygiene and health, and provide efficient protection against the rigors of the climate and the effects of the war.

In no case shall permanent places of internment be situated in unhealthy areas or in districts the climate of which is injurious to the internees.

In all cases where the district, in which a protected person is temporarily interned, is in an unhealthy area or has a climate which is harmful to his health, he shall be removed to a more suitable place of internment as rapidly as circumstances permit.

The premises shall be fully protected from dampness, adequately heated and lighted, in particular between dusk and lights out.

The sleeping quarters shall be sufficiently spacious and well ventilated, and the internees shall have suitable bedding and sufficient blankets, account being taken of the climate, and the age, sex, and state of health of the internees.

Internees shall have for their use, day and night, sanitary conveniences which conform to the rules of hygiene and are constantly maintained in a state of cleanliness. They shall be provided with sufficient water and soap for their daily personal toilet and for washing their personal laundry; installations and facilities necessary for this purpose shall be granted to them.

Showers or baths shall also be available. The necessary time shall be set aside for washing and for cleaning.

Whenever it is necessary, as an exceptional and temporary measure, to accommodate women internees who are not members of a family unit in the same place of internment as men, the provision of separate sleeping quarters and sanitary conveniences for the use of such women internees shall be obligatory.

Article 86

The Detaining Power shall place at the disposal of interned persons, of whatever denomination, premises suitable for the holding of their religious services.

Article 87

Canteens shall be installed in every place of internment, except where other suitable facilities are available.

Their purpose shall be to enable internees to make purchases, at prices not higher than local market prices, of foodstuffs and articles of everyday use, including soap and tobacco, such as would increase their personal well-being and comfort.

Profits made by canteens shall be credited to a welfare fund to be set up for each place of internment, and administered for the benefit of the internees attached to such place of internment.

The Internee Committee provided for in Article 102 shall have the right to check the management of the canteen and of the said fund.

When a place of internment is closed down, the balance of the welfare fund shall be transferred to the welfare fund of a place of internment for internees of the same nationality, or, if such a place does not exist, to a central welfare fund which shall be administered for the benefit of all internees remaining in the custody of the Detaining Power.

In case of a general release, the said profits shall be kept by the Detaining Power, subject to any agreement to the contrary between the Powers concerned.

Article 88

In all places of internment exposed to air raids and other hazards of war, shelters adequate in number and structure to ensure the necessary protection shall be installed.

In case of alarms, the internees shall be free to enter such shelters as quickly as possible, excepting those who remain for the protection of their quarters against the aforesaid hazards.

Any protective measures taken in favor of the population shall also apply to them. All due precautions must be taken in places of internment against the danger of fire.

Chapter III

FOOD AND CLOTHING

Article 89

Daily food rations for internees shall be sufficient in quantity, quality and variety to keep internees in a good state of health and prevent the development of nutritional deficiencies.

Account shall also be taken of the customary diet of the internees. Internees shall also be given the means by which they can prepare for themselves any additional food in their possession.

Sufficient drinking water shall be supplied to internees.

The use of tobacco shall be permitted. Internees who work shall receive additional rations in proportion to the kind of labor which they perform.

Expectant and nursing mothers and children under fifteen years of age shall be given additional food, in proportion to their physiological needs.

Article 90

When taken into custody, internees shall be given all facilities to provide themselves with the necessary clothing, footwear and change of underwear, and later on, to procure further supplies if required.

Should any internees not have sufficient clothing, account being taken of the climate, and be unable to procure any, it shall be provided free of charge to them by the Detaining Power.

The clothing supplied by the Detaining Power to internees and the outward markings placed on their own clothes shall not be ignominious nor expose them to ridicule.

Workers shall receive suitable working outfits, including protective clothing, whenever the nature of their work so requires.

Chapter IV

HYGIENE AND MEDICAL ATTENTION

Article 91

Every place of internment shall have an adequate infirmary, under the direction of a qualified doctor, where internees may have the attention they require, as well as an appropriate diet.

Isolation wards shall be set aside for cases of contagious or mental diseases.

Maternity cases and internees suffering from serious diseases, or whose condition requires special treatment, a surgical operation or hospital care, must be admitted to any institution where adequate treatment can be given and shall receive care not inferior to that provided for the general population.

Internees shall, for preference, have the attention of medical personnel of their own nationality.

Internees may not be prevented from presenting themselves to the medical authorities for examination.

The medical authorities of the Detaining Power shall, upon request, issue to every internee who has undergone treatment an official certificate showing the nature of his illness or injury, and the duration and nature of the treatment given. A duplicate of this certificate shall be forwarded to the Central Agency provided for in Article 140.

Treatment, including the provision of any apparatus necessary for the maintenance of internees in good health, particularly dentures and other artificial appliances and spectacles, shall be free of charge to the internee.

Article 92

Medical inspections of internees shall be made at least once a month. Their purpose shall be, in particular, to supervise the general state of health, nutrition and cleanliness of internees, and to detect contagious diseases, especially tuberculosis, malaria, and venereal diseases. Such inspections shall include, in particular, the checking of weight of each internee and, at least once a year, radioscopic examination.

Chapter V

RELIGIOUS, INTELLECTUAL AND PHYSICAL ACTIVITIES

Article 93

Internees shall enjoy complete latitude in the exercise of their religious duties, including attendance at the services of their faith, on condition that they comply with the disciplinary routine prescribed by the detaining authorities.

Ministers of religion who are interned shall be allowed to minister freely to the members of their community.

For this purpose, the Detaining Power shall ensure their equitable allocation amongst the various places of internment in which there are internees speaking the same language and belonging to the same religion.

Should such ministers be too few in number, the Detaining Power shall provide them with the necessary facilities, including means of transport, for moving from one place to another, and they shall be authorized to visit any internees who are in hospital.

Ministers of religion shall be at liberty to correspond on matters concerning their ministry with the religious authorities in the country of detention and, as far as possible, with the international religious organizations of their faith. Such correspondence shall not be considered as forming a part of the quota mentioned in Article 107. It shall, however, be subject to the provisions of Article 112.

When internees do not have at their disposal the assistance of ministers of their faith, or should these latter be too few in number, the local religious authorities of the same faith may appoint, in agreement with the Detaining Power, a minister of the internees' faith or, if such a course is feasible from a denominational point of view, a minister of similar religion or a qualified layman. The latter shall enjoy the facilities granted to the ministry he has assumed. Persons so appointed shall comply with all regulations laid down by the Detaining Power in the interests of discipline and security.

Article 94

The Detaining Power shall encourage intellectual, educational and recreational pursuits, sports and games amongst internees, whilst leaving them free to take part in them or not.

It shall take all practicable measures to ensure the exercise thereof, in particular by providing suitable premises.

All possible facilities shall be granted to internees to continue their studies or to take up new subjects.

The education of children and young people shall be ensured; they shall be allowed to attend schools either within the place of internment or outside.

Internees shall be given opportunities for physical exercise, sports and outdoor games. For this purpose, sufficient open spaces shall be set aside in all places of internment.

Special playgrounds shall be reserved for children and young people.

Article 95

The Detaining Power shall not employ internees as workers, unless they so desire.

Employment which, if undertaken under compulsion by a protected person not in internment, would involve a breach of Articles 40 or 51 of the present Convention, and employment on work which is of a degrading or humiliating character are in any case prohibited. After a working period of six weeks, internees shall be free to give up work at any moment, subject to eight days' notice.

These provisions constitute no obstacle to the right of the Detaining Power to employ interned doctors, dentists and other medical personnel in their professional capacity on behalf of their fellow internees, or to employ internees for administrative and maintenance work in places of internment and to detail such persons for work in the kitchens or for other domestic tasks, or to require such persons to undertake duties connected with the protection of internees against aerial bombardment or other war risks.

No internee may, however, be required to perform tasks for which he is, in the opinion of a medical officer, physically unsuited. The Detaining Power shall take entire responsibility for all working conditions, for medical attention, for the payment of wages, and for ensuring that all employed internees receive compensation for occupational accidents and diseases.

The standards prescribed for the said working conditions and for compensation shall be in accordance with the national laws and regulations, and with the existing practice; they shall in no case be inferior to those obtaining for work of the same nature in the same district.

Wages for work done shall be determined on an equitable basis by special agreements between the internees, the Detaining Power, and, if the case arises, employers other than the Detaining Power, due regard being paid to the obligation of the Detaining Power to provide for free maintenance of internees and for the medical attention which their state of health may require. Internees permanently detailed for categories of work mentioned in the third paragraph of this Article shall be paid fair wages by the Detaining Power.

The working conditions and the scale of compensation for occupational accidents and diseases to internees thus detailed shall not be inferior to those applicable to work of the same nature in the same district.

Article 96

All labor detachments shall remain part of and dependent upon a place of internment.

The competent authorities of the Detaining Power and the commandant of a place of internment shall be responsible for the observance in a labor detachment of the provisions of the present Convention.

The commandant shall keep an up-to-date list of the labor detachments subordinate to him and shall communicate it to the delegates of the Protecting Power, of the International Committee of the Red Cross and of other humanitarian organizations who may visit the places of internment.

Chapter VI

PERSONAL PROPER AND FINANCIAL RESOURCES

Article 97

Internees shall be permitted to retain articles of personal use. Monies, cheques, bonds, etc., and valuables in their possession may not be taken from them except in accordance with established procedure. Detailed receipts shall be given therefore.

The amounts shall be paid into the account of every internee as provided for in Article 98. Such amounts may not be converted into any other currency unless legislation in force in the territory in which the owner is interned so requires or the internee gives his consent.

Articles which have above all a personal or sentimental value may not be taken away.

A woman internee shall not be searched except by a woman.

On release or repatriation, internees shall be given all articles, monies or other valuables taken from them during internment and shall receive in currency the balance of any credit to their accounts kept in accordance with Article 98, with the exception of any articles or amounts withheld by the Detaining Power by virtue of its legislation in force.

If the property of an internee is so withheld, the owner shall receive a detailed receipt.

Family or identity documents in the possession of internees may not be taken away without a receipt being given.

At no time shall internees be left without identity documents. If they have none, they shall be issued with special documents drawn up by the detaining authorities, which will serve as their identity papers until the end of their internment.

Internees may keep on their persons a certain amount of money, in cash or in the shape of purchase coupons, to enable them to make purchases.

Article 98

All internees shall receive regular allowances, sufficient to enable them to purchase goods and articles, such as tobacco, toilet requisites, etc. Such allowances may take the form of credits or purchase coupons.

Furthermore, internees may receive allowances from the Power to which they owe allegiance, the Protecting Powers, the organizations which may assist them, or their families, as well as the income on their property in accordance with the law of the Detaining Power.

The amount of allowances granted by the Power to which they owe allegiance shall be the same for each category of internees (infirm, sick, pregnant women, etc.) but may not be allocated by that Power or distributed by the Detaining Power on the basis of discrimination between internees which are prohibited by Article 27 of the present Convention.

The Detaining Power shall open a regular account for every internee, to which shall be credited the allowances named in the present Article, the wages earned and the remittances received, together with such sums taken from him as may be available under the legislation in force in the territory in which he is interned.

Internees shall be granted all facilities consistent with the legislation in force in such territory to make remittances to their families and to other dependants. They may draw from their accounts the amounts necessary for their personal expenses, within the limits fixed by the Detaining Power. They shall at all times be afforded reasonable facilities for consulting and obtaining copies of their accounts. A statement of accounts shall be furnished to the Protecting Power on request, and shall accompany the internee in case of transfer.

Chapter VII

ADMINISTRATION AND DISCIPLINE

Article 99

Every place of internment shall be put under the authority of a responsible officer, chosen from the regular military forces or the regular civil administration of the Detaining Power.

The officer in charge of the place of internment must have in his possession a copy of the present Convention in the official language, or one of the official languages, of his country and shall be responsible for its application.

The staff in control of internees shall be instructed in the provisions of the present Convention and of the administrative measures adopted to ensure its application. The text of the present Convention and the texts of special agreements concluded under the said Convention shall be posted inside the place of internment, in a language which the internees understand, or shall be in the possession of the Internee Committee.

Regulations, orders, notices and publications of every kind shall be communicated to the internees and posted inside the places of internment, in a language which they understand.

Every order and command addressed to internees individually must likewise be given in a language which they understand.

Article 100

The disciplinary regime in places of internment shall be consistent with humanitarian principles, and shall in no circumstances include regulations imposing on internees any physical exertion dangerous to their health or involving physical or moral victimization.

Identification by tattooing or imprinting signs or markings on the body is prohibited.

In particular, prolonged standing and roll-calls, punishment drill, military drill and maneuvers, or the reduction of food rations, are prohibited.

Article 101

Internees shall have the right to present to the authorities in whose power they are any petition with regard to the conditions of internment to which they are subjected. They shall also have the right to apply without restriction through the Internee Committee or, if they consider it necessary, direct to the representatives of the Protecting Power, in order to indicate to them any points on which they may have complaints to make with regard to the conditions of internment. Such petitions and complaints shall be transmitted forthwith and without alteration, and even if the latter are recognized to be unfounded, they may not occasion any punishment.

Periodic reports on the situation in places of internment and as to the needs of the internees may be sent by the Internee Committees to the representatives of the Protecting Powers.

Article 102

In every place of internment, the internees shall freely elect by secret ballot every six months, the members of a Committee empowered to represent them before the

Detaining and the Protecting Powers, the International Committee of the Red Cross and any other organization which may assist them.

The members of the Committee shall be eligible for re-election. Internees so elected shall enter upon their duties after their election has been approved by the detaining authorities. The reasons for any refusals or dismissals shall be communicated to the Protecting Powers concerned.

Article 103

The Internee Committees shall further the physical, spiritual and intellectual well-being of the internees.

In case the internees decide, in particular, to organize a system of mutual assistance amongst themselves, this organization would be within the competence of the Committees in addition to the special duties entrusted to them under other provisions of the present Convention.

Article 104

Members of Internee Committees shall not be required to perform any other work, if the accomplishment of their duties is rendered more difficult thereby.

Members of Internee Committees may appoint from amongst the internees such assistants as they may require.

All material facilities shall be granted to them, particularly a certain freedom of movement necessary for the accomplishment of their duties (visits to labor detachments, receipt of supplies, etc.).

All facilities shall likewise be accorded to members of Internee Committees for communication by post and telegraph with the detaining authorities, the Protecting Powers, the International Committee of the Red Cross and their delegates, and with the organizations which give assistance to internees.

Committee members in labor detachments shall enjoy similar facilities for communication with their Internee Committee in the principal place of internment.

Such communications shall not be limited, nor considered as forming a part of the quota mentioned in Article 107.

Members of Internee Committees who are transferred shall be allowed a reasonable time to acquaint their successors with current affairs.

Chapter VIII

RELATIONS WITH THE EXTERIOR

Article 105

Immediately upon interning protected persons, the Detaining Power shall inform them, the Power to which they owe allegiance and their Protecting Power of the measures taken for executing the provisions of the present Chapter.

The Detaining Power shall likewise inform the Parties concerned of any subsequent modifications of such measures.

Article 106

As soon as he is interned, or at the latest not more than one week after his arrival in a place of internment, and likewise in cases of sickness or transfer to another place of internment or to a hospital, every internee shall be enabled to send direct to his family, on the one hand, and to the Central Agency provided for by Article 140, on the other, an internment card similar, if possible, to the model annexed to the present Convention, informing his relatives of his detention, address and state of health. The said cards shall be forwarded as rapidly as possible and may not be delayed in any way.

Article 107

Internees shall be allowed to send and receive letters and cards.

If the Detaining Power deems it necessary to limit the number of letters and cards sent by each internee, the said number shall not be less than two letters and four cards monthly; these shall be drawn up so as to conform as closely as possible to the models annexed to the present Convention.

If limitations must be placed on the correspondence addressed to internees, they may be ordered only by the Power to which such internees owe allegiance, possibly at the request of the Detaining Power.

Such letters and cards must be conveyed with reasonable dispatch; they may not be delayed or retained for disciplinary reasons.

Internees who have been a long time without news, or who find it impossible to receive news from their relatives, or to give them news by the ordinary postal route, as well as those who are at a considerable distance from their homes, shall be allowed to send telegrams, the charges being paid by them in the currency at their disposal.

They shall likewise benefit by this provision in cases which are recognized to be urgent.

As a rule, internees' mail shall be written in their own language.

The Parties to the conflict may authorize correspondence in other languages.

Article 108

Internees shall be allowed to receive, by post or by any other means, individual parcels or collective shipments containing in particular foodstuffs, clothing, medical supplies, as well as books and objects of a devotional, educational or recreational character which may meet their needs.

Such shipments shall in no way free the Detaining Power from the obligations imposed upon it by virtue of the present Convention.

Should military necessity require the quantity of such shipments to be limited, due notice thereof shall be given to the Protecting Power and to the International Committee of the Red Cross, or to any other organization giving assistance to the internees and responsible for the forwarding of such shipments.

The conditions for the sending of individual parcels and collective shipments shall, if necessary, be the subject of special agreements between the Powers concerned, which may in no case delay the receipt by the internees of relief supplies.

Parcels of clothing and foodstuffs may not include books. Medical relief supplies shall, as a rule, be sent in collective parcels.

Article 109

In the absence of special agreements between Parties to the conflict regarding the conditions for the receipt and distribution of collective relief shipments, the regulations concerning collective relief which are annexed to the present Convention shall be applied.

The special agreements provided for above shall in no case restrict the right of Internee Committees to take possession of collective relief shipments intended for internees, to undertake their distribution and to dispose of them in the interests of the recipients.

Nor shall such agreements restrict the right of representatives of the Protecting Powers, the International Committee of the Red Cross, or any other organization giving assistance to internees and responsible for the forwarding of collective shipments, to supervise their distribution to the recipients.

Article 110

All relief shipments for internees shall be exempt from import, customs and other dues.

All matter sent by mail, including relief parcels sent by parcel post and remittances of money, addressed from other countries to internees or dispatched by them through the post office, either direct or through the Information Bureaus provided for in Article 136 and the Central Information Agency provided for in Article 140, shall be exempt from all postal dues both in the countries of origin and destination and in intermediate countries. To this end, in particular, the exemption provided by the Universal Postal Convention of 1947 and by the agreements of the Universal Postal Union in favor of civilians of enemy nationality detained in camps or civilian prisons shall be extended to the other interned persons protected by the present Convention.

The countries not signatory to the above-mentioned agreements shall be bound to grant freedom from charges in the same circumstances.

The cost of transporting relief shipments which are intended for internees and which, by reason of their weight or any other cause, cannot be sent through the post office, shall be borne by the Detaining Power in all the territories under its control.

Other Powers which are Parties to the present Convention shall bear the cost of transport in their respective territories.

Costs connected with the transport of such shipments, which are not covered by the above paragraphs, shall be charged to the senders.

The High Contracting Parties shall endeavor to reduce, so far as possible, the charges for telegrams sent by internees, or addressed to them.

Article 111

Should military operations prevent the Powers concerned from fulfilling their obligation to ensure the conveyance of the mail and relief shipments provided for in Articles 106, 107, 108 and 113, the Protecting Powers concerned, the International Committee of the

Red Cross or any other organization duly approved by the Parties to the conflict may undertake the conveyance of such shipments by suitable means (rail, motor vehicles, vessels or aircraft, etc.).

For this purpose, the High Contracting Parties shall endeavor to supply them with such transport, and to allow its circulation, especially by granting the necessary safe-conducts. Such transport may also be used to convey:

(a) Correspondence lists and reports exchanged between the Central Information Agency referred to in Article 140 and the National Bureaus referred to in Article 136;

(b) Correspondence and reports relating to internees which the Protecting Powers, the International Committee of the Red Cross or any other organization assisting the internees exchange either with their own delegates or with the Parties to the conflict.

These provisions in no way detract from the right of any Party to the conflict to arrange other means of transport if it should so prefer, nor preclude the granting of safe-conducts, under mutually agreed conditions, to such means of transport.

The costs occasioned by the use of such means of transport shall be borne, in proportion to the importance of the shipments, by the Parties to the conflict whose nationals are benefited thereby.

Article 112

The censoring of correspondence addressed to internees or dispatched by them shall be done as quickly as possible.

The examination of consignments intended for internees shall not be carried out under conditions that will expose the goods contained in them to deterioration. It shall be done in the presence of the addressee, or of a fellow-internee duly delegated by him.

The delivery to internees of individual or collective consignments shall not be delayed under the pretext of difficulties of censorship. Any prohibition of correspondence ordered by the Parties to the conflict, either for military or political reasons, shall be only temporary and its duration shall be as short as possible.

Article 113

The Detaining Powers shall provide all reasonable facilities for the transmission, through the Protecting Power or the Central Agency provided for in Article 140, or as otherwise required, of wills, powers of attorney letters of authority, or any other documents intended for internees or dispatched by them.

In all cases the Detaining Power shall facilitate the execution and authentication in due legal form of such documents on behalf of internees, in particular by allowing them to consult a lawyer.

Article 114

The Detaining Power shall afford internees all facilities to enable them to manage their property, provided this is not incompatible with the conditions of internment and the law which is applicable. For this purpose, the said Power may give them permission to leave the place of internment in urgent cases and if circumstances allow.

Article 115

In all cases where an internee is a party to proceedings in any court, the Detaining Power shall, if he so requests, cause the court to be informed of his detention and shall, within legal limits, ensure that all necessary steps are taken to prevent him from being in any way prejudiced, by reason of his internment, as regards the preparation and conduct of his case or as regards the execution of any judgment of the court.

Article 116

Every internee shall be allowed to receive visitors, especially near relatives, at regular intervals and as frequently as possible. As far as is possible, internees shall be permitted to visit their homes in urgent cases, particularly in cases of death or serious illness of relatives.

Chapter IX

PENAL AND DISCIPLINARY SANCTIONS

Article 117

Subject to the provisions of the present Chapter, the laws in force in the territory in which they are detained will continue to apply to internees who commit offences during internment. If general laws, regulations or orders declare acts committed by internees to be punishable, whereas the same acts are not punishable when committed by persons who are not internees, such acts shall entail disciplinary punishments only. No internee may be punished more than once for the same act, or on the same count.

Article 118

The courts or authorities shall in passing sentence take as far as possible into account the fact that the defendant is not a national of the Detaining Power. They shall be free to reduce the penalty prescribed for the offence with which the internee is charged and shall not be obliged, to this end, to apply the minimum sentence prescribed.

Imprisonment in premises without daylight, and, in general, all forms of cruelty without exception are forbidden.

Internees who have served disciplinary or judicial sentences shall not be treated differently from other internees.

The duration of preventive detention undergone by an internee shall be deducted from any disciplinary or judicial penalty involving confinement to which he may be sentenced.

Internee Committees shall be informed of all judicial proceedings instituted against internees whom they represent, and of their result.

Article 119

The disciplinary punishments applicable to internees shall be the following:

1. A fine which shall not exceed 50 per cent of the wages which the internee would otherwise receive under the provisions of Article 95 during a period of not more than thirty days.

2. Discontinuance of privileges granted over and above the treatment provided for by the present Convention.

3. Fatigue duties, not exceeding two hours daily, in connection with the maintenance of the place of internment.

4. Confinement. In no case shall disciplinary penalties be inhuman, brutal or dangerous for the health of internees.

Account shall be taken of the internee's age, sex and state of health.

The duration of any single punishment shall in no case exceed a maximum of thirty consecutive days, even if the internee is answerable for several breaches of discipline when his case is dealt with, whether such breaches are connected or not.

Article 120

Internees who are recaptured after having escaped or when attempting to escape shall be liable only to disciplinary punishment in respect of this act, even if it is a repeated offence.

Article 118, paragraph 3, notwithstanding, internees punished as a result of escape or attempt to escape, may be subjected to special surveillance, on condition that such surveillance does not affect the state of their health, that it is exercised in a place of internment and that it does not entail the abolition of any of the safeguards granted by the present Convention.

Internees who aid and abet an escape, or attempt to escape, shall be liable on this count to disciplinary punishment only.

Article 121

Escape, or attempt to escape, even if it is a repeated offence, shall not be deemed an aggravating circumstance in cases where an internee is prosecuted for offences committed during his escape.

The Parties to the conflict shall ensure that the competent authorities exercise leniency in deciding whether punishment inflicted for an offence shall be of a disciplinary or judicial nature, especially in respect of acts committed in connection with an escape, whether successful or not.

Article 122

Acts which constitute offences against discipline shall be investigated immediately. This rule shall be applied, in particular, in cases of escape or attempt to escape.

Recaptured internees shall be handed over to the competent authorities as soon as possible. In case of offences against discipline, confinement awaiting trial shall be reduced to an absolute minimum for all internees, and shall not exceed fourteen days. Its duration shall in any case be deducted from any sentence of confinement.

The provisions of Articles 124 and 125 shall apply to internees who are in confinement awaiting trial for offences against discipline.

Article 123

Without prejudice to the competence of courts and higher authorities, disciplinary punishment may be ordered only by the commandant of the place of internment, or by a responsible officer or official who replaces him, or to whom he has delegated his disciplinary powers.

Before any disciplinary punishment is awarded, the accused internee shall be given precise information regarding the offences of which he is accused, and given an opportunity of explaining his conduct and of defending himself.

He shall be permitted, in particular, to call witnesses and to have recourse, if necessary, to the services of a qualified interpreter.

The decision shall be announced in the presence of the accused and of a member of the Internee Committee.

The period elapsing between the time of award of a disciplinary punishment and its execution shall not exceed one month.

When an internee is awarded a further disciplinary punishment, a period of at least three days shall elapse between the execution of any two of the punishments, if the duration of one of these is ten days or more.

A record of disciplinary punishments shall be maintained by the commandant of the place of internment and shall be open to inspection by representatives of the Protecting Power.

Article 124

Internees shall not in any case be transferred to penitentiary establishments (prisons, penitentiaries, convict prisons, etc.) to undergo disciplinary punishment therein.

The premises in which disciplinary punishments are undergone shall conform to sanitary requirements; they shall in particular be provided with adequate bedding. Internees undergoing punishment shall be enabled to keep themselves in a state of cleanliness.

Women internees undergoing disciplinary punishment shall be confined in separate quarters from male internees and shall be under the immediate supervision of women.

Article 125

Internees awarded disciplinary punishment shall be allowed to exercise and to stay in the open air at least two hours daily.

They shall be allowed, if they so request, to be present at the daily medical inspections.

They shall receive the attention which their state of health requires and, if necessary, shall be removed to the infirmary of the place of internment or to a hospital.

They shall have permission to read and write, likewise to send and receive letters. Parcels and remittances of money, however, may be withheld from them until the completion of their punishment; such consignments shall meanwhile be entrusted to the Internee Committee, who will hand over to the infirmary the perishable goods contained in the parcels. No internee given a disciplinary punishment may be deprived of the benefit of the provisions of Articles 107 and 143 of the present Convention.

Article 126

The provisions of Articles 71 to 76 inclusive shall apply, by analogy, to proceedings against internees who are in the national territory of the Detaining Power.

Chapter X

TRANSFERS OF INTERNEES

Article 127

The transfer of internees shall always be effected humanely.

As a general rule, it shall be carried out by rail or other means of transport, and under conditions at least equal to those obtaining for the forces of the Detaining Power in their changes of station.

If, as an exceptional measure, such removals have to be effected on foot, they may not take place unless the internees are in a fit state of health, and may not in any case expose them to excessive fatigue.

The Detaining Power shall supply internees during transfer with drinking water and food sufficient in quantity, quality and variety to maintain them in good health, and also with the necessary clothing, adequate shelter and the necessary medical attention.

The Detaining Power shall take all suitable precautions to ensure their safety during transfer, and shall establish before their departure a complete list of all internees transferred.

Sick, wounded or infirm internees and maternity cases shall not be transferred if the journey would be seriously detrimental to them, unless their safety imperatively so demands.

If the combat zone draws close to a place of internment, the internees in the said place shall not be transferred unless their removal can be carried out in adequate conditions of safety, or unless they are exposed to greater risks by remaining on the spot than by being transferred.

When making decisions regarding the transfer of internees, the Detaining Power shall take their interests into account and, in particular, shall not do anything to increase the difficulties of repatriating them or returning them to their own homes.

Article 128

In the event of transfer, internees shall be officially advised of their departure and of their new postal address. Such notification shall be given in time for them to pack their luggage and inform their next of kin.

They shall be allowed to take with them their personal effects, and the correspondence and parcels which have arrived for them.

The weight of such baggage may be limited if the conditions of transfer so require, but in no case to less than twenty-five kilograms per internee.

Mail and parcels addressed to their former place of internment shall be forwarded to them without delay.

The commandant of the place of internment shall take, in agreement with the Internee Committee, any measures needed to ensure the transport of the internees' community property and of the luggage the internees are unable to take with them in consequence of restrictions imposed by virtue of the second paragraph. ...

SECTION V

INFORMATION BUREAUX AND CENTRAL AGENCY

Article 136

Upon the outbreak of a conflict and in all cases of occupation, each of the Parties to the conflict shall establish an official Information Bureau responsible for receiving and transmitting information in respect of the protected persons who are in its power.

Each of the Parties to the conflict shall, within the shortest possible period, give its Bureau information of any measure taken by it concerning any protected persons who are kept in custody for more than two weeks, who are subjected to assigned residence or who are interned.

It shall, furthermore, require its various departments concerned with such matters to provide the aforesaid Bureau promptly with information concerning all changes pertaining to these protected persons, as, for example, transfers, release, repatriations, escapes, admittances to hospitals, births and deaths.

Article 137

Each national Bureau shall immediately forward information concerning protected persons by the most rapid means to the Powers of whom the aforesaid persons are nationals, or to Powers in whose territory they resided, through the intermediary of the Protecting Powers and likewise through the Central Agency provided for in Article 140.

The Bureaus shall also reply to all enquiries which may be received regarding protected persons.

Information Bureaus shall transmit information concerning a protected person unless its transmission might be detrimental to the person concerned or to his or her relatives. Even in such a case, the information may not be withheld from the Central Agency which, upon being notified of the circumstances, will take the necessary precautions indicated in Article 140.

All communications in writing made by any Bureau shall be authenticated by a signature or a seal.

Article 138

The information received by the national Bureau and transmitted by it shall be of such a character as to make it possible to identify the protected person exactly and to advise his next of kin quickly.

The information in respect of each person shall include at least his surname, first names, place and date of birth, nationality, last residence and distinguishing characteristics, the first name of the father and the maiden name of the mother, the date, place and nature of the action taken with regard to the individual, the address at which correspondence may be sent to him and the name and address of the person to be informed.

Likewise, information regarding the state of health of internees who are seriously ill or seriously wounded shall be supplied regularly and if possible every week.

Article 139

Each national Information Bureau shall, furthermore, be responsible for collecting all personal valuables left by protected persons mentioned in Article 136, in particular those who have been repatriated or released, or who have escaped or died; it shall forward the said valuables to those concerned, either direct, or, if necessary, through the Central Agency.

Such articles shall be sent by the Bureau in sealed packets which shall be accompanied by statements giving clear and full identity particulars of the person to whom the articles belonged, and by a complete list of the contents of the parcel. Detailed records shall be maintained of the receipt and dispatch of all such valuables.

Article 140

A Central Information Agency for protected persons, in particular for internees, shall be created in a neutral country.

The International Committee of the Red Cross shall, if it deems necessary, propose to the Powers concerned the organization of such an Agency, which may be the same as that provided for in Article 123 of the Geneva Convention relative to the Treatment of Prisoners of War of August 12, 1949.

The function of the Agency shall be to collect all information of the type set forth in Article 136 which it may obtain through official or private channels and to transmit it as rapidly as possible to the countries of origin or of residence of the persons concerned, except in cases where such transmissions might be detrimental to the persons whom the said information concerns, or to their relatives. It shall receive from the Parties to the conflict all reasonable facilities for effecting such transmissions.

The High Contracting Parties, and in particular those whose nationals benefit by the services of the Central Agency, are requested to give the said Agency the financial aid it may require.

The foregoing provisions shall in no way be interpreted as restricting the humanitarian activities of the International Committee of the Red Cross and of the relief Societies described in Article 142.

Article 141

The national Information Bureaus and the Central Information Agency shall enjoy free postage for all mail, likewise the exemptions provided for in Article 110, and further, so far as possible, exemption from telegraphic charges or, at least, greatly reduced rates.

PART IV

EXECUTION OF THE CONVENTION SECTION I GENERAL PROVISIONS

Article 142

Subject to the measures which the Detaining Powers may consider essential to ensure their security or to meet any other reasonable need, the representatives of religious organizations, relief societies, or any other organizations assisting the protected persons, shall receive from these Powers, for themselves or their duly accredited agents, all facilities for visiting the protected persons, for distributing relief supplies and material from any source, intended for educational, recreational or religious purposes , or for assisting them in organizing their leisure time within the places of internment. Such societies or organizations may be constituted in the territory of the Detaining Power, or in any other country, or they may have an international character.

The Detaining Power may limit the number of societies and organizations whose delegates are allowed to carry out their activities in its territory and under its supervision, on condition, however, that such limitation shall not hinder the supply of effective and adequate relief to all protected persons.

The special position of the International Committee of the Red Cross in this field shall be recognized and respected at all times.

Article 143

Representatives or delegates of the Protecting Powers shall have permission to go to all places where protected persons are, particularly to places of internment, detention and work.

They shall have access to all premises occupied by protected persons and shall be able to interview the latter without witnesses, personally or through an interpreter. Such visits may not be prohibited except for reasons of imperative military necessity, and then only as an exceptional and temporary measure.

Their duration and frequency shall not be restricted.

Such representatives and delegates shall have full liberty to select the places they wish to visit.

The Detaining or Occupying Power, the Protecting Power and when occasion arises the Power of origin of the persons to be visited, may agree that compatriots of the internees shall be permitted to participate in the visits.

The delegates of the International Committee of the Red Cross shall also enjoy the above prerogatives.

The appointment of such delegates shall be submitted to the approval of the Power governing the territories where they will carry out their duties.

Article 144

The High Contracting Parties undertake, in time of peace as in time of war, to disseminate the text of the present Convention as widely as possible in their respective countries, and, in particular, to include the study thereof in their programs of military and, if possible, civil instruction, so that the principles thereof may become known to the entire population.

Any civilian, military, police or other authorities, who in time of war assume responsibilities in respect of protected persons, must possess the text of the Convention and be specially instructed as to its provisions.

Article 145

The High Contracting Parties shall communicate to one another through the Swiss Federal Council and, during hostilities, through the Protecting Powers, the official translations of the present Convention, as well as the laws and regulations which they may adopt to ensure the application thereof.

Article 146

The High Contracting Parties undertake to enact any legislation necessary to provide effective penal sanctions for persons committing, or ordering to be committed, any of the grave breaches of the present Convention defined in the following Article.

Each High Contracting Party shall be under the obligation to search for persons alleged to have committed, or to have ordered to be committed, such grave breaches, and shall bring such persons, regardless of their nationality, before its own courts.

It may also, if it prefers, and in accordance with the provisions of its own legislation, hand such persons over for trial to another High Contracting Party concerned, provided such High Contracting Party has made out a prima facie case.

Each High Contracting Party shall take measures necessary for the suppression of all acts contrary to the provisions of the present Convention other than the grave breaches defined in the following Article.

In all circumstances, the accused persons shall benefit by safeguards of proper trial and defense, which shall not be less favorable than those provided by Article 105 and those following of the Geneva Convention relative to the Treatment of Prisoners of War of August 12, 1949.

Article 147

Grave breaches to which the preceding Article relates shall be those involving any of the following acts, if committed against persons or property protected by the present Convention: willful killing, torture or inhuman treatment, including biological experiments, willfully causing great suffering or serious injury to body or health, unlawful deportation or transfer or unlawful confinement of a protected person, compelling a protected person to serve in the forces of a hostile Power, or willfully depriving a protected person of the rights of fair and regular trial prescribed in the present Convention, taking of hostages and extensive destruction and appropriation of property, not justified by military necessity and carried out unlawfully and wantonly.

Article 148

No High Contracting Party shall be allowed to absolve itself or any other High Contracting Party of any liability incurred by itself or by another High Contracting Party in respect of breaches referred to in the preceding Article.

Article 149

At the request of a Party to the conflict, an enquiry shall be instituted, in a manner to be decided between the interested Parties, concerning any alleged violation of the Convention.

If agreement has not been reached concerning the procedure for the enquiry, the Parties should agree on the choice of an umpire who will decide upon the procedure to be followed. Once the violation has been established, the Parties to the conflict shall put an end to it and shall repress it with the least possible delay.

SECTION II

FINAL PROVISIONS

Article 150

The present Convention is established in English and in French. Both texts are equally authentic.

The Swiss Federal Council shall arrange for official translations of the Convention to be made in the Russian and Spanish languages.

Article 151

The present Convention, which bears the date of this day, is open to signature until 12 February 1950, in the name of the Powers represented at the Conference which opened at Geneva on 21 April 1949.

Article 152

The present Convention shall be ratified as soon as possible and the ratifications shall be deposited at Berne.

A record shall be drawn up of the deposit of each instrument of ratification and certified copies of this record shall be transmitted by the Swiss Federal Council to all the Powers in whose name the Convention has been signed, or whose accession has been notified.

Article 153

The present Convention shall come into force six months after not less than two instruments of ratification have been deposited.

Thereafter, it shall come into force for each High Contracting Party six months after the deposit of the instrument of ratification.

Article 154

In the relations between the Powers who are bound by the Hague Conventions respecting the Laws and Customs of War on Land, whether that of 29 July 1899, or that of 18 October 1907, and who are parties to the present Convention, this last Convention shall be supplementary to Sections II and III of the Regulations annexed to the above-mentioned Conventions of The Hague.

Article 155

From the date of its coming into force, it shall be open to any Power in whose name the present Convention has not been signed, to accede to this Convention.

Article 156

Accessions shall be notified in writing to the Swiss Federal Council, and shall take effect six months after the date on which they are received.

The Swiss Federal Council shall communicate the accessions to all the Powers in whose name the Convention has been signed, or whose accession has been notified.

Article 157

The situations provided for in Articles 2 and 3 shall effective immediate effect to ratifications deposited and accessions notified by the Parties to the conflict before or after the beginning of hostilities or occupation. The Swiss Federal Council shall communicate by the quickest method any ratifications or accessions received from Parties to the conflict.

Article 158

Each of the High Contracting Parties shall be at liberty to denounce the present Convention.

The denunciation shall be notified in writing to the Swiss Federal Council, which shall transmit it to the Governments of all the High Contracting Parties.

The denunciation shall take effect one year after the notification thereof has been made to the Swiss Federal Council. However, a denunciation of which notification has been made at a time when the denouncing Power is involved in a conflict shall not take effect until peace has been concluded, and until after operations connected with the release, repatriation and re-establishment of the persons protected by the present Convention have been terminated.

The denunciation shall have effect only in respect of the denouncing Power. It shall in no way impair the obligations which the Parties to the conflict shall remain bound to fulfil by virtue of the principles of the law of nations, as they result from the usages established among civilized peoples, from the laws of humanity and the dictates of the public conscience.

Article 159

The Swiss Federal Council shall register the present Convention with the Secretariat of the United Nations. The Swiss Federal Council shall also inform the Secretariat of the United Nations of all ratifications, accessions and denunciations received by it with respect to the present Convention.

In witness whereof the undersigned, having deposited their respective full powers, have signed the present Convention.

Done at Geneva this twelfth day of August 1949, in the English and French languages. The original shall be deposited in the Archives of the Swiss Confederation. The Swiss Federal Council shall transmit certified copies thereof to each of the signatory and acceding States.

Excerpts from the Protocol Additional to the Geneva Conventions of 12 August 1949, and relating to the Protection of Victims of International Armed Conflicts (Protocol I), 8 June 1977

1125 *U.N.T.S.* 3, entered into force 7 December 1978

Article 1

General principles and scope of application

1. The High Contracting Parties undertake to respect and to ensure respect for this Protocol in all circumstances.

2. In cases not covered by this Protocol or by other international agreements, civilians and combatants remain under the protection and authority of the principles of international law derived from established custom, from the principles of humanity and from dictates of public conscience.

3. This Protocol, which supplements the Geneva Conventions of 12 August 1949 for the protection of war victims, shall apply in the situations referred to in Article 2 common to those Conventions.

4. The situations referred to in the preceding paragraph include armed conflicts which peoples are fighting against colonial domination and alien occupation and against racist regimes in the exercise of their right of self-determination, as enshrined in the Charter of the United Nations and the Declaration on Principles of International Law concerning Friendly Relations and Co-operation among States in accordance with the Charter of the United Nations....

Article 4

Legal status of the Parties to the conflict

The application of the Conventions and of this Protocol, as well as the conclusion of the agreements provided for therein, shall not affect the legal status of the Parties to the conflict. Neither the occupation of a territory nor the application of the Conventions and this Protocol shall affect the legal status of the territory in question....

Article 6

Qualified persons

1. The High Contracting Parties shall, also in peacetime, endeavour, with the assistance of the national Red Cross (Red Crescent, Red Lion and Sun) Societies, to train qualified personnel to facilitate the application of the Conventions and of this Protocol, and in particular the activities of the Protecting Powers.

2. The recruitment and training of such personnel are within domestic jurisdiction.

3. The International Committee of the Red Cross shall hold at the disposal of the High Contracting Parties the lists of persons so trained which the High Contracting Parties may have established and may have transmitted to it for that purpose.

4. The conditions governing the employment of such personnel outside the national territory shall, in each case, be the subject of special agreements between the Parties concerned.

Article 10

Protection and care

1. All the wounded, sick and shipwrecked, to whichever Party they belong, shall be respected and protected.

2. In all circumstances they shall be treated humanely and shall receive, to the fullest extent practicable and with the least possible delay, the medical care and attention required by their condition. There shall be no distinction among them founded on any grounds other than medical ones.

Article 11

Protection of persons

1. The physical or mental health and integrity of persons who are in the power of the adverse Party or who are interned, detained or otherwise deprived of liberty as a result of a situation referred to in Article 1 shall not be endangered by any unjustified act or omission. Accordingly, it is prohibited to subject the persons described in this Article to any medical procedure which is not indicated by the state of health of the person concerned and which is not consistent with generally accepted medical standards which would be applied under similar medical circumstances to persons who are nationals of the Party conducting the procedure and who are in no way deprived of liberty.

2. It is, in particular, prohibited to carry out on such persons, even with their consent:

(a) physical mutilations;

(b) medical or scientific experiments;

(c) removal of tissue or organs for transplantation, except where these acts are justified in conformity with the conditions provided for in paragraph 1.

3. Exceptions to the prohibition in paragraph 2 (c) may be made only in the case of donations of blood for transfusion or of skin for grafting, provided that they are given voluntarily and without any coercion or inducement, and then only for therapeutic purposes, under conditions consistent with generally accepted medical standards and controls designed for the benefit of both the donor and the recipient.

4. Any wilful act or omission which seriously endangers the physical or mental health or integrity of any person who is in the power of a Party other than the one on which he depends and which either violates any of the prohibitions in paragraphs 1 and 2 or fails to comply with the requirements of paragraph 3 shall be a grave breach of this Protocol.

5. The persons described in paragraph 1 have the right to refuse any surgical operation. In case of refusal, medical personnel shall endeavour to obtain a written statement to that effect, signed or acknowledged by the patient.

6. Each Party to the conflict shall keep a medical record for every donation of blood for transfusion or skin for grafting by persons referred to in paragraph 1, if that donation is made under the responsibility of that Party. In addition, each Party to the conflict shall endeavour to keep a record of all medical procedures undertaken with respect to any person who is interned, detained or otherwise deprived of liberty as a result of a situation referred to in Article 1. These records shall be available at all times for inspection by the Protecting Power.

Article 12

Protection of medical units

1. Medical units shall be respected and protected at all times and shall not be the object of attack.

2. Paragraph 1 shall apply to civilian medical units, provided that they:

(a) belong to one of the Parties to the conflict;

(b) are recognized and authorized by the competent authority of one of the Parties to the conflict; or

(c) are authorized in conformity with Article 9, paragraph 2, of this Protocol or Article 27 of the First Convention.

3. The Parties to the conflict are invited to notify each other of the location of their fixed medical units. The absence of such notification shall not exempt any of the Parties from the obligation to comply with the provisions of paragraph 1.

4. Under no circumstances shall medical units be used in an attempt to shield military objectives from attack....

Article 13

Discontinuance of protection of civilian medical units

1. The protection to which civilian medical units are entitled shall not cease unless they are used to commit, outside their humanitarian function, acts harmful to the enemy. Protection may, however, cease only after a warning has been given setting, whenever appropriate, a reasonable time-limit, and after such warning has remained unheeded.

2. The following shall not be considered as acts harmful to the enemy:

(a) that the personnel of the unit are equipped with light individual weapons for their own defence or for that of the wounded and sick in their charge;

(b) that the unit is guarded by a picket or by sentries or by an escort;

(c) that small arms and ammunition taken from the wounded and sick, and not yet handed to the proper service, are found in the units;

(d) that members of the armed forces or other combatants are in the unit for medical reasons.

Article 14

Limitations on requisition of civilian medical units

1. The Occupying Power has the duty to ensure that the medical needs of the civilian population in occupied territory continue to be satisfied....

Article 15

Protection of civilian medical and religious personnel

1. Civilian medical personnel shall be respected and protected.

2. If needed, all available help shall be afforded to civilian medical personnel in an area where civilian medical services are disrupted by reason of combat activity.

3. The Occupying Power shall afford civilian medical personnel in occupied territories every assistance to enable them to perform, to the best of their ability, their humanitarian functions. The Occupying Power may not require that, in the performance of those functions, such personnel shall give priority to the treatment of any person except on medical grounds. They shall not be compelled to carry out tasks which are not compatible with their humanitarian mission.

4. Civilian medical personnel shall have access to any place where their services are essential, subject to such supervisory and safety measures as the relevant Party to the conflict may deem necessary.

5. Civilian religious personnel shall be respected and protected. The provisions of the Conventions and of this Protocol concerning the protection and identification of medical personnel shall apply equally to such persons.

Article 16

General protection of medical duties

1. Under no circumstances shall any person be punished for carrying out medical activities compatible with medical ethics, regardless of the person benefiting therefrom.

2. Persons engaged in medical activities shall not be compelled to perform acts or to carry out work contrary to the rules of medical ethics or to other medical rules designed for the benefit of the wounded and sick or to the provisions of the Conventions or of this Protocol, or to refrain from performing acts or from carrying out work required by those rules and provisions.

3. No person engaged in medical activities shall be compelled to give to anyone belonging either to an adverse Party, or to his own Party except as required by the law of the latter Party, any information concerning the wounded and sick who are, or who have been, under his care, if such information would, in his opinion, prove harmful to the patients concerned or to their families. Regulations for the compulsory notification of communicable diseases shall, however, be respected.

Article 17

Role of the civilian population and of aid societies

1. The civilian population shall respect the wounded, sick and shipwrecked, even if they belong to the adverse Party, and shall commit no act of violence against them. The civilian population and aid societies, such as national Red Cross (Red Crescent, Red Lion and Sun) Societies, shall be permitted, even on their own initiative, to collect and care for the wounded, sick and shipwrecked, even in invaded or occupied areas. No one shall be harmed, prosecuted, convicted or punished for such humanitarian acts....

Article 20

Prohibition of reprisals

Reprisals against the persons and objects protected by this Part are prohibited...

Article 32

General principle

In the implementation of this Section, the activities of the High Contracting Parties, of the Parties to the conflict and of the international humanitarian organizations mentioned in the Conventions and in this Protocol shall be prompted mainly by the right of families to know the fate of their relatives.

Article 33

Missing persons

1. As soon as circumstances permit, and at the latest from the end of active hostilities, each Party to the conflict shall search for the persons who have been reported missing by an adverse Party. Such adverse Party shall transmit all relevant information concerning such persons in order to facilitate such searches....

Part III

Methods and Means of Warfare Combatant and Prisoners-Of-War

Section I. Methods and Means of Warfare

Article 35

Basic rules

1. In any armed conflict, the right of the Parties to the conflict to choose methods or means of warfare is not unlimited.

2. It is prohibited to employ weapons, projectiles and material and methods of warfare of a nature to cause superfluous injury or unnecessary suffering.

3. It is prohibited to employ methods or means of warfare which are intended, or may be expected, to cause widespread, long-term and severe damage to the natural environment.

Article 36

New weapons

In the study, development, acquisition or adoption of a new weapon, means or method of warfare, a High Contracting Party is under an obligation to determine whether its employment would, in some or all circumstances, be prohibited by this Protocol or by any other rule of international law applicable to the High Contracting Party.

Article 37

Prohibition of Perfidy

1. It is prohibited to kill, injure or capture an adversary by resort to perfidy. Acts inviting the confidence of an adversary to lead him to believe that he is entitled to, or is obliged to accord, protection under the rules of international law applicable in armed conflict, with intent to betray that confidence, shall constitute perfidy. The following acts are examples of perfidy:

(a) the feigning of an intent to negotiate under a flag of truce or of a surrender;

(b) the feigning of an incapacitation by wounds or sickness;

(c) the feigning of civilian, non-combatant status; and

(d) the feigning of protected status by the use of signs, emblems or uniforms of the United Nations or of neutral or other States not Parties to the conflict.

2. Ruses of war are not prohibited. Such ruses are acts which are intended to mislead an adversary or to induce him to act recklessly but which infringe no rule of international law applicable in armed conflict and which are not perfidious because they do not invite the confidence of an adversary with respect to protection under that law. The following are examples of such ruses: the use of camouflage, decoys, mock operations and misinformation....

Article 40

Quarter

It is prohibited to order that there shall be no survivors, to threaten an adversary therewith or to conduct hostilities on this basis.

Article 41

Safeguard of an enemy hors de combat

1. A person who is recognized or who, in the circumstances should be recognized to be hors de combat shall not be made the object of attack.

2. A person is hors de combat if:

(a) he is in the power of an adverse Party;

(b) he clearly expresses an intention to surrender; or

(c) he has been rendered unconscious or is otherwise incapacitated by wounds or sickness, and therefore is incapable of defending himself; provided that in any of these cases he abstains from any hostile act and does not attempt to escape.

Part IV

Civilian Population

Section I

General Protection Against Effects of Hostilities

Chapter I

Basic rule and field of application

Art 48. Basic rule

In order to ensure respect for and protection of the civilian population and civilian objects, the Parties to the conflict shall at all times distinguish between the civilian population and combatants and between civilian objects and military objectives and accordingly shall direct their operations only against military objectives.

Article 49

Definition of attacks and scope of application

1. "Attacks" means acts of violence against the adversary, whether in offence or in defence.

2. The provisions of this Protocol with respect to attacks apply to all attacks in whatever territory conducted, including the national territory belonging to a Party to the conflict but under the control of an adverse Party.

3. The provisions of this section apply to any land, air or sea warfare which may affect the civilian population, individual civilians or civilian objects on land. They further apply to all attacks from the sea or from the air against objectives on land but do not otherwise affect the rules of international law applicable in armed conflict at sea or in the air.

4. The provisions of this section are additional to the rules concerning humanitarian protection contained in the Fourth Convention, particularly in part II thereof, and in

other international agreements binding upon the High Contracting Parties, as well as to other rules of international law relating to the protection of civilians and civilian objects on land, at sea or in the air against the effects of hostilities...

Article 50

Definition of civilians and civilian population

1. A civilian is any person who does not belong to one of the categories of persons referred to in Article 4 (A) (1), (2), (3) and (6) of the Third Convention and in Article 43 of this Protocol. In case of doubt whether a person is a civilian, that person shall be considered to be a civilian.

2. The civilian population comprises all persons who are civilians.

3. The presence within the civilian population of individuals who do not come within the definition of civilians does not deprive the population of its civilian character.

Article 51

Protection of the civilian population

1. The civilian population and individual civilians shall enjoy general protection against dangers arising from military operations. To give effect to this protection, the following rules, which are additional to other applicable rules of international law, shall be observed in all circumstances.

2. The civilian population as such, as well as individual civilians, shall not be the object of attack. Acts or threats of violence the primary purpose of which is to spread terror among the civilian population are prohibited.

3. Civilians shall enjoy the protection afforded by this section, unless and for such time as they take a direct part in hostilities.

4. Indiscriminate attacks are prohibited. Indiscriminate attacks are:

(a) those which are not directed at a specific military objective;

(b) those which employ a method or means of combat which cannot be directed at a specific military objective; or

(c) those which employ a method or means of combat the effects of which cannot be limited as required by this Protocol; and consequently, in each such case, are of a nature to strike military objectives and civilians or civilian objects without distinction.

5. Among others, the following types of attacks are to be considered as indiscriminate:

(a) an attack by bombardment by any methods or means which treats as a single military objective a number of clearly separated and distinct military objectives located in a city, town, village or other area containing a similar concentration of civilians or civilian objects; and

(b) an attack which may be expected to cause incidental loss of civilian life, injury to civilians, damage to civilian objects, or a combination thereof, which would be excessive in relation to the concrete and direct military advantage anticipated.

6. Attacks against the civilian population or civilians by way of reprisals are prohibited.

7. The presence or movements of the civilian population or individual civilians shall not be used to render certain points or areas immune from military operations, in particular in attempts to shield military objectives from attacks or to shield, favour or impede military operations. The Parties to the conflict shall not direct the movement of the civilian population or individual civilians in order to attempt to shield military objectives from attacks or to shield military operations.

8. Any violation of these prohibitions shall not release the Parties to the conflict from their legal obligations with respect to the civilian population and civilians, including the obligation to take the precautionary measures provided for in Article 57...

Article 52

General Protection of civilian objects

1. Civilian objects shall not be the object of attack or of reprisals. Civilian objects are all objects which are not military objectives as defined in paragraph 2.

2. Attacks shall be limited strictly to military objectives. In so far as objects are concerned, military objectives are limited to those objects which by their nature, location, purpose or use make an effective contribution to military action and whose total or partial destruction, capture or neutralization, in the circumstances ruling at the time, offers a definite military advantage.

3. In case of doubt whether an object which is normally dedicated to civilian purposes, such as a place of worship, a house or other dwelling or a school, is being used to make an effective contribution to military action, it shall be presumed not to be so used.

Article 53

Protection of cultural objects and of places of worship

Without prejudice to the provisions of the Hague Convention for the Protection of Cultural Property in the Event of Armed Conflict of 14 May 1954, and of other relevant international instruments, it is prohibited:

(a) to commit any acts of hostility directed against the historic monuments, works of art or places of worship which constitute the cultural or spiritual heritage of peoples;

(b) to use such objects in support of the military effort;

(c) to make such objects the object of reprisals.

Article 54

Protection of objects indispensable to the survival of the civilian population

1. Starvation of civilians as a method of warfare is prohibited.

2. It is prohibited to attack, destroy, remove or render useless objects indispensable to the survival of the civilian population, such as food-stuffs, agricultural areas for the production of food-stuffs, crops, livestock, drinking water installations and supplies and irrigation works, for the specific purpose of denying them for their sustenance

value to the civilian population or to the adverse Party, whatever the motive, whether in order to starve out civilians, to cause them to move away, or for any other motive.

3. The prohibitions in paragraph 2 shall not apply to such of the objects covered by it as are used by an adverse Party:

(a) as sustenance solely for the members of its armed forces; or

(b) if not as sustenance, then in direct support of military action, provided, however, that in no event shall actions against these objects be taken which may be expected to leave the civilian population with such inadequate food or water as to cause its starvation or force its movement.

4. These objects shall not be made the object of reprisals.

5. In recognition of the vital requirements of any Party to the conflict in the defence of its national territory against invasion, derogation from the prohibitions contained in paragraph 2 may be made by a Party to the conflict within such territory under its own control where required by imperative military necessity.

Article 55

Protection of the natural environment

1. Care shall be taken in warfare to protect the natural environment against widespread, long-term and severe damage. This protection includes a prohibition of the use of methods or means of warfare which are intended or may be expected to cause such damage to the natural environment and thereby to prejudice the health or survival of the population.

2. Attacks against the natural environment by way of reprisals are prohibited.

Article 56

Protection of works and installations containing dangerous forces

1. Works or installations containing dangerous forces, namely dams, dykes and nuclear electrical generating stations, shall not be made the object of attack, even where these objects are military objectives, if such attack may cause the release of dangerous forces and consequent severe losses among the civilian population. Other military objectives located at or in the vicinity of these works or installations shall not be made the object of attack if such attack may cause the release of dangerous forces from the works or installations and consequent severe losses among the civilian population.

2. The special protection against attack provided by paragraph 1 shall cease:

(a) for a dam or a dyke only if it is used for other than its normal function and in regular, significant and direct support of military operations and if such attack is the only feasible way to terminate such support;

(b) for a nuclear electrical generating station only if it provides electric power in regular, significant and direct support of military operations and if such attack is the only feasible way to terminate such support;

(c) for other military objectives located at or in the vicinity of these works or installations only if they are used in regular, significant and direct support of military operations and if such attack is the only feasible way to terminate such support.

3. In all cases, the civilian population and individual civilians shall remain entitled to all the protection accorded them by international law, including the protection of the precautionary measures provided for in Article 57. If the protection Ceases and any of the works, installations or military objectives mentioned in paragraph 1 is attacked, all practical precautions shall be taken to avoid the release of the dangerous forces.

4. It is prohibited to make any of the works, installations or military objectives mentioned in paragraph 1 the object of reprisals.

5. The Parties to the conflict shall endeavour to avoid locating any military objectives in the vicinity of the works or installations mentioned in paragraph 1. Nevertheless, installations erected for the sole purpose of defending the protected works or installations from attack are permissible and shall not themselves be made the object of attack, provided that they are not used in hostilities except for defensive actions necessary to respond to attacks against the protected works or installations and that their armament is limited to weapons capable only of repelling hostile action against the protected works or installations.

6. The High Contracting Parties and the Parties to the conflict are urged to conclude further agreements among themselves to provide additional protection for objects containing dangerous forces.

7. In order to facilitate the identification of the objects protected by this article, the Parties to the conflict may mark them with a special sign consisting of a group of three bright orange circles placed on the same axis, as specified in Article 16 of Annex I to this Protocol [Article 17 of Amended Annex]. The absence of such marking in no way relieves any Party to the conflict of its obligations under this Article.

Article 57

Precautions in attack

1. In the conduct of military operations, constant care shall be taken to spare the civilian population, civilians and civilian objects.

2. With respect to attacks, the following precautions shall be taken:

(a) those who plan or decide upon an attack shall:

(i) do everything feasible to verify that the objectives to be attacked are neither civilians nor civilian objects and are not subject to special protection but are military objectives within the meaning of paragraph 2 of Article 52 and that it is not prohibited by the provisions of this Protocol to attack them;

(ii) take all feasible precautions in the choice of means and methods of attack with a view to avoiding, and in any event to minimizing, incidental loss or civilian life, injury to civilians and damage to civilian objects;

(iii) refrain from deciding to launch any attack which may be expected to cause incidental loss of civilian life, injury to civilians, damage to civilian objects, or a combination thereof, which would be excessive in relation to the concrete and direct military advantage anticipated;

(b) an attack shall be cancelled or suspended if it becomes apparent that the objective is not a military one or is subject to special protection or that the attack may be expected to cause incidental loss of civilian life, injury to civilians, damage to civilian objects, or a combination thereof, which would be excessive in relation to the concrete and direct military advantage anticipated;

(c) effective advance warning shall be given of attacks which may affect the civilian population, unless circumstances do not permit.

3. When a choice is possible between several military objectives for obtaining a similar military advantage, the objective to be selected shall be that the attack on which may be expected to cause the least danger to civilian lives and to civilian objects.

4. In the conduct of military operations at sea or in the air, each Party to the conflict shall, in conformity with its rights and duties under the rules of international law applicable in armed conflict, take all reasonable precautions to avoid losses of civilian lives and damage to civilian objects.

5. No provision of this article may be construed as authorizing any attacks against the civilian population, civilians or civilian objects.

Article 58

Precautions against the effects of attacks

The Parties to the conflict shall, to the maximum extent feasible:

(a) without prejudice to Article 49 of the Fourth Convention, endeavour to remove the civilian population, individual civilians and civilian objects under their control from the vicinity of military objectives;

(b) avoid locating military objectives within or near densely populated areas;

(c) take the other necessary precautions to protect the civilian population, individual civilians and civilian objects under their control against the dangers resulting from military operations.

Article 59

Non-defended localities

1. It is prohibited for the Parties to the conflict to attack, by any means whatsoever, non-defended localities....

Article 60

Demilitarized zones

1. It is prohibited for the Parties to the conflict to extend their military operations to zones on which they have conferred by agreement the status of demilitarized zone, if such extension is contrary to the terms of this agreement.

2. The agreement shall be an express agreement, may be concluded

Chapter VI
Civil defence

Article 61
Definitions and scope

For the purpose of this Protocol:

(1) "Civil defence" means the performance of some or all of the undermentioned humanitarian tasks intended to protect the civilian population against the dangers,

and to help it to recover from the immediate effects, of hostilities or disasters and also to provide the conditions necessary for its survival. These tasks are:

(a) warning;

(b) evacuation;

(c) management of shelters;

(d) management of blackout measures;

(e) rescue;

(f) medical services, including first aid, and religious assistance;

(g) fire-fighting;

(h) detection and marking of danger areas;

(i) decontamination and similar protective measures;

(j) provision of emergency accommodation and supplies;

(k) emergency assistance in the restoration and maintenance of order in distressed areas;

(l) emergency repair of indispensable public utilities;

(m) emergency disposal of the dead;

(n) assistance in the preservation of objects essential for survival;

(o) complementary activities necessary to carry out any of the tasks mentioned above, including, but not limited to, planning and organization;

(2) "Civil defence organizations" means those establishments and other units which are organized or authorized by the competent authorities of a Party to the conflict to perform any of the tasks mentioned under (1), and which are assigned and devoted exclusively to such tasks; (3) "Personnel" of civil defence organizations means those persons assigned by a Party to the conflict exclusively to the performance of the tasks mentioned under (1), including personnel assigned by the competent authority of that Party exclusively to the administration of these organizations;

(4) "Matériel" of civil defence organizations means equipment, supplies and transports used by these organizations for the performance of the tasks mentioned under (1).

Article 62

General protection

1. Civilian civil defence organizations and their personnel shall be respected and protected, subject to the provisions of this Protocol, particularly the provisions of this section. They shall be entitled to perform their civil defence tasks except in case of imperative military necessity....

Article 69

Basic needs in occupied territories

1. In addition to the duties specified in Article 55 of the Fourth Convention concerning food and medical supplies, the Occupying Power shall, to the fullest extent of the means available to it and without any adverse distinction, also ensure the provision of clothing, bedding, means of shelter, other supplies essential to the survival of the civilian population of the occupied territory and objects necessary for religious worship.

2. Relief actions for the benefit of the civilian population of occupied territories are governed by Articles 59, 60, 61, 62, 108, 109, 110 and 111 of the Fourth Convention, and by Article 71 of this Protocol, and shall be implemented without delay.

Article 70

Relief actions

1. If the civilian population of any territory under the control of a Party to the conflict, other than occupied territory, is not adequately provided with the supplies mentioned in Article 69, relief actions which are humanitarian and impartial in character and conducted without any adverse distinction shall be undertaken, subject to the agreement of the Parties concerned in such relief actions. Offers of such relief shall not be regarded as interference in the armed conflict or as unfriendly acts. In the distribution of relief consignments, priority shall be given to those persons, such as children, expectant mothers, maternity cases and nursing mothers, who, under the Fourth Convention or under this Protocol, are to be accorded privileged treatment or special protection....

Article 73

Refugees and stateless persons

Persons who, before the beginning of hostilities, were considered as stateless persons or refugees under the relevant international instruments accepted by the Parties concerned or under the national legislation of the State of refuge or State of residence shall be protected persons within the meaning of Parts I and III of the Fourth Convention, in all circumstances and without any adverse distinction.

Article 75

Fundamental guarantees

1. In so far as they are affected by a situation referred to in Article 1 of this Protocol, persons who are in the power of a Party to the conflict and who do not benefit from more favourable treatment under the Conventions or under this Protocol shall be treated humanely in all circumstances and shall enjoy, as a minimum, the protection provided by this Article without any adverse distinction based upon race, colour, sex, language, religion or belief, political or other opinion, national or social origin, wealth, birth or other status, or on any other similar criteria. Each Party shall respect the person, honour, convictions and religious practices of all such persons.

2. The following acts are and shall remain prohibited at any time and in any place whatsoever, whether committed by civilian or by military agents:

(a) violence to the life, health, or physical or mental well-being of persons, in particular:

   (i) murder;

   (ii) torture of all kinds, whether physical or mental;

   (iii) corporal punishment; and

   (iv) mutilation;

(b) outrages upon personal dignity, in particular humiliating and degrading treatment, enforced prostitution and any form or indecent assault;

(c) the taking of hostages;

(d) collective punishments; and

(e) threats to commit any of the foregoing acts.

3. Any person arrested, detained or interned for actions related to the armed conflict shall be informed promptly, in a language he understands, of the reasons why these measures have been taken. Except in cases of arrest or detention for penal offences, such persons shall be released with the minimum delay possible and in any event as soon as the circumstances justifying the arrest, detention or internment have ceased to exist.

4. No sentence may be passed and no penalty may be executed on a person found guilty of a penal offence related to the armed conflict except pursuant to a conviction pronounced by an impartial and regularly constituted court respecting the generally recognized principles of regular judicial procedure, which include the following:

(a) the procedure shall provide for an accused to be informed without delay of the particulars of the offence alleged against him and shall afford the accused before and during his trial all necessary rights and means of defence;

(b) no one shall be convicted of an offence except on the basis of individual penal responsibility;

(c) no one shall be accused or convicted of a criminal offence on account or any act or omission which did not constitute a criminal offence under the national or international law to which he was subject at the time when it was committed; nor shall a heavier penalty be imposed than that which was applicable at the time when the criminal offence was committed; if, after the commission of the offence, provision is made by law for the imposition of a lighter penalty, the offender shall benefit thereby;

(d) anyone charged with an offence is presumed innocent until proved guilty according to law;

(e) anyone charged with an offence shall have the right to be tried in his presence;

(f) no one shall be compelled to testify against himself or to confess guilt;

(g) anyone charged with an offence shall have the right to examine, or have examined, the witnesses against him and to obtain the attendance and examination of witnesses on his behalf under the same conditions as witnesses against him;

(h) no one shall be prosecuted or punished by the same Party for an offence in respect of which a final judgement acquitting or convicting that person has been previously pronounced under the same law and judicial procedure;

(i) anyone prosecuted for an offence shall have the right to have the judgement pronounced publicly; and

(j) a convicted person shall be advised on conviction or his judicial and other remedies and of the time-limits within which they may be exercised.

5. Women whose liberty has been restricted for reasons related to the armed conflict shall be held in quarters separated from men's quarters. They shall be under the immediate supervision of women. Nevertheless, in cases where families are detained or interned, they shall, whenever possible, be held in the same place and accommodated as family units.

6. Persons who are arrested, detained or interned for reasons related to the armed conflict shall enjoy the protection provided by this Article until their final release, repatriation or re-establishment, even after the end of the armed conflict.

7. In order to avoid any doubt concerning the prosecution and trial of persons accused of war crimes or crimes against humanity, the following principles shall apply:

(a) persons who are accused or such crimes should be submitted for the purpose of prosecution and trial in accordance with the applicable rules of international law; and

(b) any such persons who do not benefit from more favourable treatment under the Conventions or this Protocol shall be accorded the treatment provided by this Article, whether or not the crimes of which they are accused constitute grave breaches of the Conventions or of this Protocol.

8. No provision of this Article may be construed as limiting or infringing any other more favourable provision granting greater protection, under any applicable rules of international law, to persons covered by paragraph 1.

Chapter II

Measures in favour of women and children

Art 76

Protection of women

1. Women shall be the object of special respect and shall be protected in particular against rape, forced prostitution and any other form of indecent assault.

2. Pregnant women and mothers having dependent infants who are arrested, detained or interned for reasons related to the armed conflict, shall have their cases considered with the utmost priority.

3. To the maximum extent feasible, the Parties to the conflict shall endeavour to avoid the pronouncement of the death penalty on pregnant women or mothers having dependent infants, for an offence related to the armed conflict. The death penalty for such offences shall not be executed on such women.

Article 77

Protection of children

1. Children shall be the object of special respect and shall be protected against any form of indecent assault. The Parties to the conflict shall provide them with the care and aid they require, whether because of their age or for any other reason.

2. The Parties to the conflict shall take all feasible measures in order that children who have not attained the age of fifteen years do not take a direct part in hostilities and, in particular, they shall refrain from recruiting them into their armed forces. In recruiting among those persons who have attained the age of fifteen years but who have not attained the age of eighteen years the Parties to the conflict shall endeavour to give priority to those who are oldest.

3. If, in exceptional cases, despite the provisions of paragraph 2, children who have not attained the age of fifteen years take a direct part in hostilities and fall into the power of an adverse Party, they shall continue to benefit from the special protection accorded by this Article, whether or not they are prisoners of war.

4. If arrested, detained or interned for reasons related to the armed conflict, children shall be held in quarters separate from the quarters of adults, except where families are accommodated as family units as provided in Article 75, paragraph 5.

5 . The death penalty for an offence related to the armed conflict shall not be executed on persons who had not attained the age of eighteen years at the time the offence was committed...

Article 79

Measures or protection for journalists

1. Journalists engaged in dangerous professional missions in areas of armed conflict shall be considered as civilians within the meaning of Article 50, paragraph 1.

2. They shall be protected as such under the Conventions and this Protocol, provided that they take no action adversely affecting their status as civilians, and without prejudice to the right of war correspondents accredited to the armed forces to the status provided for in Article 4 (A) (4) of the Third Convention.

3. They may obtain an identity card similar to the model in Annex II of this Protocol. This card, which shall be issued by the government of the State of which the Journalist is a national or in whose territory he resides or in which the news medium employing him is located, shall attest to his status as a journalist.

Article 82

Legal advisers in armed forces

The High Contracting Parties at all times, and the Parties to the conflict in time of armed conflict, shall ensure that legal advisers are available, when necessary, to advise military commanders at the appropriate level on the application of the Conventions and this Protocol and on the appropriate instruction to be given to the armed forces on this subject....

Article 83

Dissemination

1. The High Contracting Parties undertake, in time of peace as in time of armed conflict, to disseminate the Conventions and this Protocol as widely as possible in their respective countries and, in particular, to include the study thereof in their programmes of military instruction and to encourage the study thereof by the civilian population, so that those instruments may become known to the armed forces and to the civilian population.

2. Any military or civilian authorities who, in time of armed conflict, assume responsibilities in respect of the application of the Conventions and this Protocol shall be fully acquainted with the text thereof.

Article 84

Rules of application

The High Contracting Parties shall communicate to one another, as soon as possible, through the depositary and, as appropriate, through the Protecting Powers, their official translations of this Protocol, as well as the laws and regulations which they may adopt to ensure its application.

Section II

Repression of Breaches of the Conventions and of this Protocol

Article 85

Repression of breaches of this Protocol

1. The provisions of the Conventions relating to the repression of breaches and grave breaches, supplemented by this Section, shall apply to the repression of breaches and grave breaches of this Protocol.

2. Acts described as grave breaches in the Conventions are grave breaches of this Protocol if committed against persons in the power of an adverse Party protected by Articles 44, 45 and 73 of this Protocol, or against the wounded, sick and shipwrecked of the adverse Party who are protected by this Protocol, or against those medical or religious personnel, medical units or medical transports which are under the control of the adverse Party and are protected by this Protocol.

3. In addition to the grave breaches defined in Article 11, the following acts shall be regarded as grave breaches of this Protocol, when committed wilfully, in violation of the relevant provisions of this Protocol, and causing death or serious injury to body or health:

(a) making the civilian population or individual civilians the object of attack;

(b) launching an indiscriminate attack affecting the civilian population or civilian objects in the knowledge that such attack will cause excessive loss of life, injury to civilians or damage to civilian objects, as defined in Article 57, paragraph 2 (a)(iii);

(c) launching an attack against works or installations containing dangerous forces in the knowledge that such attack will cause excessive loss of life, injury to civilians or damage to civilian objects, as defined in Article 57, paragraph 2 (a)(iii);

(d) making non-defended localities and demilitarized zones the object of attack;

(e) making a person the object of attack in the knowledge that he is hors de combat;

(f) the perfidious use, in violation of Article 37, of the distinctive emblem of the red cross, red crescent or red lion and sun or of other protective signs recognized by the Conventions or this Protocol.

4. In addition to the grave breaches defined in the preceding paragraphs and in the Conventions, the following shall be regarded as grave breaches of this Protocol, when committed wilfully and in violation of the Conventions or the Protocol:

(a) the transfer by the occupying Power of parts of its own civilian population into the territory it occupies, or the deportation or transfer of all or parts of the population of the occupied territory within or outside this territory, in violation of Article 49 of the Fourth Convention;

(b) unjustifiable delay in the repatriation of prisoners of war or civilians;

(c) practices of apartheid and other inhuman and degrading practices involving outrages upon personal dignity, based on racial discrimination;

(d) making the clearly-recognized historic monuments, works of art or places of worship which constitute the cultural or spiritual heritage of peoples and to which special protection has been given by special arrangement, for example, within the framework of a competent international organization, the object of attack, causing as a result extensive destruction thereof, where there is no evidence of the violation by the adverse Party of Article 53, subparagraph (b), and when such historic monuments, works of art and places of worship are not located in the immediate proximity of military objectives;

(e) depriving a person protected by the Conventions or referred to in paragraph 2 or this Article of the rights of fair and regular trial.

5. Without prejudice to the application of the Conventions and of this Protocol, grave breaches of these instruments shall be regarded as war crimes.

Article 86

Failure to act

1. The High Contracting Parties and the Parties to the conflict shall repress grave breaches, and take measures necessary to suppress all other breaches, of the Conventions or of this Protocol which result from a failure to act when under a duty to do so.

2. The fact that a breach of the Conventions or of this Protocol was committed by a subordinate does not absolve his superiors from penal disciplinary responsibility, as the case may be, if they knew, or had information which should have enabled them

to conclude in the circumstances at the time, that he was committing or was going to commit such a breach and if they did not take all feasible measures within their power to prevent or repress the breach.

Article 87

Duty of commanders

1. The High Contracting Parties and the Parties to the conflict shall require military commanders, with respect to members of the armed forces under their command and other persons under their control, to prevent and, where necessary, to suppress and to report to competent authorities breaches of the Conventions and of this Protocol.

2. In order to prevent and suppress breaches, High Contracting Parties and Parties to the conflict shall require that, commensurate with their level of responsibility, commanders ensure that members of the armed forces under their command are aware of their obligations under the Conventions and this Protocol.

3. The High Contracting Parties and Parties to the conflict shall require any commander who is aware that subordinates or other persons under his control are going to commit or have committed a breach of the Conventions or of this Protocol, to initiate such steps as are necessary to prevent such violations of the Conventions or this Protocol, and, where appropriate, to initiate disciplinary or penal action against violators thereof.

Article 88

Mutual assistance in criminal matters

1. The High Contracting Parties shall afford one another the greatest measure of assistance in connexion with criminal proceedings brought in respect of grave breaches of the Conventions or of this Protocol.

2. Subject to the rights and obligations established in the Conventions and in Article 85, paragraph 1 of this Protocol, and when circumstances permit, the High Contracting Parties shall co-operate in the matter of extradition. They shall give due consideration to the request of the State in whose territory the alleged offence has occurred.

3. The law of the High Contracting Party requested shall apply in all cases. The provisions of the preceding paragraphs shall not, however, affect the obligations arising from the provisions of any other treaty of a bilateral or multilateral nature which governs or will govern the whole or part of the subject of mutual assistance in criminal matters.

Article 89

Co-operation

In situations of serious violations or the Conventions or of this Protocol, the High Contracting Parties undertake to act jointly or individually, in co-operation with the United Nations and in conformity with the United Nations Charter.

Article 90

International Fact-Finding Commission

1. (a) An International Fact-Finding Commission (hereinafter referred to as "the Commission") consisting of 15 members of high moral standing and acknowledged impartiality shall be established;

(b) When not less than 20 High Contracting Parties have agreed to accept the competence of the Commission pursuant to paragraph 2, the depositary shall then, and at intervals of five years thereafter, convene a meeting of representatives of those High Contracting Parties for the purpose of electing the members of the Commission. At the meeting, the representatives shall elect the members of the Commission by secret ballot from a list of persons to which each of those High Contracting Parties may nominate one person;

(c) The members of the Commission shall serve in their personal capacity and shall hold office until the election of new members at the ensuing meeting;

(d) At the election, the High Contracting Parties shall ensure that the persons to be elected to the Commission individually possess the qualifications required and that, in the Commission as a whole, equitable geographical representation is assured;

(e) In the case of a casual vacancy, the Commission itself shall fill the vacancy, having due regard to the provisions of the preceding subparagraphs;

(f) The depositary shall make available to the Commission the necessary administrative facilities for the performance of its functions.

2. (a) The High Contracting Parties may at the time of signing, ratifying or acceding to the Protocol, or at any other subsequent time, declare that they recognize ipso facto and without special agreement, in relation to any other High Contracting Party accepting the same obligation, the competence of the Commission to inquire into allegations by such other Party, as authorized by this Article;

(b) The declarations referred to above shall be deposited with the depositary, which shall transmit copies thereof to the High Contracting Parties;

(c) The Commission shall be competent to:

(i) inquire into any facts alleged to be a grave breach as defined in the Conventions and this Protocol or other serious violation of the Conventions or of this Protocol;

(ii) facilitate, through its good offices, the restoration of an attitude of respect for the Conventions and this Protocol;

(d) In other situations, the Commission shall institute an inquiry at the request of a Party to the conflict only with the consent of the other Party or Parties concerned;

(e) Subject to the foregoing provisions or this paragraph, the provisions of Article 52 of the First Convention, Article 53 of the Second Convention, Article 132 or the Third Convention and Article 149 of the Fourth Convention shall continue to apply to any alleged violation of the Conventions and shall extend to any alleged violation of this Protocol.

3. (a) Unless otherwise agreed by the Parties concerned, all inquiries shall be undertaken by a Chamber consisting of seven members appointed as follows:

(i) five members of the Commission, not nationals of any Party to the conflict, appointed by the President of the Commission on the basis of equitable representation of the geographical areas, after consultation with the Parties to the conflict;

(ii) two ad hoc members, not nationals of any Party to the conflict, one to be appointed by each side;

(b) Upon receipt of the request for an inquiry, the President of the Commission shall specify an appropriate time-limit for setting up a Chamber. If any ad hoc member has not been appointed within the time-limit, the President shall immediately appoint such additional member or members of the Commission as may be necessary to complete the membership of the Chamber.

4. (a) The Chamber set up under paragraph 3 to undertake an inquiry shall invite the Parties to the conflict to assist it and to present evidence. The Chamber may also seek such other evidence as it deems appropriate and may carry out an investigation of the situation in loco;

(b) All evidence shall be fully disclosed to the Parties, which shall have the right to comment on it to the Commission;

(c) Each Party shall have the right to challenge such evidence.

5. (a) The Commission shall submit to the Parties a report on the findings of fact of the Chamber, with such recommendations as it may deem appropriate;

(b) If the Chamber is unable to secure sufficient evidence for factual and impartial findings, the Commission shall state the reasons for that inability;

(c) The Commission shall not report its findings publicly, unless all the Parties to the conflict have requested the Commission to do so.

6. The Commission shall establish its own rules, including rules for the presidency or the Commission and the presidency of the Chamber. Those rules shall ensure that the functions of the President of the Commission are exercised at all times and that, in the case of an inquiry, they are exercised by a person who is not a national of a Party to the conflict.

7. The administrative expenses of the Commission shall be met by contributions from the High Contracting Parties which made declarations under paragraph 2, and by voluntary contributions. The Party or Parties to the conflict requesting an inquiry shall advance the necessary funds for expenses incurred by a Chamber and shall be reimbursed by the Party or Parties against which the allegations are made to the extent of 50 per cent of the costs of the Chamber. Where there are counter-allegations before the Chamber each side shall advance 50 per cent of the necessary funds.

Article 91

Responsibility

A Party to the conflict which violates the provisions of the Conventions or of this Protocol shall, if the case demands, be liable to pay compensation. It shall be responsible for all acts committed by persons forming part of its armed forces.

Part IV

Final Resolutions

Article 92

Signature

This Protocol shall be open for signature by the Parties to the Conventions six months after the signing of the Final Act and will remain open for a period or twelve months.

Article 93

Ratification

This Protocol shall be ratified as soon as possible. The instruments of ratification shall be deposited with the Swiss Federal Council, depositary of the Conventions.

Article 94

Accession

This Protocol shall be open for accession by any Party to the Conventions which has not signed it. The instruments of accession shall be deposited with the depositary.

Article 95

Entry into force

1. This Protocol shall enter into force six months after two instruments of ratification or accession have been deposited.

2. For each Party to the Conventions thereafter ratifying or acceding to this Protocol, it shall enter into force six months after the deposit by such Party of its instrument of ratification or accession.

Article 96

Treaty relations upon entry into force or this Protocol

1. When the Parties to the Conventions are also Parties to this Protocol, the Conventions shall apply as supplemented by this Protocol.

2. When one of the Parties to the conflict is not bound by this Protocol, the Parties to the Protocol shall remain bound by it in their mutual relations. They shall furthermore be bound by this Protocol in relation to each of the Parties which are not bound by it, if the latter accepts and applies the provisions thereof.

3. The authority representing a people engaged against a High Contracting Party in an armed conflict of the type referred to in Article 1, paragraph 4, may undertake to apply the Conventions and this Protocol in relation to that conflict by means of a unilateral declaration addressed to the depositary. Such declaration shall, upon its receipt by the depositary, have in relation to that conflict the following effects:

(a) the Conventions and this Protocol are brought into force for the said authority as a Party to the conflict with immediate effect;

(b) the said authority assumes the same rights and obligations as those which have been assumed by a High Contracting Party to the Conventions and this Protocol; and

(c) the Conventions and this Protocol are equally binding upon all Parties to the conflict.

Article 97

Amendment

1. Any High Contracting Party may propose amendments to this Protocol. The text of any proposed amendment shall be communicated to the depositary, which shall decide, after consultation with all the High Contracting Parties and the International Committee of the Red Cross, whether a conference should be convened to consider the proposed amendment.

2. The depositary shall invite to that conference all the High Contracting Parties as well as the Parties to the Conventions, whether or not they are signatories or this Protocol.

Article 98

Revision of Annex I

1. Not later than four years after the entry into force of this Protocol and thereafter at intervals of not less than four years, the International Committee of the Red Cross shall consult the High Contracting Parties concerning Annex I to this Protocol and, if it considers it necessary, may propose a meeting of technical experts to review Annex I and to propose such amendments to it as may appear to be desirable. Unless, within six months of the communication of a proposal for such a meeting to the High Contracting Parties, one third of them object, the International Committee of the Red Cross shall convene the meeting, inviting also observers of appropriate international organizations. Such a meeting shall also be convened by the International Committee of the Red Cross at any time at the request of one third of the High Contracting Parties.

2. The depositary shall convene a conference of the High Contracting Parties and the Parties to the Conventions to consider amendments proposed by the meeting of technical experts if, after that meeting, the International Committee of the Red Cross or one third of the High Contracting Parties so request.

3. Amendments to Annex I may be adopted at such a conference by a two-thirds majority of the High Contracting Parties present and voting.

4. The depositary shall communicate any amendment so adopted to the High Contracting Parties and to the Parties to the Conventions. The amendment shall be considered to have been accepted at the end of a period of one year after it has been so communicated, unless within that period a declaration of non-acceptance of the amendment has been communicated to the depositary by not less than one third of the High Contracting Parties.

5. An amendment considered to have been accepted in accordance with paragraph 4 shall enter into force three months after its acceptance for all High Contracting Parties other than those which have made a declaration of non-acceptance in accordance with that paragraph. Any Party making such a declaration may at any time withdraw it and the amendment shall then enter into force for that Party three months thereafter.

6. The depositary shall notify the High Contracting Parties and the Parties to the Conventions of the entry into force of any amendment, of the Parties bound thereby, of the date of its entry into force in relation to each Party, of declarations of non-acceptance made in accordance with paragraph 4, and of withdrawals of such declarations.

Article 99

Denunciation

1. In case a High Contracting Party should denounce this Protocol, the denunciation shall only take effect one year after receipt of the instrument of denunciation. If, however, on the expiry of that year the denouncing Party is engaged in one of the situations referred to in Article I, the denunciation shall not take effect before the end of the armed conflict or occupation and not, in any case, before operations connected with the final release, repatriation or re-establishment of the persons protected by the Convention or this Protocol have been terminated.

2. The denunciation shall be notified in writing to the depositary, which shall transmit it to all the High Contracting Parties.

3. The denunciation shall have effect only in respect of the denouncing Party.

4. Any denunciation under paragraph 1 shall not affect the obligations already incurred, by reason of the armed conflict, under this Protocol by such denouncing Party in respect of any act committed before this denunciation becomes effective.

Article 100

Notifications

The depositary shall inform the High Contracting Parties as well as the Parties to the Conventions, whether or not they are signatories of this Protocol, of:

(a) signatures affixed to this Protocol and the deposit of instruments of ratification and accession under Articles 93 and 94;

(b) the date of entry into force of this Protocol under Article 95;

(c) communications and declarations received under Articles 84, 90 and 97;

(d) declarations received under Article 96, paragraph 3, which shall be communicated by the quickest methods; and

(e) denunciations under Article 99.

Article 101

Registration

1. After its entry into force, this Protocol shall be transmitted by the depositary to the Secretariat of the United Nations for registration and publication, in accordance with Article 102 of the Charter of the United Nations.

2. The depositary shall also inform the Secretariat of the United Nations of all ratifications, accessions and denunciations received by it with respect to this Protocol.

Article 102

Authentic texts

The original of this Protocol, of which the Arabic, Chinese, English, French, Russian and Spanish texts are equally authentic, shall be deposited with the depositary, which shall transmit certified true copies thereof to all the Parties to the Conventions.

Convention on the Prevention and Punishment of the Crime of Genocide

Adopted by Resolution 260 (III) A of the United Nations
General Assembly on 9 December 1948.

Article 1

The Contracting Parties confirm that genocide, whether committed in time of peace or in time of war, is a crime under international law which they undertake to prevent and to punish.

Article 2

In the present Convention, genocide means any of the following acts committed with intent to destroy, in whole or in part, a national, ethnical, racial or religious group, as such: (a) Killing members of the group; (b) Causing serious bodily or mental harm to members of the group; (c) Deliberately inflicting on the group conditions of life calculated to bring about its physical destruction in whole or in part; (d) Imposing measures intended to prevent births within the group; (e) Forcibly transferring children of the group to another group.

Article 3

The following acts shall be punishable: (a) Genocide; (b) Conspiracy to commit genocide; (c) Direct and public incitement to commit genocide; (d) Attempt to commit genocide; (e) Complicity in genocide.

Article 4

Persons committing genocide or any of the other acts enumerated in Article 3 shall be punished, whether they are constitutionally responsible rulers, public officials or private individuals.

Article 5

The Contracting Parties undertake to enact, in accordance with their respective Constitutions, the necessary legislation to give effect to the provisions of the present Convention and, in particular, to provide effective penalties for persons guilty of genocide or any of the other acts enumerated in Article 3.

Article 6

Persons charged with genocide or any of the other acts enumerated in Article 3 shall be tried by a competent tribunal of the State in the territory of which the act was committed, or by such international penal tribunal as may have jurisdiction with respect to those Contracting Parties which shall have accepted its jurisdiction.

Article 7

Genocide and the other acts enumerated in Article 3 shall not be considered as political crimes for the purpose of extradition. The Contracting Parties pledge themselves in such cases to grant extradition in accordance with their laws and treaties in force.

Article 8

Any Contracting Party may call upon the competent organs of the United Nations to take such action under the Charter of the United Nations as they consider appropriate for the prevention and suppression of acts of genocide or any of the other acts enumerated in Article 3.

Article 9

Disputes between the Contracting Parties relating to the interpretation, application or fulfillment of the present Convention, including those relating to the responsibility of a State for genocide or any of the other acts enumerated in Article 3, shall be submitted to the International Court of Justice at the request of any of the parties to the dispute.

Article 10

The present Convention, of which the Chinese, English, French, Russian and Spanish texts are equally authentic, shall bear the date of 9 December 1948.

Article 11

The present Convention shall be open until 31 December 1949 for signature on behalf of any Member of the United Nations and of any non-member State to which an invitation to sign has been addressed by the General Assembly.

The present Convention shall be ratified, and the instruments of ratification shall be deposited with the Secretary-General of the United Nations. After 1 January 1950, the present Convention may be acceded to on behalf of any Member of the United Nations and of any non-member State which has received an invitation as aforesaid. Instruments of accession shall be deposited with the Secretary-General of the United Nations.

Article 12

Any Contracting Party may at any time, by notification addressed to the Secretary-General of the United Nations, extend the application of the present Convention to all or any of the territories for the conduct of whose foreign relations that Contracting Party is responsible.

Article 13

On the day when the first twenty instruments of ratification or accession have been deposited, the Secretary-General shall draw up a proces-verbal and transmit a copy of it to each Member of the United Nations and to each of the non-member States contemplated in Article 11. The present Convention shall come into force on the ninetieth day following the date of deposit of the twentieth instrument of ratification or accession.

Any ratification or accession effected subsequent to the latter date shall become effective on the ninetieth day following the deposit of the instrument of ratification or accession.

Article 14

The present Convention shall remain in effect for a period of ten years as from the date of its coming into force. It shall thereafter remain in force for successive periods of five years for such Contracting Parties as have not denounced it at least six months before the expiration of the current period. Denunciation shall be effected by a written notification addressed to the Secretary-General of the United Nations.

Article 15

If, as a result of denunciations, the number of Parties to the present Convention should become less than sixteen, the Convention shall cease to be in force as from the date on which the last of these denunciations shall become effective.

Article 16

A request for the revision of the present Convention may be made at any time by any Contracting Party by means of a notification in writing addressed to the Secretary-General. The General Assembly shall decide upon the steps, if any, to be taken in respect of such request.

Article 17

The Secretary-General of the United Nations shall notify all Members of the United Nations and the non-member States contemplated in Article 11 of the following: (a) Signatures, ratifications and accessions received in accordance with Article 11; (b) Notifications received in accordance with Article 12; (c) The date upon which the present Convention comes into force in accordance with Article 13; (d) Denunciations received in accordance with Article 14; (e) The abrogation of the Convention in accordance with Article 15; (f) Notifications received in accordance with Article 16.

Article 18

The original of the present Convention shall be deposited in the archives of the United Nations. A certified copy of the Convention shall be transmitted to all Members of the United Nations and to the non-member States contemplated in Article 11.

Article 19

The present Convention shall be registered by the Secretary-General of the United Nations on the date of its coming into force.

Index

Explosive Projectiles, 8, 41, 38
Sandoz, Y., 20
Second Additional Protocol, 50, 51
Second Geneva Convention, 10, 60
  art. 12, 50, 26
  art. 42, 53
  art. 44(2), 31
  art. 51, 65
  artt. 19, 36, 39, 42 and 43, 98–136
Serbia and Montenegro, 51
sexual mutilation, 6
sexual slavery, 37
shipwrecked, 24
shipwrecked persons, 27
sick and wounded combatants, 8, 17–18
soldiers, 23
Solferino, 6
Somalia, 27
Spain, 35
special military commissions, 34
spies
  treatment of, 35
spirit of humanity, 10, 219
starvation, 27
state and individual responsibility, 9
stateless persons, 66–68
state practice, 17
state responsibility, 66–68
  attributability, 55
  basic rules, 5
  duties to restore the situation, 37
  international obligation, 60
Statute and the resolutions of International
    Conferences of the Red Cross and
    Red Crescent, 8
Statute of the ICC
  Art. 8, 6
Statute of the ICTR
  genocide, 63

T

Prosecutor v. Dusko Tadiç, 19
Tadiç Case, 49
taking of hostages, 40
temperamenta belli, 9
The Art of War, 6

The Treaty relating to the Use of Sub-
    marines and Noxious Gases in
    Warfare, 21
Third Geneva Convention, 93–135
  art. 4, 37
  art. 12, 52, 97
  art. 13, 52
  art. 14, 50
  art. 16, 50
  art. 17, 52
  art. 18, 52
  art. 19, 52
  art. 25, 52
  art. 26 and 28, 52
  art. 27, 52
  art. 28, 52
  art. 38, 52
  art. 49-51, 52
  art. 57, 119
  art. 84, 123
  art. 99, 52
  art. 118, 52
  art. 130, 50–51
  artt. 29-31, 52
  artt. 34 and 35, 52
  artt. 42 and 91-93, 52
  artt. 59-62, 52
  artt. 71, 74, 76 and 77, 52
  artt. 72, 74 and 75, 52
torture, 70

U

UNESCO, 6, 10
United Kingdom, 26
United Nations
  General Assembly, 34
United Nations General Assembly Resolu-
    tion 2444 (XXIII), 70
United States, 70
unity, 71
universality, 71
University Centre for International Hu-
    manitarian Law in Geneva, 57
University of Geneva, 57
unlawful transfer. *See unlawful deporta-
    tion*

About the Author

Dr. Curtis F.J. Doebbler is an international human rights lawyer who practices before international human rights tribunals. He also represents and advises individuals, non-governmental organizations, and governmental entities on issues of peacemaking, human rights, humanitarian law, constitutional law, and humanitarian assistance, and international criminal law. He frequently lectures and teaches in a variety of settings ranging from universities to projects for homeless persons. He has held academic posts at the London School of Economics, Khartoum University, Tuzla University, The American University in Cairo, Tashkent State Institute of Law, and the University of Pristina in Kosovo. He is currently Professor of Law at An-Najah National University in Nablus, Palestine.

His other publications are in the field of international human rights law, international law concerning refugees, stateless and displaced persons, peace building, humanitarian assistance, international criminal law, health and human rights, and public international law. He is a frequently contributor and commentator to newspapers in more than two dozen countries. His most recent books are *International Human Rights Law: Cases and Materials*, CD Publishing: Washington D.C. (2004) and *Introduction to International Human Rights Law*, CD Publishing: Washington D.C. (2006).

Additional Publications by Dr. Curtis F.J. Doebbler

Doebbler, C.F.J., *International Human Rights Law: Cases and Materials*, CD Publishing: Washington, DC, USA, ISBN 0-9743570-0-6 (2004). Paperback: US$49.49 and electronic book format: US$10.50.

Doebbler, C.F.J., (Добблер, К.Ф.Д.), *Изучение Международного Права Прав Человека* (Russian), ABA CEELI and Tashkent State Institute of Law: Tashkent, Uzbekistan, ISBN 0-9743570-1-4 (2004). Paperback: US$15.00 and electronic book format: US$6.50.

Doebbler, C.F.J., (compiled by), *Selected Human Rights Treaties in Russian and English* (2004). Paperback: US$17.00 and electronic book format: US$7.95.

Doebbler, C.F.J., (compiled by), *Selected Human Rights Treaties in Albanian and English* (2003). Paperback: US$12.00 and electronic book format: US$5.95.

International Study Team, (containing contributions by C.F.J. Doebbler), *Our Common Responsibility: The Impact of a New War on Iraqi Children* (2003). Paperback: US$15.00 and electronic book format: US$6.50.

Doebbler, C.F.J., (compiled by), *Selected Human Rights Treaties in Arabic and English* (2002). Paperback: US$12.50 and electronic book format: US$5.

Doebbler, C.F.J., (with the collaboration of Ahmed, J., and Dabhoiwala, M.), *Handbook for Using the Internet for Teaching and Research in Political Science* (2002). Paperback (spiral bound): US$10.00 and electronic book format: US$4.

Doebbler, C.F.J., *Handbook on the Human Rights Approach to Health* (2002). Paperback: US$10.00 and electronic book format: US$4.50.

[postage & handling additional.]

All of these publications can be purchased in printed or electronic form from:

CD Publishing
http://cdpublishing.com
email: Sales@cdpublishing.com
fax: +1-206-984-4734

www.ingramcontent.com/pod-product-compliance
Lightning Source LLC
Chambersburg PA
CBHW031506270326
41930CB00006B/279